Reading Under Control

Now in an updated third edition, this best-selling textbook from the English Education team at Roehampton University introduces students and primary teachers to key issues in the teaching of reading. The authors know that reading is of profound importance for the learning, personal fulfilment and pleasure of individuals. They also know that to be a teacher of reading is to enter a complex and contentious arena. Their aim is to provide comprehensive and balanced guidance to ensure that students and teachers feel 'in control'.

Strongly rooted in the classroom, the book provides comprehensive coverage of reading practices and resources. Key features include:

- historical and philosophical perspectives;
- the typical journey a reader undertakes;
- EAL, ICT and gender issues in reading;
- a detailed inspection of the phonics debate;
- reading routines and related resources;
- assessment issues;
- individual needs;
- literacy difficulties.

Incorporating new literacy developments and curriculum changes, *Reading Under Control* is essential reading for both trainee teachers and qualified teachers interested in continuing their professional development.

Judith Graham recently retired as a Principal Lecturer from Roehampton University.

Alison Kelly is Senior Lecturer in English Education at Roehampton University.

Related titles

**WRITING UNDER CONTROL
(SECOND EDITION)**

Judith Graham and Alison Kelly
978-1-84312-017-9

**LANGUAGE KNOWLEDGE FOR PRIMARY TEACHERS
(THIRD EDITION)**

Angela Wilson
978-1-84312-207-4

THE PRIMARY ENGLISH ENCYCLOPAEDIA
The heart of the curriculum

Margaret Mallet
978-1-84312-372-9

Reading Under Control

Teaching Reading in the Primary School

Third Edition

Edited by

Judith Graham and Alison Kelly

Routledge
Taylor & Francis Group

LONDON AND NEW YORK

First published 1997 by David Fulton Publishers
Second edition published 2000

This edition published 2008 by Routledge
2 Park Square, Milton Park, Abingdon, Oxon, OX14 4RN

Simultaneously published in the USA and Canada by Routledge
270 Madison Ave, New York, NY 10016

Routledge is an imprint of the Taylor & Francis Group, an informa business

Typeset in ITC Garamond by GreenGate Publishing Services, Tonbridge, Kent
Printed and bound in Great Britain by T J International Ltd, Padstow, Cornwall

British Library Cataloguing in Publication Data
A catalogue record for this book is available from the British Library

Library of Congress Cataloging in Publication Data
Reading under control : teaching reading in the primary school / [edited by] Judith Graham and Alison Kelly. -- 3rd ed.
       p. cm.
  Includes bibliographical references and index.
  ISBN 978-1-84312-461-0 (alk. paper)
  1. Reading (Elementary)--Great Britain. I. Graham, Judith. II. Kelly, Alison.
  LB1573.R2932 2008
  372.41--dc22
                                        2007023603

ISBN-10: 1–84312–461–0
ISBN-13: 978–1–84312–461–0

Contents

Illustrations

FIGURES

TABLES

Notes on contributors

Fiona M. Collins is Principal Lecturer and subject leader of English Education at Roehampton University. Her research interests are children's literature with a particular interest in children's responses to narrative, historical fiction and children's literature in performance. She is co-editor of *Historical Fiction for Children: Capturing the Past* (David Fulton), and of *Turning the Page: Children's Literature in Performance and the Media* (Peter Lang). In addition, she was co-author of the *Bookstart* evaluation: *Bookstart: Planting a Seed for Life*.

Judith Graham taught in London schools, at the Institute of Education, at the University of Greenwich, at Roehampton University and the University of Cambridge, where, in retirement, she still makes a small contribution. Her publications include *Pictures on the Page, Cracking Good Books* and *Cracking Good Picture Books* (all NATE). For David Fulton, she has edited and contributed to *Writing Under Control* and *Historical Fiction for Children*. She has also written several publications on authors and their books for Scholastic and PCET, and written chapters, mainly on literacy, children's books and illustration, for many other edited books and journals.

Alison Kelly is Senior Lecturer in English Education at Roehampton University. She worked for many years as a primary school teacher in London. At Roehampton she teaches on undergraduate and postgraduate courses, and her current research interests include poetry. She is co-editor of *Writing Under Control* (David Fulton; now Routledge), has written several books of teaching materials for Scholastic Publications and acts as an educational consultant to Usborne Publishing.

Liz Laycock is now retired after several decades' involvement in primary education, as a classroom teacher and an advisory teacher, in higher education and ITE. She was Programme Convener for the Primary PGCE and Director of Programmes in the Faculty of Education at Roehampton University. She is a contributor to *Writing Under Control* (David Fulton; now Routledge) and *The Literate Classroom, Historical Fiction for Children, Literacy Through Creativity* and *Education in the United Kingdom* (all David Fulton). She has also written several books for teachers on aspects of literacy teaching for Scholastic Publications.

Kimberly Safford is Senior Lecturer in English Education. Before moving to Roehampton University, she was Research Officer at the Centre for Literacy in Primary Education, where she co-authored *Boys on the Margin*, *Many Routes to Meaning* and *Animating Literacy* (all published by CLPE). She has carried out research for *Creative Partnerships* into the role of the arts in children's language and literacy learning, and she works with the National Association for Language Development in the Curriculum on supporting bilingual pupils and multilingualism in education.

Cathy Svensson is the Master's Programme Convenor for Special and Inclusive Education at Roehampton University. She has a particular interest in communication difficulties, early years and policy issues related to inclusion. She is co-author of the *Bookstart: Planting a Seed for Life* evaluation. She also contributes to the undergraduate teaching programme but the majority of her teaching relates to the Master's programme.

Anne Washtell is Senior Lecturer in English Education at Roehampton University. She was a primary school teacher in London and also worked as an advisory teacher for English. She now teaches on postgraduate and undergraduate courses as well as working with graduate teachers. She is particularly interested in the role of children's names in early literacy and student teachers' experiences of teaching synthetic phonics. She is a contributor to *Writing Under Control* and has written teaching materials for Scholastic Publications.

Preface

Reading Under Control was first published in 1997. Our hope was that the book would be principled, informative and practical, and leave its readers feeling empowered to be good teachers of reading. The team who wrote the book had all spent many years in the classroom teaching children to read and many more years in training teachers, making their experience 'count' for the next generation of teachers. In 1997, the 'new' *National Curriculum* had been in place for two years (published with a promise that it would remain unchanged for five years) and there were additional demands for comprehensive record-keeping and assessment. We wanted to respond to our students' needs for guidance in these areas as well as to give a firm foundation for the teaching of reading, whatever directives issued from governments. We also hoped that the book would be useful and interesting to teachers and this proved to be the case.

We wrote a second edition of the book in 2000, partly because professional feedback from teachers and students and our own continuing research had heightened certain issues and partly because, again, we needed to make a response to new governmental demands. The *National Literacy Strategy* had been published in 1998 and at least three directives landed on early years specialists before the comprehensive *Curriculum Guidance for the Foundation Stage* was published in early 2000. We recognised that students were obliged to find a way through these documents whilst remaining clear-sighted about what mattered in the teaching of reading.

A third edition is now appropriate. Our convictions about how literacy is learned have not changed but it is unrealistic to believe that the climate in which students and teachers work has been left untouched by the onslaught of government directives. (Onslaught is not too strong a word; there have been 142 literacy documents in the last ten years – more than one a month!) The avalanche of documents culminates (but perhaps does not cease) with the publication of the *Rose Report*, which has much within its pages with which we would agree but which privileges one way of teaching reading in the early stages, a course of action which we would wish to problematise, given what we know about teachers' needs for ownership of their teaching methods, children's different learning styles and the need for further and rigorous research. Nevertheless, students must know about these developments so we have included a new chapter in this edition, Chapter 3, 'Getting to Grips with Phonics', which offers ample and clear guidance so that students can hold their own.

This is not the only new chapter. There are two other totally new chapters (Chapters 4 and 9) and all the others have been rewritten to bring them up to date. Here is a brief summary of each chapter.

Chapter 1 puts all recent developments into a philosophical and historical context. How to define literacy, how we learn to read, how we teach reading are topics that have always intrigued people but the theories developed to explain these are extraordinarily diverse and often contradictory. The last thirty years in the history of the teaching of reading have seen ideas about how children learn to read come and go and we hope that you will gain a sense of perspective from this chapter.

Chapter 2 looks at four key issues which influence children's development as readers. All preoccupy us in the twenty-first century. Gender differences and preferences, widely diverse language and cultural backgrounds, the impact of ICT and an emphasis on the freedom to be creative have all been shown by research to be significant in children's literacy progress and are not to be neglected. These key areas merit a chapter to themselves, which they did not have in the previous edition.

Chapter 3 is all about phonics. English, with its forty-four identifiable vowel and consonant sounds and its mere twenty-six letters to represent them, is always going to be a challenge in the decoding stage. Countries with more regular sound/symbol correlations do not get themselves quite so excited by the topic (and, incidentally, leave the decoding until much later in the child's life than we do in this country), but we cannot avoid the complexities in our grapho-phonic system and this chapter, with its accompanying glossary, clears a path through for you. Certainly, if the *Rose Report* is absorbed into a new version of the (statutory) *National Curriculum*, this chapter will be an excellent reference point for you.

Chapter 4 is another new chapter which we have called 'The Reading Journey', as it traces the typical development of a child from her earliest forays into language and literacy through to fluent and reflective reading and writing, beyond the risk of failure. We acknowledge that the journey is not the same for everybody and certainly arduous for some but the chapter highlights those factors (such as reading-like behaviour, good experiences of play, drawing) that are deemed highly significant on the journey.

Chapter 5 looks at the classroom practices that teachers use to teach reading. We have called these practices 'routines' though we would not like you to imagine that they have the negative connotations of that word. Classrooms are at their most enabling when there are recognisable patterns and expectations and the best teachers have an underlying structure to their lessons even if they vary the surface imaginatively. Many of these routines are time-honoured but some are relatively new and owe their arrival to the *National Literacy Strategy* and the *Primary National Strategy*. Detailed and exemplified accounts are given of, amongst other routines, guided and shared reading, and there are many activities worked through in detail to bring these routines to life. You may think that you could restrict your reading to official documents and to websites but our belief is that because official documentation often issues from committees with, commonly, a narrow brief, the wider picture gets lost and, in particular, that these documents lack the personal voice that we hope you detect in our book. That said, there is much in, for instance, the renewed *Primary National Strategy* that is truly enlightened and encouraging.

Chapter 6 helps to chart a way through the abundant resources – books, of course, but not only books – that are available for the teaching of reading. We have re-ordered this chapter so that, after an introductory section where we make a case for narrative whilst also recognising the place of non-fiction, resources are mapped onto the routines as described in Chapter 5. We have retained the emphasis on range and variety, bearing in mind the *National Curriculum* but also what we know about children's widely differing tastes. In the first and second editions, we included much information on reading schemes but schools do not make the same use of these as in the past, so this section has shrunk. If your school uses a reading scheme, seek out the first or second edition of *Reading Under Control.*

Chapter 7, on monitoring and assessing reading, enables you to identify and plan appropriate teaching for all your pupils. We have included a shorter (but equally telling) miscue analysis, a diagnostic tool which so many teachers report opens their eyes to the strategies that pupils are (or are not) using as they read. This chapter will also guide you through informal and formal assessment arrangements and explain assessment for learning (AfL) and assessment of learning (AoL).

Chapter 8 deals with those children at either end of the reading spectrum. Those who give us cause for concern as they struggle to decode or to derive sense from the words on the page occupy most of this chapter but we do not ignore those very able readers, who need to be remembered also. Special Educational Needs become complex as there are numerous government initiatives to be understood and followed but, through the maze of waves, School Action, School Action Plus, and early, additional and further support materials, we hope there is a clear message about what struggling readers do and do not need.

The final chapter is another new chapter. Dyslexia is a term which students hear frequently in school; indeed, many students who have struggled themselves with literacy have wondered whether they are or could be 'dyslexic'. The term is defined for you in this chapter and we share some of the research, particularly on the place of phonological awareness, which is helping us understand children's severe reading difficulties.

Every chapter suggests further reading, as even in a one-topic book such as this there is still plenty more to learn about. (Reading is apparently the most-researched area in the history of educational research.)

Throughout the book, we have given you examples of good teaching, mini case studies, useful checklists and ideas which we hope will stimulate your thinking. We hope that the package we offer leaves you feeling in control of reading because you understand its history and its complexities. It is an irony that we now talk about the 'simple' view of reading when in fact reading is extraordinarily complicated. Until we can see into readers' brains as they read (and we can to a limited extent already), we will never quite know what it is we do as we read. As a team, we do not think it is in the best interests of children that teaching approaches are narrowed or set one against another. We have seen teachers working in many different and balanced ways in the interests of each child in their classroom and we know that, when teachers are good (i.e. well informed, observant, sensitive, efficient and enthusiastic readers themselves who like reading aloud), they get results whatever the method (or, despite the method!). Good teachers have pupils who get lost in books, who respond with heart and mind to what they have read and who are sufficiently confident to question and debate their reading. Reading for these pupils is never merely a mechanical exercise.

The wolf in the children's book *A Cultivated Wolf* (Pascal Biet and Becky Bloom) is perplexed when he encounters a pig, a duck and a cow who are engaged in 'silent reading' in the sun. The wolf is inspired to learn to read and write but his initial efforts do not impress the trio of farm animals. Ultimately, having progressed through various dull scheme books, the wolf buys his first storybook. He reads to pig, duck and cow, one story after another, and he reads with 'confidence and passion'. 'He's a master,' the animals declare and the wolf joins this band of readers.

Teaching and reading with 'confidence and passion' would seem to us to say it all. It is our hope that this book sets you on your path to reaching these goals.

Judith Graham and Alison Kelly
April 2007

PS Personal pronouns 'he' and 'she' are a nuisance. When we talk about the generic teacher or child, we vary the use of 'he' and 'she' throughout the book.

Acknowledgements

The contributors have been able to include accounts of teachers and children at work thanks to examples supplied by their students, their colleagues and classroom teachers with whom they have worked. In addition to those who contributed to the first and second editions of this book, they would like to thank Jane Ferguson, Rosemary Kelly, Suzanne Maile, Matt Mair, Mary Martin, David Montgomerie, Sue Smedley and Lavinia Spong for their advice and contributions to this third edition. Our thanks go also to the students who contributed the reading profile in Chapter 4 and the reading re-enactment in Chapter 7, and finally to Conrad Guettler and Mark Pawley for their enduring patience, support and interest.

Chapter 1

How We Got to Where We Are

Alison Kelly

INTRODUCTION

There has never been a shortage of books about the teaching of reading. There have always been discussions and debates about how children learn to read and the best way to teach them. These debates are often passionate and polarised, sometimes even vitriolic. The difficulty is that there is no one definitive all-encompassing theory or method, so one of the things all teachers of reading have to do in order to feel in control is to inform themselves. Teachers need to have a balanced, historical perspective on the issues so that their developing understanding of the theories can inform practice.

This book is written at a time of significant change in the educational landscape, and governmental control of the teaching of reading has never been tighter. The year 1988 saw the publication of the first version of the *National Curriculum* (NC) that laid down the content of the English curriculum. Ten years later (1998), in a drive to raise standards, the *National Literacy Strategy* (NLS) expanded on this content and prescribed its delivery via a daily literacy hour. However, despite almost 15 per cent more pupils achieving the target level in reading expected at the end of Key Stage 2 (KS2) (level 4 in the NC) by 2005, there were still 95,000 children not reaching this level. Former Deputy Chief Inspector of Schools Jim Rose was commissioned to review the teaching of early reading. His report – the *Independent Review of the Teaching of Early Reading* (DfES, 2006a, the *Rose Report*) – is controversial in that it is tightly (some would say narrowly) prescriptive about the type of phonics teaching that should go on. However, it also endorses the importance of a very rich learning environment in which to embed such teaching.

This chapter offers a foundation for you to develop your understanding of reading: controversies about the subject relate to beliefs about what reading is, what it is that readers have to do, how reading is to be taught and the books that should be used. As we shall show, these beliefs are tied up with understandings about the nature of literacy and about how children learn; these understandings have changed across the years. In this chapter we will map out some of these changes.

LITERACY

Any discussion about reading has to be located in our understanding of what literacy is. At a tangible level, the tools of reading and writing have been transformed and have multiplied, so that the days of slates, chalk and quill pens have been superseded by screens and hundreds of different writing implements to choose from. Reading from the page is still the norm but consider the range of reading you do away from the page in any one day. You read from print in the environment; you may read emails from your computer screen, text messages from your mobile, information from the internet … the list is end-less. And it is not just text-based print that you engage with; think of the many symbols, logos and other visual representations with which you are surrounded and which you 'read' and interpret continuously.

Charting the evolution of the tools of literacy is not so hard; what is much more com-plex is getting hold of what is actually meant by 'literacy'. For many years this was unproblematic. The recitation of passages and rote learning that characterised classrooms of the late nineteenth century was underpinned by a narrow concept of literacy, and teachers were judged (and offered payment accordingly) if they taught in this restricted way. In the 1950s a definition from the Ministry of Education stated that being literate means someone is 'able to read and write for practical purposes of daily life' (in DES, 1975:10). A little later, UNESCO offered the following definition: 'A person is literate who can, with understanding, both read and write a short simple sentence on his everyday life' (in DES, 1975:10).

However, the ethnographer Brian Street (1997) argues that definitions like these are unsatisfactory, restricting and over-simplified. They assume that literacy is a set of skills and attributes that are transparent, universal and assessable. Wherever you are, literacy is straightforward and static. Because such definitions stand alone and are independent of particular cultural or social settings, Street calls this view of literacy an 'autonomous' one. He prefers to see literacy from an 'ideological' viewpoint – one that acknowledges social and cultural dimensions and refuses to separate literacy events from the prevail-ing set of beliefs and values of the culture from which they spring.

This ideological perspective is powerfully illustrated in a fascinating study (Gregory and Williams, 2000) of different generations of children growing up in the Spitalfields area of London. One of the groups that they worked with comprised Bangladeshi–British children. The table below shows the early out-of-school literacy-related experiences these children were having. Note the different languages with which these children were operating – Arabic, Bengali, English and Hindi – and then how wide-ranging the purposes for using these languages were – from formal religious learning about the Qur'an to informal watching of television. This description of the children's literacies, which includes oral language, sits comfortably within Street's ideo-logically based model of literacy.

An ideological perspective on literacy suggests that there is more than one literacy and challenges assumptions that lie behind words like 'illiteracy'. Teachers working with the

Table 1.1 Out-of-school literacy-related experiences of a group of Bangladeshi–British children (adapted from Gregory and Williams, 2000:168)

Activity	Context	Purpose	Language
Qur'anic class	Formal	Religious	Arabic
Bengali class	Formal	Cultural	Bengali
Reading with older sibling	Informal	Homework	English
Video/TV	Informal	Pleasure	Hindi and English

Travellers' community in London in the 1980s found families often living in the restricted space offered by just one trailer and with none of the traditional trappings of literacy apparent – to all intents and purposes they were 'illiterate'. However, oral storytelling was a strong part of these children's lives and they were at ease with road signs and other environmental print: literacy for these children was different from those of their counterparts in school. Skilful teachers will recognise and build on children's early, socially learnt experiences of literacy and in Chapter 4 we look more closely at these early, socially embedded experiences.

WHAT IS READING?

In formulating the principles that underpin the NC, Brian Cox, chair of the working party, offered the following definition of reading. It is one that still holds good today:

> Reading is much more than the decoding of black marks upon a page; it is a quest for meaning and one which requires the reader to be an active participant.
>
> (Cox, 1991:133)

There are three key ideas here. First of all, reading is quite clearly about decoding. In order to get at the printed word the reader has to crack the code needed to decipher the print. But, as reading a piece of nonsense text, or decoding a text in a language you do not understand, would show, there is much more to it than this. Reading is about making sense and the drive to make sense is what powers young children's learning. As our discussion of literacy showed, making sense is, to a certain extent, culturally shaped and we need to hold firmly on to our understanding of children's social and cultural identities. Finally, Cox's definition includes the notion of active participation. Theories about children's learning show them to be active constructors of meaning. So, reading is the bringing together of a text to be decoded and understood and a reader who has to engage actively with both these processes. How the reader does this has been the source of debate and research for many years.

MODELS OF READING

Approaches to the teaching of reading are determined by prevailing understandings about the reading process: the beliefs that educators hold (about how readers manage to turn the black marks into meaningful text) are what govern approaches. Over the years different models and frameworks have been offered to explain this complex cognitive process.

One-dimensional model

Until the twentieth century the view was that reading was a simple matter of decoding the black marks and was therefore just about seeing and hearing sounds and words. The neglect of meaning in this enterprise is brought sharply home when we read in Annual Reports of 1866 that inspectors asked pupils to read backwards from their reading primers in order to be sure that they had not memorised the texts in advance of the tests (Rapple, 1994). It follows logically from such a view that reading can be easily taught through the graded introduction of sounds and words. It is a model that accords with the pedagogy of the Victorian classroom, in which rote learning of sounds and words was the norm.

Orchestration models

In the twentieth century a broader view of reading developed and this can be illustrated through what we can call 'orchestration' models. The idea of orchestration comes from Bussis *et al.*, who propose that 'reading is the act of orchestrating diverse knowledge' (1985:40).

The first and most famous of these models is one in which different cue-systems are orchestrated. It was developed during the 1970s and 1980s by psycholinguist Kenneth Goodman (1982), who, along with other researchers (e.g. Frank Smith, 1978), brought together the disciplines of psychology and linguistics. This led to a broader view of reading than had been seen before: whilst words and letters were still important, the model now included other information that children bring to reading. This model shows what children need to draw on and pull together when they read.

This 'other information' is contained in three cue-systems. The first of these is the semantic cue-system, in which readers draw on meaning from the text itself but also from what they know of the situation they are reading about, from life experience and from other texts. A child who knows that 'ice creams *melt* in the sun' is unlikely to mis-cue and read that 'ice creams *meet* in the sun'. Next – and it is important to note that these are not staged – is the syntactic cue-system in which readers draw on what they know of language and grammar (spoken and written) to predict what is coming next. A child who knows that what ice creams do in the sun is *melt* is unlikely to miscue and read that 'ice creams *meal* in the sun', as she implicitly knows that a verb needs to fill that slot. The third cue-system is grapho-phonic in which readers use what they know of sound–symbol correspondences, visual knowledge of letter combinations and sight vocabulary. Thus, a child meeting 'melt' for the first time could blend its four constituent phonemes together: 'm' - 'e' - 'l' - 't'.

Unlike the one-dimensional model or the cognitive psychological ones that are discussed below, psycholinguists assumed that 'there was only one reading process, that is that all readers, whether beginner/inexperienced or fluent/experienced use the same process, although they differ in the control they have over the process. They assumed a non-stage reading process' (Hall, 2003:40).

More recently, the NLS adapted this theoretical model to a teaching model which depicted reading as a process of shedding light on the text by means of a range of 'searchlights'. With four searchlights mapping directly on to the cue-systems (graphic and phonic cues were split into two) this model governed the teaching of reading from 1998 to 2006. Teaching objectives for reading were split into levels which covered the searchlights. The three levels were text, sentence and word: at text level, the focus was on meaning and context, at sentence level on grammar and at word level on phonics and graphic knowledge.

Cognitive psychological views

Models that draw on multi-level orchestration were challenged by critics. Drawing from cognitive psychology, these critics argued that such models reflect what it is that skilled, rather than beginner, readers do. They believed that the importance of phonic strategies in the early stages of reading was marginalised. A cognitive psychological stance (e.g. Frith, 1985; Ehri, 1987) sees learning to read as a staged, linear process with decoding as the first step.

The difference between these models and the one-dimensional model is that they take account of comprehension as well as decoding. However, the emphasis is different from that of the psycholinguists. For psycholinguists, meaning is privileged as the primary driver and such a model is often described as offering a 'top-down' teaching approach. Cognitive psychologists on the other hand place the emphasis on word recognition, thus offering the reverse – a 'bottom-up' approach. As Hall so aptly puts it: 'both schools of thought … agree on the destination … but disagree on the journey to that destination' (Hall, 2003:69).

The *Rose Report* recommended that the NLS searchlight model be replaced with a framework drawn from cognitive psychology – the 'simple view of reading' – and this has been adopted by the *Primary National Strategy* (PNS) (DfES, 2006b). The 'simple view' makes a clear distinction between beginning reading (learning to read) and the longer process of 'reading to learn'. In contrast to orchestration models, the 'simple' model views learning to read as starting with an early short, focused delivery of phonics teaching, which then gives way to lifelong work on comprehension: 'Obviously, in order to comprehend written texts children must first learn to recognise, that is decode, the words on the page' (DfES, 2006a:53). The simple view is represented as shown in Figure 1.1.

You will see that two different sets of processes are identified here: word recognition processes, which focus on decoding, and language comprehension processes, which are about understanding texts and spoken language. The model shows four quadrants into which children may fall. For instance, a child with weak decoding skills but strengths in understanding and interpreting texts could be positioned in the top left

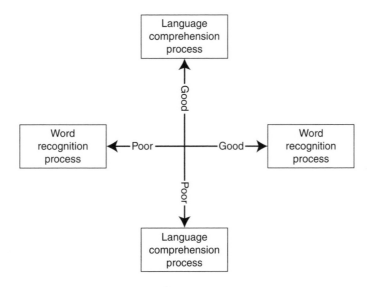

Figure 1.1 The simple view of reading (DfES, 2006a:77)

quadrant, thus helping the teacher determine what kind of support she needs next. It is highly likely that progress in these dimensions will be uneven and teachers will need to monitor children's learning needs closely in relation to both sets of processes. It is important to note that the *Rose Report* makes it clear that this model of reading needs to be 'securely embedded within a broad and language-rich curriculum' (DfES, 2006a:16) and that oral development is emphasised as key to underpinning progress in both word recognition and language comprehension.

At this stage you might find it useful to pause and consider these different models of how we learn to become readers. There is a diagram for the simple view – could you devise one for the other perspectives? Try listing the similarities and differences between the models. What arguments could you put for and against each of them? The simple view is the model that is meant to be implemented in schools but are there insights from the other models that you will find useful to remember?

HISTORICAL OVERVIEW

With different models of reading come different kinds of reading lessons. The following section offers a brief historical overview of approaches to the teaching of reading. You might find it helpful to consider where you, your parents or your grandparents fit into this history, so, before you read any further, spend five minutes jotting down anything at all that you remember about learning to read either at school or home: a book maybe, or a significant memory of reading with another adult. Whether you learnt to read in Britain or another country, you may find that you remember texts that are described or ones that were similar to them, or maybe there are teaching approaches mentioned here that chime with your own memories.

The alphabetic method

As the section about one-dimensional models described, for many years people thought that reading was simply about seeing and hearing letters, sounds and words. This view leads to a particular kind of teaching where reading can be broken down into little bits to be taught in sequence. An early example was the 'alphabetic method' that was used in England from medieval times. In this approach, the very few children who had reading lessons learnt the names of the letters of the alphabet and spelled out combinations of them. In museums, there are examples of seventeenth-century horn books, so called because they were constructed out of wood with a sheet of paper protected by a layer of transparent horn. These early reading books were not much bigger than a child's hand and could be tied on to the child's belt so that they did not get lost. They usually comprised the alphabet, the Lord's Prayer (which was of course a very well known text) and columns of syllables for the children to read.

The phonic approach

In the mid-nineteenth century the alphabetic method was challenged by an increasing interest in phonics (although it is interesting to note that phonic methods are to be found in an alphabet book published as early as 1570 (Avery, in Hunt, 1995)). The difference between these two approaches is that phonics is about decoding using the letter *sounds* (or phonemes) rather than their *names*, so the child who meets the word 'cat' for the first time will blend the phonemes together rather than pronouncing the separate letter names. So the horn book, with its alphabet and syllables, was superseded by texts such as *Petherick's Progressive Phonic Primer* (in Beard, 1987) which required the children to blend a sequence of phonemes (e.g. 'o/f of, o/n on, o/x ox'). There were vigorous debates about the efficiency of this method, as shown by the title of another primer, *Reading Made Easy in Spite of the Alphabet* (in Diack, 1965). Winston Churchill recalls learning to read with one such book called *Reading Without Tears*. He says that 'It certainly did not justify its title in my case … We toiled each day. My nurse pointed with a pen at different letters. I thought it all very tiresome' (in Diack, 1965: 30). These early phonic primers taught children through carefully graded sequences of sounds but, as we shall show, one of the difficulties with phonic approaches lies in the nature of the English language, which is not completely phonically regular. To overcome this, *Reading Without Tears* omitted irregular words whilst another, *The Pronouncing Reading Book* (1862, in Diack), used different colours to show different vowel sounds such as the 'a' in 'apple', 'was' and 'are'.

A more recent initiative in 1960 attempted to regularise the sound–symbol system through the introduction of a so-called 'Initial Teaching Alphabet' (ITA). To the twenty-six letters of the alphabet, an additional twenty symbols were added. It was a short-lived initiative: a paucity of texts using ITA (and a lack of any ITA symbols in the environment) restricted the range of reading, and children with reading difficulties found the transfer back to the conventional alphabet enormously challenging.

The hugely popular *Bangers and Mash* (1975) series featuring two mischievous chimps introduced children to phonics by means of graded presentation of the main phonemes (or 'sounds', as they were then described). Despite some qualms about their potentially racist elements, these books are still to be found in schools today and their humour, format and safe formula seem to provide a useful comfort zone for some reluctant readers. From the same era, the *Letterland* (1973) scheme was an enormously popular phonics-based programme. Its distinctive personalised pictograms (*Dippy Duck* and *Clever Cat*, to name two) guided phonics instruction for many young readers at that time.

The 'look and say' approach

Another approach, 'look and say', is often described as being more recent than phonics but it too was being promoted in the mid-nineteenth century. Unlike phonics, 'look and say' starts with words (or sometimes whole sentences) which children learn from flash cards before meeting them in a book. A contemporary advocate of this approach claimed that 'a child would learn to name any twenty-six familiar words much sooner than twenty-six unknown, unheard and unthought of letters of the alphabet' (Horace Mann, 1838, quoted in Diack, 1965: 42). Just as phonic approaches introduced children to sounds in a carefully graded way, so too with 'look and say', where key words, written on cards and held up by the teacher, were gradually taught and reinforced through books containing much repetition and carefully controlled vocabulary. As with phonics, traditional teaching of this method involved lots of rote learning, drills and whole-class work; such routines were well suited to the organisation of the large classes so typical of elementary schools from 1870 onwards and gave teachers a sense of control in very difficult circumstances.

Both phonics and 'look and say' were taking hold at a time when behaviourism was a prominent and popular learning theory. This theory portrays the child as a 'clean slate' and sees new learning coming about as a matter of stimulus and response, the idea being that learning is goal-directed, with appropriate behaviour being reinforced and inappropriate being ignored (Skinner, 1953). Advocates of 'look and say' made claims for the centrality of meaning in their approach whilst supporters of phonics argued that phonic knowledge enabled children to 'attack' unfamiliar words. The 'look and say' emphasis on the whole word owes something to Gestalt theory, which stresses the importance of the 'whole' to which the 'parts' are subordinate.

Many famous reading schemes from the twentieth century have their origins in 'look and say' principles: *Janet and John, Ladybird Key Words, 1, 2, 3 and Away*, to name but a few. So the lives of Peter and Jane, the protagonists of the Ladybird series, were structured by the careful introduction of a number of 'key words' that were sequentially ordered.

The 'language experience' approach

Phonics and 'look and say' approaches, and sometimes a combination of the two, were dominant through to the 1970s, with many published reading schemes reflecting these views of reading.

At about the same time that teachers were becoming increasingly aware of the impact some of these reading schemes could have on the self-esteem of children from ethnic minorities and on girls, new thoughts about children's learning began to impinge on teaching pedagogy. These led to the idea of 'language experience', where the children's own experiences and language were seen to be important starting points for literacy learning. With these ideas came the *Breakthrough to Literacy* materials (McKay, 1970), which gave children the opportunity to base reading texts on their own experience. These materials comprised personal banks of words and 'sentence makers' (stands rather like those used in Scrabble) from which the children constructed their own sentences, which became their first reading matter. The publishers also produced reading books that made an attempt to present children with familiar language and situations. Some teachers continue to use *Breakthrough* materials today and find them especially useful for drawing children's attention to words and sentences.

Theories about children's learning shifted considerably between the 1960s and 1980s and this was also the era when the psycholinguistic model of reading began to have an impact on classroom practice. In terms of children's talk, the advent of the tape recorder meant that researchers were able to listen to children over longer stretches of time and in far more systematic ways than previously. They showed children to be much more active and creative in their learning than behaviourism had acknowledged them to be and went on to look at how teachers might build on these understandings about children's oral language to bridge their move into literacy. This was also the time when the social nature of learning was being brought vividly to light as the work of Lev Vygotsky and Jerome Bruner became increasingly influential amongst educationalists. Vygotsky's 'zone of proximal development' (1978) and

Bruner's 'scaffolding' (in Wood *et al.*, 1976) emerged as powerful ways of understanding the role of the teacher and of the text itself in children's learning. It is to the role of texts in learning to read that we turn now.

Text-based approaches

In 1988 Margaret Meek published a seminal booklet, *How Texts Teach What Readers Learn*. In it she describes the reading lessons to be gleaned from a child's interaction with the author/illustrator and she demonstrates this through close analysis of *Rosie's Walk* (Pat Hutchins), where a fox pursues an apparently oblivious hen who is taking a walk around the farmyard. What is notable is the fact that the fox is not mentioned at all in the brief, thirty-two-word-long sentence that comprises the whole text. Meek's claim is that books like this (see Eileen Browne's *Handa's Surprise* for a more recent book written in the same tradition but with a multicultural setting) teach children about layers of meaning, about irony and about viewpoint and she suggests that it is the interactions children have with such texts that lay foundations for the reading they will encounter in later years.

This deeper understanding about the role of the text itself in learning to read coincided with criticisms of some of the older reading schemes (such as those mentioned above) from the 1970s and 80s, both on equal opportunities grounds and for their language, which emerged as stilted because of the graded introduction of words and sounds. Such language sounded like nothing children had heard before and made it difficult for them to draw on what they already knew of language to help them read. Concerns like these and the influence of the cue-system model of reading led to the publication in the 1980s of new reading schemes (such as *Story Chest*, 1981, and *Oxford Reading Tree*, 1985) that tried to take some of these recent understandings on board by using more natural language, giving attention to more meaningful plots and relevant themes, and trying to address equal opportunities issues through, for example, the inclusion of more characters from ethnic minorities: all this without losing sight of teaching graphic and phonic skills – a tall order!

There was also some disquiet about the rigidity imposed by the use of just one scheme, and one criticism of some of the early reading schemes was that they created a so-called 'reading ladder' with only a narrow progression of books to be worked through. Such a structure can work against the development of children's choosing skills and can also restrict the range of books they read. It was partly in response to this difficulty that the idea of 'individualised reading' was first developed in the late 1960s by Cliff Moon. The intention was to provide children with broad, colour-coded bands of books that were within their reading grasp. It is an organisational device still used by many schools although many now use, especially for Guided Reading, the more recently devised Book Bands (Hobsbaum, 2000), which offer colour-coded collections of books mapped against the NC level descriptions. See Chapter 6 for further discussion of Book Bands.

The early 1980s saw the impact of the so-called 'real books' movement: some teachers were so concerned about the ways in which they perceived reading schemes as narrowing children's choices that they stopped using reading schemes altogether and chose 'real books' instead. Primary school teacher Liz Waterland wrote an influential booklet recounting how she changed from using reading schemes to 'real books'. Her publication, *Read with Me* (1985), was criticised for the lack of attention paid to phonic work and for the implication that little systematic teaching of reading is needed. The 'real books' approach suffered because it became associated with certain false assumptions which were not part of its well intentioned origins. These assumptions included myths such as: reading can be learned 'osmotically' without direct teaching; phonic teaching is not necessary; all books that are not part of a scheme are 'good' (and, vice versa, that all reading-scheme books are not); and reading can only be taught *either* through reading schemes *or* through 'real books'. Huge public controversy about these issues led to a number of government-initiated surveys (e.g. House of Commons Select Committee Report 1990) which found that very few teachers operated according to any of these erroneous assumptions. What the surveys did find was that effectively taught reading was due to coherent and well understood school policies which were properly implemented by the head, the English coordinator and the classroom teachers.

Resources: books and extracts

The arrival of the NC (1988) and, ten years later, the NLS, had a significant impact on the range of books in the classroom. The need for children to be reading widely was clearly stated in both these documents, with the NLS listing the different kinds of fiction and non-fiction that should be read in each term. Booster funding went into schools to support the implementation of the NLS, enabling them to strengthen and widen classroom and library collections. The searchlight model was in place, so classroom collections were developed to ensure that they contained the required range of reading but also books for early readers which allowed them to draw fully on all four searchlights. Phonic and graphic regularity were important and so too were the considerations of meaningful language and context that had first been highlighted by the cue-system model.

Despite this enrichment, there were criticisms of the way in which the structure of the literacy hour tended to fragment reading, particularly for more experienced children who need sustained opportunities for reading. Too many children fell prey to the 'extract culture' of this time whereby their experience of novels and short stories was in danger of being reduced to just four or five sections from the text to be analysed at text, sentence and word level but never fully experienced. Some notable children's authors went so far as to publish *Meetings with the Minister*, in which they defend their writing against such stultifying treatment (Ashley *et al.*, 2003).

Decodable books

The 'simple' view of reading offers a much more tightly focused conceptual framework for teachers, which has implications for book choice for beginner readers. Because of its early emphasis on word recognition the *Rose Report*'s recommendation is that 'decodable books' should be used at this stage. Rose explains that these are 'early reading books specially designed to incorporate regular text, which children can decode using the phonic skills they have secured' (DfES, 2006a:27) and is quick to emphasise that these should in no way preclude reading other books. Indeed, he cites ongoing research from Warwick University (Solity and Vousden in DfES, 2006a) that shows how many 'recognised favourite children's books' offer the same benefits as books that have been written specifically for decoding purposes. It is important to remember that the emphasis of the 'simple' view is on word recognition over and above other cue-systems and this makes it all the more important that children are experiencing a rich and varied diet of reading, particularly through a well developed read-aloud programme (see Chapter 6).

LEARNING STYLES

So far, this chapter has focused on models, approaches, texts and the ways in which theory about learning has influenced these. Early in the chapter we talked about bringing together the book and the reader. Developing theories about learning have altered the lens through which we view this reader – from the empty, passive vessel of the behaviourist model through to the active, social learner that more recent thinking describes.

Research carried out in the 1980s added a new layer to these understandings. Bussis and her colleagues (1985) carried out longitudinal studies over six years, observing children's progress in reading (and other curriculum areas). Particularly interesting were their findings about children's preferred ways of going about learning. For one group, momentum and fluency were all-important and they drew heavily on semantic and syntactic cues. Drawing on these 'big shapes' (Barrs and Thomas, 1991), these learners read for meaning, predicting with confidence, moving backwards and forwards in the text and exhibiting parallel thought processing. By contrast, the learning style for a second cluster of children was one that favoured the 'smaller units' (Barrs and Thomas, 1991); working from the sounds and words and with a preference for accuracy, this group approached tasks in a linear and methodical way. Although this research dates back to the 1980s, its findings are still fresh and relevant today; indeed, the journal *Literacy* featured a discussion about the study between two eminent scholars (Barrs and Meek Spencer, 2005).

There are links to be made here between this research and the very popular notions of children as visual, auditory or kinaesthetic learners (VAK). Emanating from work in the 1970s about neurolinguistic programming, VAK approaches increasingly inform teachers' planning as they seek to take these different styles into account. What we, as teachers of reading, need to take from these different areas of research is that children may learn in different ways and our planning should do all it can to ensure there are no barriers to learning in place. Understanding about children's preferred learning styles should not close down options for them; rather, it should open them up: readers need approaches that appeal to all the senses (see Chapter 5 on reading routines for many examples of these) and approaches that encourage fluency and momentum in reading as well as word recognition skills. The delicate balance that teachers have to find lies between what is known about the subject being taught and what is known about the reader: our task is to weave these two strands of knowledge together in richly provisioned classrooms and through planning for focused, multi-sensory teaching.

CURRENT GOVERNMENT DOCUMENTATION

The Early Years Foundation Stage (EYFS)

The *Curriculum Guidance for the Foundation Stage* (CGFS, DfES, 2000) has been combined with *Birth to Three Matters* (DfES, 2002) and re-presented as the *Early Years Foundation Stage* (DfES, 2007a). This will be implemented from September 2008 and will cover care as well as learning and development for children from birth to five years old. Included in this document are the Early Learning Goals for 'communication, language and literacy' which were in the original CGFS. The intention is that children will have met these by the end of their reception year. With regard to reading, there are Early Learning Goals that contribute towards young children's understanding of the big shapes (e.g. retell narratives; use language to recreate roles; listen and respond to stories) and the smaller units (e.g. 'hear and say sounds in words in the order in which they occur'; 'link sounds to letters').

The *National Curriculum* (NC)

The NC (DfEE, 1999a) for English is structured in the same way as the other Core and Foundation subjects, so it starts with the programmes of study that specify what the children should be taught. These are followed by the attainment targets that describe the standards children should be meeting and are arranged in 'level descriptions of increasing difficulty'.

In common with the other programmes of study for English, general reading requirements are listed under the headings of 'knowledge, skills and understanding' and 'breadth of study'. We look at 'breadth of study' in Chapter 6 and you will see that there is an expectation that children will become acquainted with a rich array of different genres, both fiction and non-fiction. The 'knowledge, skills and understanding' section lists the range of reading strategies children should be using. The expectations for both Key Stages 1 and 2 cover the word recognition and language comprehension processes of the 'simple' view and also include recommendations that draw from orchestration models (using 'grammatical awareness' for instance).

The *National Literacy Strategy* (NLS) and the *Primary National Strategy* (PNS)

In 1998 the NLS *Framework for Teaching* (DfEE, 1998) was introduced. This document, which was non-statutory, expanded the NC Programmes of Study and provided teaching objectives for children from Reception to Year 6. It was controversial in that it prescribed not only what should be taught but how, in the form of a daily literacy hour. In terms of reading, the searchlight model underpinned teaching objectives at text, sentence and word level.

The year 2006 saw the publication of a renewed version of the Framework in the form of the PNS *Primary Framework for Literacy and Mathematics* (DfES, 2006b). Incorporated into this document are the Early Learning Goals for 'communication, language and literacy' as well as refurbished objectives that show progression from Year 6 to Year 7. The objectives from the NLS have been clustered into twelve strands. This document is underpinned by the recommendations of the *Rose Report*, so, in line with that report's emphasis on the centrality of oral language, the scope of the objectives has been broadened to include four strands for speaking and listening. Out of the twelve strands, there are three for reading: strand 5, which focuses on word recognition, with strands 7 and 8 addressing language comprehension. Following Rose's recommendations, the searchlight model of reading is replaced by the 'simple' view, and a 'synthetic' approach to phonics is prescribed (see discussion of this in Chapter 3).

In many ways, the renewed PNS *Framework* is a more flexible document than the NLS, with a huge store of online resources to support teachers' planning (by means of an interactive planning tool). What is contentious though is its insistence on adherence to one specific approach to phonics. In suggesting that one method only must be used there is a danger that teachers' professional decision-making is eroded with a consequent loss of enthusiasm and confidence. In addition, the 'one method and one method only' approach can blind teachers to the individual strengths, weaknesses and ways of learning of the children in front of them.

CONCLUSION

Research into the teaching of reading and its practice is never static. It will be evident from this chapter how complex and subtle the reading process is and how vital it is to avoid over-simplifying descriptions of how we read and how we should teach reading to others. The important thing is not to be daunted by the volume of research but rather to see it as ultimately helpful to us in giving children the very best possible teaching. The worry is that the volume of directives might result in our reflecting less on principles than we ought to if we are to remain creative and innovative teachers; going back to theories and thinking about them enables us to achieve real progress in reading in our classrooms and to keep the teaching of reading under our own control. Reading is not, in Street's words, an 'autonomous' skill that can be easily handed over: it is a reciprocal and dynamic activity which has to take account of the reading process and of the learner's needs and identity.

Further reading and website

Barrs, M. and Thomas, A. (eds) (1991) *The Reading Book.* London: CLPE.

Barrs, M. and Meek Spencer, M. (2005) 'Essay review, inquiry into meaning', *Literacy* 39 (1), 46–53.

Hall, K. (2005) *Listening to Stephen Read.* Buckingham: Open University Press.

Riley, J. (2006) *Language and Literacy: Creative Approaches to Teaching.* London: Paul Chapman.

DFES Standards: http://www.standards.dfes.gov.uk/

Chapter 2

Reading Differences, Reading Diversity
Kimberly Safford

INTRODUCTION

Research in classrooms, schools, homes and communities has contributed to our grow-ing awareness and understanding of factors that influence children's development as readers. Certain topics have emerged as key areas of interest, and also of contention and concern. These include:

- the reasons behind apparently entrenched gender disparity in literacy attainment;
- the ways in which children's ethnic backgrounds and home languages can be acknowledged in the literacy curriculum and provision;
- the growth and impact of ICT, and children's enthusiasm for this mode of communi-cation;
- the official promotion of 'creativity', and how this may have an impact on literacy learning and teaching.

These areas of educational research have inspired numerous government inquiries, reports and advisory publications for schools; however, as a teacher you will be aware that your school and your classroom may look very different from the national picture.

THE GENDER GAP

There is now a recognised gender gap in reading and writing attainment and this situa-tion cannot be accounted for in a straightforward way. Gender inequalities have been a concern of educators since the 1960s, primarily with regard to the expectations and achievements of girls. Today, however, concerns about girls in education have virtually disappeared; the underachievement of boys continues to be a priority since OFSTED raised the alarm about a 'persistent vein of low achievement' amongst boys and their negative attitudes towards reading (1993:127).

Boys and girls in primary school attain virtually equal scores in end of Key Stage maths and science tests (see Table 2.1). However, there is a large gender gap in read-ing and especially in writing attainment (see Table 2.2).

Table 2.1 Year 6 test scores (*National Curriculum* Assessments): percentage of children achieving Level 4 and above in maths and science (DfES, 2006c)

2006 Year 6 National Curriculum Assessments	Girls achieving Level 4 and above	Boys achieving Level 4 and above
Maths	75%	77%
Science	87%	86%

Table 2.2 Year 6 test scores (*National Curriculum* Assessments): percentage of children achieving Level 4 and above in reading, writing and combined English (DfES, 2006c)

Year	Boys' reading	Boys' writing	Girls' reading	Girls' writing	Combined English	
					Boys	*Girls*
2002	77	52	83	68	70	79
2003	73	52	84	69	70	81
2004	79	56	87	71	72	83
2005	82	55	87	72	74	84
2006	79	59	87	75	74	85

This gap has persisted in spite of attempts to make tests more 'boy-friendly' with the introduction of shorter writing tasks on topics such as 'Outer Space Boots' and genres such as a police report on a crime scene (QCA, 2003a). As you can see from Tables 2.1 and 2.2, in 2006 there was an 8 per cent gender gap in reading attainment, a 16 per cent gender gap in writing and an 11 per cent gap in overall English attainment. These British gender inequalities in reading reflect an international trend. In a major study entitled *Reading All Over the World* (Twist *et al.*, 2003), which examined reading attainment of over 140,000 ten-year-olds internationally, girls performed better than boys in all of the thirty-five countries surveyed.

How has this gender gap in reading been studied? In England, interviews with 1,512 pupils in primary, middle and secondary schools (National Literacy Trust, 2005) found that girls enjoy reading more than boys do. Girls are also significantly more likely than boys to rate themselves as 'good readers'. Many more boys than girls think that reading is 'boring' and that reading is for girls only. Girls are more likely than boys to read fiction, magazines, text messages and emails (note the communicative aspect of the last two forms of reading, both of which use ICT). Boys are more likely than girls to read websites, newspapers, graphic novels and comics. Girls are more likely to read in a variety of settings: at school, at home, in the library, on the bus, with friends. More boys than girls report reading only in school. This last piece of data has significant implications for teachers; if boys are reading mainly, or only, in school, it is even more vital to get reading provision and approaches right.

Millard (1997) and Barrs (2000) have argued persuasively that the very act of reading is perceived as a gendered occupation and preoccupation: there are more women readers than men, especially of fiction; the primary teaching profession is overwhelmingly female and it is mostly mothers who read with their children and help them with their homework. Furthermore, it is observable that girls tend to socialise around reading: they recommend and share books and magazines more often than boys do, and this youthful literacy habit is reflected in overwhelmingly female adult book groups which, more often than not, are engaged in reading and discussing narrative fiction.

Girls also tend to play around reading, actively choosing to spend time creating and exchanging booklets of stories, magazines, birthday cards, menus, shopping lists, letters and party invitations. They enact the roles of reader and writer as they play. This play around reading is often in line with school expectations, helping to make many girls

experienced, confident readers. Boys' play interests, however, are often perceived neg-
atively in schools. Research in the Foundation Stage (Holland, 2003) and in Key Stage 2
(Anderson, 2003) has pointed to the ways in which boys' narrative fantasy play (which
may involve fighting, killing, guns, swords or lasers) is often quashed for appearing
'inappropriate'; this research suggests that negative attitudes to narrative fantasy on
such 'taboo play themes' may cause boys to lose interest in reading.

It is sometimes assumed that boys prefer to read non-fiction rather than narrative
texts. Gemma Moss (1999a, 1999b), in her studies of reading patterns in primary schools,
found that boys are often drawn to non-fiction texts because they are not part of schools'
graded reading schemes; boys choose these texts in order to evade teachers' judgements
of their reading abilities. Moss also identified boys who are 'can but don't' readers; they
can read but are reluctant, or embarrassed, to read in the classroom. They avoid reading
and perceive it as 'un-cool'. These 'can but don't' readers are at risk of underachieving
because they are not getting enough practice to improve their reading skills. Girls, on
the other hand, are far less concerned about their status as readers. They are more com-
pliant in accepting teachers' evaluations of their reading abilities and teachers' selection
of texts for them to read. Teachers themselves may have stereotyped attitudes which
influence their expectations of what boys and girls enjoy reading and are capable of
achieving (Holden, 1999; Myhill, 1999).

Teaching approaches, choice of text and length of time are key elements in creating an
inclusive reading classroom; as a teacher, you can develop a range of speaking and listening, reading and writing around a strong poem, short story or novel. Safford *et al.*
(2004) have illustrated how a longer teaching sequence involving interactive, social
approaches to reading and writing, in-depth work around powerful texts, and the purposeful use of ICT for exploration and communication all play a role in engaging
underachieving boy readers. For example, a half-term teaching sequence around the traditional tale *The Seal Wife* began with oral retellings of the story and moved on to engage
children in discussions, drawings, improvised dialogues in role, dramatic re-enactments,
reading similar tales and poetry digitally and on the internet, writing letters in role, writing prequels and sequels to the tale, and children writing and publishing their own
versions of the story on a website as well as on paper. This rich way of working had particularly noticeable effects on the progress of boys. The researchers concluded: 'This
project demonstrates that underachieving boys, with time and preparation, can and do
engage with reading in school, they can and do imaginatively enter the world of a text,
they can and do enjoy a range of narrative fiction' (Safford *et al.*, 2004:105).

Ethnicity and class intersect with gender (Gilborn and Gipps, 1996; Gilborn and
Mirza, 2000; Reay, 1991). OFSTED (2005) has noted the persistent underachievement of
white working-class boys. Traveller pupils are 'the group most at risk in the education
system' (OFSTED, 1999:7). The performance of Bangladeshi and Pakistani pupils in the
early years of schooling remains too low. African and Caribbean heritage children start
school with high scores in baseline tests but by age eleven many of them, particularly
boys, experience a 'marked decline' and in secondary schools they are amongst 'the
lowest performing group at GCSE level' (OFSTED, 1999:11).

As you read the following conversation between a Year 6 boy and his Teaching
Assistant (TA), you can reflect on some of the issues which can impact on ethnic minority children's attitudes to and achievement in reading:

TA: What books do you like to read?

B: None! I don't like to read any books.

TA: And what sort of reading do you like to do?

B: Nothing. At home my mum or my sister tell [read to] me – 'cause they know I hate it – I'm like my dad. He doesn't read.

TA: I've seen you reading comics.

B: Home's not like school is it? At home my mum reads to me. I like that ... She [the class teacher] sends me out of class with J. I hate going out of class. People look at me. They cuss you at play ... In reading time I only pretend to read my library book, although some of it I can read ... My reading book is *Chip and Kipper*. No way I'm reading that! It has easy words like 'the', 'a', 'when' ... I can't believe they gave me that ... I did like reading *The Cat in the Hat* – that was easy ... I like song-books ... and poetry by Benjamin Zephaniah. He's a black man like me ... I like stories, but I can't read them.

(Bunting, 2005:10)

This picture can, of course, differ considerably and positively. Research in effective schools (McKenley *et al.*, 2003) attributes high attainment of ethnic minority pupils to a 'mesmerising', inclusive curriculum which reflects pupils' identities and interests: a curriculum 'rich in other aspects that are not covered by the *National Curriculum*' where teachers are encouraged to use their 'creative intuition' to deepen the quality of children's learning. In such schools, children's heritages and ethnicities are embraced, enjoyed and (most importantly) used for learning. Teachers choose relevant and interesting authors for study and organise visits and writing workshops with poets, storytellers and writers (such as Benjamin Zephaniah, Jan Blake and Valerie Bloom). As a teacher, you will need to consider how what 'counts' as literacy in school relates to the lived experiences of the children in your class.

Further reading and website

Barrs, M. and Pigeon, S. (eds) (1998) *Boys and Reading*. London: CLPE.

Frater, G. (2000) *Securing Boys' Literacy: A Survey of Effective Practice in Primary Schools*. London: Basic Skills Agency.

Millard, E. (1997) *Differently Literate: Boys, Girls and the Schooling of Literacy*. London: Falmer Press.

Younger, M. and Warrington, M. (2005) *Raising Boys' Achievement*. London: DfES.

Literacy Trust: www.literacytrust.org.uk

CHILDREN LEARNING AND USING ENGLISH AS AN ADDITIONAL LANGUAGE (EAL)

You should expect to have pupils who are learning EAL in your classrooms. In England, 686,000 pupils are recorded as having a mother tongue other than English and more than 200 languages are spoken in the homes of children attending school. Ethnic minority children account for 33 per cent of pupils in all British primary and secondary schools, and the number of pupils identified as having EAL has increased by 35 per cent since 1997 (DfES, 2005a).

Children who are non-native speakers of English face great challenges in the main-stream classroom. They must learn English at the same time as they learn the academic content of the curriculum. These two strands of learning must happen simultaneously: children with EAL cannot defer learning the curriculum until they have mastered a sufficient amount of English.

Pupils learning EAL are not a homogeneous group. They may be bilingual (knowing two languages) or multilingual. They range from new arrivals and refugees, to British-born children who grow up hearing and speaking one or more languages besides English. In the mainstream school, children with EAL are learning in and through another language and may come from cultural backgrounds and communities with different understandings and expectations of education, language and learning. These pupils of course have many of the same learning needs as native English speakers, but they also have distinct and different learning requirements, particularly in reading a new or an unfamiliar language.

The distinctiveness of the task for pupils with EAL is to make progress from a starting point radically different from that of other pupils: they have to learn a new language, to learn the curriculum in that new language, to acquire appropriate social skills, and to accommodate a new language, values, culture and expectations alongside existing ones learned at home (South, 1999).

Good practice in supporting children who are learning EAL involves differentiating tasks, taking into account these different starting points and children's prior language and learning experiences. Is the child a new arrival with no previous experience of school, or a new arrival who can read and write in her home language? Is the child a 'low-key British bilingual' (Harris, 1997) who may hear and understand a language other than English at home, but who claims no expertise in that language? Or is the child a 'high-achieving multilingual' (Harris, 1997) who attends Saturday school to study and progress in her home language?

Research with large cohorts of children over many years (Collier, 1995; Collier and Thomas, 2001) has shown that children who are new to English quickly learn 'play-ground' English within two to four years, enabling them to communicate effectively in most social situations. But it takes ten to twelve more years to become competent in 'academic' English: the type of higher-level language, reading and writing that is vital for success in school. Fluency in 'social' English often masks misunderstandings and difficulties in 'academic' English. This 'language gap' between what Cummins (2000) describes as Basic Interpersonal Communicative Skills (BICS) and Cognitive Academic Language Proficiency (CALP) is a key factor in the underachievement of children with EAL and also for many children identified as native speakers of English. Therefore, pedagogy and provision for children with EAL will also broadly benefit all children.

Cummins has described how children with EAL require learning situations that are 'context-embedded' and 'cognitively demanding', and this, again, applies to all children – not just those who are learning English. Children with EAL learn through oral interaction, where language is modelled, used and repeated in a meaningful way (e.g. in reading: 'I can see a … What can you see?'; in games: 'Now it's your turn'; in classroom routines: 'Now it's time to …'). Children learn through activities that offer a practical framework which allows them to make sense of what is going on (e.g. work with circuits in science, shapes in maths). Children with EAL (and all children) benefit from the use of gestures, key visuals (e.g. graphs, matrices), and realia (hands-on artefacts and objects). In early years and Key Stage 1 (KS1) settings, children need many opportunities to hear and retell stories with strong plots and predictable, repetitive language, such as 'Run, run as fast as you can, you can't catch me, I'm the gingerbread man'. In KS2, poetry can provide this kind of strong, repetitive language. As teachers, you will need to consider the extent to which texts and content are made accessible through language modelling, physical gesture and enactment, visuals, vocabulary and props (Gravelle, 2000; Gibbons, 1993, 2002).

You should also consider how the cue-systems for reading (semantic, syntactic, grapho-phonic) might be different for bilingual learners. Native speakers of English know what to expect in terms of likely word order, and which words typically go together. For instance, expressions like 'bread and butter' and 'ride' a bike (rather than 'drive') are easy to 'read' because the words collocate. Bilingual learners may not bring such culturally acquired knowledge or such secure idiomatic confidence to their reading, although they do learn and confirm such expressions through reading (Gregory, 1996; Gregory and Williams, 2000). For children whose first language uses a different script, there is further new learning to be done in order to become familiar with a totally new set of sound symbols.

As children progress into KS2, the language, reading and writing of the curriculum become more abstract and complex. This is a particular challenge for children who are new to English in KS2, and teachers' planning should identify and explicitly address the language demands of curriculum tasks. You should be asking yourself the following questions:

- Structure: How do I say/read/write this? What syntactic features are significant? How do genre and register influence these features?
- Function: Why am I saying/reading/writing this? What is the purpose? What am I trying to achieve?
- Meaning: What am I trying to understand/communicate? Who is the audience? What vocabulary is particular to this context?

One of the key principles of good practice identified by the National Association for Language Development in the Curriculum (NALDIC) is to draw the children's attention to the relationship between form and function by making key grammatical elements explicit. As teachers, you can encourage children to make connections between spoken language and the written language they read in texts. For example, a Year 6 teacher planning work in history about the lives of Victorian children will need to identify both the vocabulary she intends to use (e.g. parlour maid, chimney sweep) and the language structures which will hold this vocabulary (e.g. The parlour maid *had to* get up early *so she could* light the fires; A chimney sweep's job *was* unhealthy *because of* the soot and ashes); it is this attention to language structures which is particularly important in supporting children learning EAL. Table 2.3 shows another example, of a Year 1 teacher's plan for children to learn about the properties of materials.

Because learning a language always involves learning about a culture, and texts are culturally specific, children learning EAL may be unfamiliar with book or story language and contexts that we take for granted. It is beneficial – and fun – for the whole class to explore the meanings of compound words ('Is a watchdog a dog with a watch?'),

Table 2.3 Year 1 teacher's plan for a lesson about the properties of materials (adapted from Mobbs, 1997)

Topic	Activities and resources	Thinking skills	Generic language structures	Specific vocabulary
Science: properties of materials	Handling a range of materials (metal, wood, glass, etc.)	Classifying Describing Comparing	This feels … This is … but this one is … This one isn't … These are similar/different because …	Shiny, smooth, hard, soft, scratchy, bumpy, reflecting, bendy, stiff, dark, light, opaque, transparent

homonyms ('The tap has sprung a leek/leak!') and idioms ('Put your best foot forward') (McWilliam, 1998). As the teacher you will need to consider how to make oral and written classroom texts accessible to all learners.

For children to feel confident in the classroom they need to know that their home languages can be used in learning. The visibility and provision of different languages and scripts through environmental print and books in the classroom make an important contribution to this. As well as conveying a message of respect and inclusion, maintenance and development of home languages play an important role in children's cognitive development (Baker, 2000). A good activity for the whole class is for children to mind-map, describe and, by interviewing family members, further investigate their own language histories, and to discuss how we all use language in a range of contexts.

Akif: You have to say 'thank you' to big people.

Aftab: I say 'arp' [polite form of 'you' in Urdu] at the temple.

Teacher: Would you say 'arp' to your friend?

Aftab: No. 'Toom'.

Sandeep: I say 'satsriacal' [greetings] to the old people. My papaji lives at my sister's house and I always say 'satsriacal' to him.

Lee: This is Chinese. I can write it.

Vijay: I can write my name in Gujerati.

Leroy: I can't. That's good.

(Boyd, in Bain *et al.*, 1992:156)

Further reading and websites

Edwards, V. (2005) *The Other Languages: A Guide to Multilingual Classrooms*. Reading: NCLL.

Franson, C. (2002) *The EAL Teacher: Descriptors of Good Practice*. Watford: NALDIC.

Leung, C. (ed.) (2002) *Language and Additional/Second Language Issues for School Education: A Reader for Teachers*. Watford: NALDIC.

Rutter, J. (2003) *Supporting Refugee Children in 21st Century Britain: A Compendium of Essential Information*. Stoke-on-Trent: Trentham Books.

Cummins, Jim: www.iteachilearn.com

DfES Standards Site ethnic minority achievement homepage: http://www.standards. dfes.gov.uk/ethnicminorities/

Multiverse: www.multiverse.ac.uk

National Association for Language Development in the Curriculum: http://www.naldic. org.uk/

USING ICT: OPPORTUNITIES FOR 'REAL' READING AND WRITING

Interviews with children in primary, middle and secondary schools (National Literacy Trust, 2005) reveal that their 'favourite reading activity' is 'designing a website'. In classroom research (Safford *et al.*, 2004), boys in Years 4 and 5 report using a computer at home between one and four hours daily for a wide range of reading including authors' homepages and homework revision sites; they also routinely word-process their homework. Even the youngest children arrive in school with in-depth knowledge about email, texting, gaming, digital cameras and video, websites, CDs and online shopping. The large-scale *Pedagogies with E-Learning Resources Project* (Somekh, 2006) finds 'a massive gap' between the way that children use ICT in school and the way they use it at home and that 30 per cent of teachers are not making good use of ICT for learning.

ICT has widened our notions of what constitutes reading. Children show a high level of interest and engagement in electronic and digital forms of literacy because they know that this is the type of 'real' reading and writing that adults do for work and for pleasure. Safford *et al.* (2004) have shown how classroom activities involving email, screen reading and web publishing motivate children to engage thoughtfully with a range of fiction. The following text is part of a lengthy email written by a boy in Year 5 to the protagonist of Louis Sacher's novel *There's a Boy in the Girls' Bathroom*. Although he knows that the character Bradley is fictional, Andrew ('the Master of the net') is fully engaged in this piece of writing:

> Dear Bradley … Here are some facts if you want to have a good image. First: have a bath every day. Secondly: hide your odd socks or try to wear matching ones. Thirdly: wear a strong, breath-taking after-shave. Fourth: take part in a sport and play for the school … These are my facts. I hope you use them. From the one and only Master of the net, Andrew.
>
> (in Safford *et al.*, 2004:72)

Becoming a reader influences a child's understanding of how to write for other readers. In a classroom research project examining language, sport and ICT (Safford *et al.*, 2007), Year 6 children contributed to a weblog (an online journal) during the 2006 World Cup football games. Their online reading and writing ('blogging') was enthusiastic, vivid and committed, whether they were interested in football or not. Their writing reflected their immersion in a wide range of football texts: poetry and fiction about football as well as newspapers, magazines, headlines and live broadcast commentary. For reluctant readers and writers, like Alan, the blog offered special opportunities. His authoritative blog entries demonstrated his knowledge and informed opinion as he addressed his Internet readership. Writing before England's match against Sweden, Alan viewed the game from two perspectives and speculated on the outcome:

> I think that if England are winning comfortably then I would put on Theo [Walcott] so he can get past the tired defenders. But if England were chasing the game then I wouldn't put him on because it puts a lot of pressure on him and he'll get frustrated and lose the ball.

In their online blog writing, these Year 6 children reflected what they were reading, watching and hearing, using the language of sport creatively to describe, question, speculate, protest, support, complain, give information, entertain and persuade. As the blog developed, children's writing took on the lively elements of football commentary, including such phrases as 'clinical finisher' and 'the defence was sleeping'.

Wegerif and Dawes (2004) have shown how the class computer or the computer suite can be used to promote opportunities for extended work in pairs, small groups or with the whole class. Examples of good practice might include using a class interactive whiteboard or laptops to:

- navigate a website;
- watch a live web-cam of animal wildlife, weather, a volcano or a city street (linked to class topic work);
- revise collaborative writing;
- work through interactive programmes on a CD;
- create multimedia presentations;
- read texts of their choice for pleasure.

ICT should be integrated into your classroom routines for reading and writing. When you look around your classroom, ask yourself whether ICT is used for exploration and communication, whether the class computer is used daily as a normal part of literacy routines, and whether class work involving ICT makes links with children's out-of-school knowledge and experiences of ICT.

There are many free website builders where you can create and manage a class website to display children's book reviews, writing and artwork, complete with a guestbook in which parents respond. You can collect and view favourite educational and authors' websites. Children can email authors or post book reviews on their websites, and often authors will email responses to children's questions which the individual child can read aloud to the class or small group.

You can set up email accounts for fictional characters so that children can email the Big Bad Wolf, the Highwayman or more contemporary characters like Alem in Benjamin Zephaniah's novel *Refugee Boy* or Marigold and Dolphin in Jacqueline Wilson's *The Illustrated Mum*. In role as that character, you can then email a response, or children could take on different roles in a story and email each other.

The simple Microsoft Office PowerPoint program can be used to create flexible, interactive presentations that tell or extend stories and poems, with branching questions that take readers down different narrative paths. Digital photographs of or by the class, and children's own artwork and writing, can be added to PowerPoint presentations, as well as links to related websites for further reading. PowerPoint presentations can be created and updated for groups or individual children to support different levels of language development and reading experience. Children can also make their own on-screen stories for others to read.

Educational journals have regular and up-to-date articles on practical uses of ICT in the classroom (e.g. *Primary English*, *English 4–11*). The official government sites are BECTA and the National Grid for Learning (NGfL). *Teachers Evaluating Multimedia* (TEEM) offers evaluations by teachers of educational multimedia for classroom use.

EMAOnline has resources for using ICT which will support ethnic minority children and children learning English as an additional language. Remember that teachers and children – not technologies – create interactivity, and the best resource for using ICT is you, the teacher.

Further reading and websites

Books on using ICT date rapidly. Some of the best resources and ideas are found online.
British Educational Communications and Technology Association (BECTA): http://www.becta.org.uk/
National Grid for Learning (NGfL): http://www.ngfl.gov.uk/
National Whiteboard Network: http://www.nwnet.org.uk/pages/
Teachers Evaluating Multimedia (TEEM): http://www.teem.org.uk/

CREATIVITY AND THE ENGLISH CURRICULUM

Since the publication of *Excellence and Enjoyment* (DfES, 2003a), the government has promoted innovative and creative approaches to teaching in a series of publications and initiatives. OFSTED (2002) noted that the most successful primary schools and teachers take ownership of national frameworks such as the *National Literacy Strategy* and adapt these to the needs of the children in their classes. In *Excellence and Enjoyment*, which heralded the launch of the *Primary National Strategy*, the DfES (2003a) stated unequivocally that teachers 'have the power to decide how they teach' and that schools should 'take control of their curriculum'. OFSTED (2003) has observed that, far from inhibiting the learning of the 'Three Rs', creativity enhances teaching, and teachers are urged to promote an atmosphere of 'expecting the unexpected'. *Creativity: Find It, Promote It!* (QCA, 2003b) offers exemplars of creative practice across the curriculum, such as a Year 2 teaching sequence using the traditional tale of Jack and the Beanstalk: the teacher goes into role as Jack and, later, as the giant, and talks with the class, who are in role as villagers. During the lesson, children develop their ideas about how to help the giant become less aggressive. Here is the teacher reflecting on the sequence of work:

> By playing the role of Jack, I would challenge the pupils about their instant reactions without dismissing their response. It wasn't the teacher, but Jack, saying, 'I don't think that's a very good idea'. This prompted an unusual degree of creative contributions from pupils. Several pupils who don't usually volunteer ideas came up with really good suggestions – being in role seemed to give them a new confidence.
>
> (QCA, 2003b)

These exploratory, oral activities led to a range of narrative and in-role writing, and this approach reflects a renewed emphasis on drama, and on speaking and listening, as ways to develop children as readers and writers (DfES, 2003b; Arts Council, 2003).

You and your class may have an opportunity to work alongside drama specialists, painters, sculptors, dancers, poets or musicians. *Creative Partnerships* is a nationally funded organisation that promotes partnerships between artists, arts organisations, teachers and schools. At the local level, agencies such as the Centre for British Teachers (CfBT), Excellence in Cities, and Education Action Zones support collaborative projects between schools and museums, orchestras, theatres and community arts centres.

These collaborative experiences, working alongside experts, inspire children and have a significant, positive impact on their attitudes to and achievement in literacy (Safford and Barrs, 2006; Ellis and Safford, 2005; Brice Heath, 2004, 2005). For example, Year 4 children who worked with a filmmaker to produce a series of short films about bullying were aware of the impact of such work on their wider language and literacy skills:

> It was a proper, proper film like a video, like in Hollywood … I've never done anything like that, properly. [It] has helped me with understanding. I've learned new words cos we did quite a lot of reading. I'm better at my reading. I'm better at everything actually.
>
> (Kree, Year 4, in Safford and Barrs, 2006:63)

There is an increasing interest in how visual and 'multimodal texts' can be used in the classroom, where children work with drawings, diagrams, photographs, film, video and other forms of representation to deepen their understanding of the many modes of reading and writing. Working with the Qualifications and Curriculum Authority (QCA, 2004), Eve Bearne and her team explicitly analysed how children's drawings communicate 'more than words' and demonstrated how the teacher can assess children's visual and oral texts using elements of the statutory writing assessment framework.

> Liam, in Year 1, who has drawn and labelled a picture entitled 'The Rainforest', chooses to make a text with images, plus labels and additional verbal information … He sequences the information following the levels of the rainforest and the floor, rather like visual 'paragraphs'. The separate pictures act as short descriptive items and he uses the white space between the images to separate ideas, rather like punctuation … The number of images and their detail is the pictorial equivalent of descriptive writing.
>
> (QCA, 2004:12)

Liam's drawing reflects the kinds of books he enjoys reading. You may notice how children's information books communicate on many levels simultaneously: they may switch between different genres and narrative voices, conveying information in collage, illustrations, diagrams, graphs, timelines, sequences and photographs. Dorling Kindersley information books can be read in any order across double-page spreads, or even read back to front or along the margins of the page. Similarly, in children's fictional picture books (such as those by Lauren Child) the writing skips, jumps and spirals across the pages, weaving in and out of pictures and collage, and the narrative voice suddenly switches to address the reader directly. Reading and creating multimodal texts will involve you and the children in your class developing a meta-language about how still and moving images convey meaning.

Children need to develop different kinds of reading skills to make meaning, not only from the array of multimedia and virtual worlds that they encounter, but also from written and spoken words (Simpson, 1996; O'Brien and Comber, 2000). Teachers need to take account of children's many 'pathways into reading' (Minns, 1999) so that 'creativity and difference are seen as normal and as productive' (Kress, 2003:120) rather than as distractions and barriers to success.

Effective approaches to the teaching of reading are underpinned by our understanding of the diverse factors that influence children's literacy learning: gender differences and preferences; the many languages that are read, written and spoken in homes and communities; how ethnicity and class are reflected, or neglected, in the English curriculum;

the use of ICT in and out of school; and the recognition of the promise and potential of creative approaches to teaching.

Further reading and websites

British Film Institute Primary Education Working Group (2003) *Look Again! A Teaching Guide to Using Film and Television with Three- to-Eleven-Year-Olds.* London: DfES and BFI.
Goodwin, P. (2004) *Literacy Through Creativity.* London: David Fulton.
Grigg, C. (2002) *Visual Paths to Literacy.* London: Tate Galleries.
Robinson, K. (1999) *All Our Futures: Creativity, Culture and Education.* London: National Advisory Committee on Creative and Cultural Education.
Creative Partnerships: www.creative-partnerships.com
Creativity: Find It, Promote It: www.qca.org.uk/creativity/

Chapter 3

Getting to Grips with Phonics

Anne Washtell

INTRODUCTION

This chapter aims to set out key principles and ideas that underpin the teaching and learning of phonics. The intention is to do this in as straightforward a way as possible whilst acknowledging the underlying complexities of the English language when it comes to mapping the spoken to the written form. It is stating the obvious to say that phonics is key to learning to read and spell (decoding and encoding print), and with the publication of the *Independent Review of the Teaching of Early Reading* (the *Rose Report*, DfES, 2006a) it has become a central tenet of the reading curriculum. However, in order to make sense of the current expectations for the teaching of phonics, we need an understanding of some of the key issues and debates.

What do we mean by 'phonics'? It is not 'phonetics', nor 'phonemes', nor 'phonology'. At its simplest, it is the relationship between letter symbol and sound, so when we read aloud the word 'man' we are able to blend its constituent sounds – 'm', 'a', 'n' – and when we want to write the word 'man' we can segment the word and hear the three sounds and represent them with three appropriate letters. The linguist David Crystal explains that 'phonic approaches are based on the principle of identifying the regular sound–letter relationships in a writing system, and teaching the child to use these to construct or decode words' (Crystal, 1987:251).

Phonics has had a long and troubled history and has been at the centre of much controversy and heated debate. Arguments have focused on the type of phonics which should be taught to children; the degree of emphasis that should be placed on phonics in relation to the other aspects of the reading process; whether or not phonics should be directly taught or left to be inferred by children; the order and pace at which phonemes are introduced; the age at which formal instruction should start; and much, much more. At times, the arguments have become vitriolic and strongly politicised, as is the case today.

Since the introduction of the *National Curriculum* (NC) in 1989, phonics has had its place in the Programmes of Study, although this in itself has proved to be contentious. Over time, with growing concerns about standards in reading, as expressed, for example, in Martin Turner's *Sponsored Reading Failure* (1990), the spotlight on phonics has burnt ever more brightly and its place in the NC has been steadily strengthened.

After ten years of the NC, only 65 per cent of children at the end of Key Stage 2 (KS2) achieved Level 4 in their reading. During this time, as you saw in Chapter 2, other worrying issues were revealed, particularly the disparity in achievement between boys and girls. In response to these disappointing trends the *National Literacy Strategy* (NLS) was launched in 1998, with phonics much more strongly placed within word level work and as part of the searchlight model of reading. In addition, the NLS provided clear direction on pedagogy such as shared and guided work and went on to produce several publications designed to strengthen phonics teaching, notably the NLS's *Phonics: Progression in Phonics* (DfEE,1999b) and the *Primary National Strategy's* (PNS) *Playing with Sounds: A Supplement to Progression in Phonics* (DfES, 2004a). However, despite improvements in the standards of reading, with 80 per cent of children achieving Level 4 at the end of KS2 in 2005, there were underlying concerns that the rise in achievement was faltering and was simply not fast enough. The nine years of the NLS made 'very little impact ... on raising standards of reading' (DfES, 2006a:11–12). Rose states that 15 per cent of children do not achieve the level for their age in reading at the end of Key Stage 1 (KS1) and that 16 per cent do not achieve the expected level for their age in KS2. This amounts to approximately 85,000 and 95,000 children respectively (DfES, 2006a:13). These figures are shocking, especially when considering costs of remediation the older the child gets, the cost to the child's self-esteem and the further challenges faced in secondary schooling and in adult life.

In recent times, people with a wide range of vested interests – politicians, professional organisations, self-appointed experts, publishers of phonics resources and teachers themselves – have entered the debate about phonics teaching. The quality of phonics teaching during the life of the NLS, after a faltering start, did show improvement. However, there were also areas for concern, as noted in the HMI report (2002). OFSTED (2004) was asked to look at the wide variation in attainment in reading and, amongst its findings, noted that schools that had low expectations about the speed at which children should acquire phonic knowledge hindered children's progress and achievement (OFSTED, 2004:4). OFSTED also felt that teachers' subject knowledge in relation to phonics needed to improve. A Phonics Seminar was convened in 2003, after which the NLS tried to address some of the criticisms levelled at its teaching materials through the production of *Playing with Sounds: A Supplement to Progression in Phonics* (DfES, 2004a). Although welcomed by many teachers, the materials were not without their critics. In particular, the Reading Reform Foundation continued to express particular concern about the teaching methods as well as the sequence and pace at which phonemes were introduced.

THE PHONICS SEMINAR

The purpose of the seminar was to look into the effective teaching of phonics in the NLS. The seminar is significant in this short history, largely because of the people who presented papers there and the arguments they put forward. Amongst them was Linnea Ehri, who made the case for systematic phonic work.

Ehri referred to the findings of the *National Reading Panel* (2000), which undertook a major review of existing research into the teaching of reading. Its conclusions were that phonemic awareness and alphabetic knowledge are strong predictors of later success in learning to read. The review also showed that code emphasis approaches are more effective in the early stages of learning to read, which bears out two earlier reviews of research undertaken by Jeanne Chall (1967) and Marilyn Jager Adams (1990). Furthermore, because English is a complex language, it was all the more important that phonics be taught systematically. The evidence suggests that children who are taught systematically become better readers. Phonic instruction is needed and it should start early. Finally, Ehri argued that children's phonic knowledge must be thorough.

A second significant figure at the conference was Rhona Johnston, whose paper 'Accelerating reading and spelling with synthetic phonics: a five year follow up' provided a detailed account of what has come to be known as the 'Clackmannanshire study' (Johnston and Watson, 1998). (Note that Johnston and Watson discuss synthetic phonics whereas Ehri argues for a 'systematic' approach to the teaching of phonics; it is important not to confuse these two terms.) This seven-year longitudinal study, despite being criticised for its flawed research methods (which included more instruction being given to the group taught by synthetic phonics), has been influential in bringing synthetic phonics to the fore (see below and glossary). The research looked at three methods of phonic instruction, with the project lasting sixteen weeks. The children, who were in Primary 1 (Reception), were split into three groups. One group was taught by analytic phonics, the second group through phonological awareness training as well as analytic phonics and the third by synthetic phonics. By the end of the project, the synthetic group had made marked gains compared with the other two groups. For example, in reading they were seven months ahead of their chronological age as well as being seven months ahead of the other two groups. Similarly, their spelling was seven months ahead of their chronological age and about eight to nine months ahead of the other groups. The children's progress was then monitored over time. By the end of Primary 7 (Year 6), the children's word reading was three years six months ahead of their chronological age, spelling was one year eight months ahead of chronological age and reading comprehension was three years five months ahead of chronological age. This final figure is of interest, as it indicates a drop in advantage compared with when it was assessed in Primary 2 as three years seven months ahead of chronological age. Could this be something to do with the balance between teaching comprehension and code-based knowledge with these children? We can only speculate. Other studies have reached similar conclusions about the gains in attainment that synthetic phonics appears to give, for example Sumbler and Willows (1996) and Stuart (1999).

A head of steam was building in relation to the role and status of phonics in the teaching of reading and it was, therefore, not surprising that, in 2005, the House of Commons Education and Skills Committee, after taking evidence from interested parties, produced their report *Teaching Children to Read*, which called for an immediate review of the teaching of early reading.

THE INDEPENDENT REVIEW OF THE TEACHING OF EARLY READING

This review was led by Professor Jim Rose, whose initial findings were presented in *The Independent Review of the Teaching of Early Reading Interim Report* (DfES, 2005d). You might find it of interest to read the responses to the Interim Report from the United Kingdom Literacy Association (UKLA) and the Reading Reform Foundation, which provide contrasting perspectives on key issues. The final report was published in March 2006.

In his report, Rose draws far-reaching conclusions, some of which will be discussed briefly here. He calls for the reconstruction of the searchlights model into what is known as the 'simple' view of reading. This is important for phonics, as word recognition processes are clearly distinguishable from language comprehension processes. A far from simple explanation of the 'simple' view can be read in Appendix 1 of the report. (For further information about the 'simple' view see Chapters 1 and 9.)

Having reviewed a body of research in Britain and other English-speaking countries, including the United States and Australia, Rose finds that researchers 'highlight the crucial importance of systematic phonic teaching for beginning readers' (DfES, 2006a:17). Rose's rationale for endorsing this view is that, because there is a complex relationship between phonemes and graphemes in English, it is 'crucial to teach phonic work systematically, regularly and explicitly, because children are highly unlikely to work out this relationship for themselves' (DfES, 2006a:18–19). There are clear messages here about classroom practice and understandings about how children learn, to which we return later on.

Rose also looked at best practice, sending inspectors out into schools to gather evidence. Part of the remit for the review was to look in particular at the merits of synthetic phonics. What his team was looking for was teaching methods that secured 'optimum progress and high achievement for all beginner readers and writers' (DfES, 2006a:15). Reflecting on this school-based evidence, as well as research evidence and the views of professionals and experts, Rose decided, despite acknowledging 'uncertainties in research findings', that synthetic phonics offers the best starting point for beginning readers. He states that 'there is much convincing evidence to show from the practice observed that, as generally understood, synthetic phonics is the form of systematic phonic work that offers the vast majority of beginners the best route to becoming skilled readers' (DfES, 2006a:19).

The historical significance of this prescriptive landmark statement should not be underestimated. As we shall see later on, it has been closely adhered to in the PNS and associated training. However, it is very important to evaluate this statement within the wider scope of the report. For example, Rose places much emphasis on the centrality of speaking and listening in facilitating early reading development. Although he calls 'strongly for the inclusion of a vigorous programme of phonic work', he adds the caveat that this work must be 'securely embedded within a broad and language-rich curriculum' (DfES, 2006a:16). This is especially significant when considering his discussion about the age at which formal phonics instruction should be introduced. Drawing on Ehri's research, which points to the advantages of an early start, Rose recommends that, for most children, the age of five, if not before, is appropriate for the commencement of a programme of systematic phonic work. Understandably, this has given rise to serious concerns amongst early years educators who feel that this is too early. However, Rose draws on evidence from the *Early Reading Development Pilot*, which involved 180 schools, to show that the increasing rate of phonics teaching did not compromise the wider principles of the *Early Years Foundation Stage* (EYFS) curriculum. He emphasises the power of play, stories, songs, rhymes and drama as ways in which children can be introduced to words and sounds. Finally, he clearly states that the decision about the introduction of systematic phonic instruction 'should be a matter of principled, professional judgement based on careful observation and robust assessment' (2006a:30).

Rose is uncompromising about the place and value of phonic work. What follows is a short summary of some of his key points, with relevant paragraphs of the report indicated in brackets for the purposes of further reading and discussion:

- Phonic work must be embedded in a 'language rich curriculum' (35).
- Phonic knowledge should be taught discretely and as the prime (first) approach to establishing word recognition (53).
- Phonic work should be 'time limited', i.e. for most children to be complete by the end of Key Stage 1 (129).
- Most of the phoneme/grapheme correspondences should be taught 'in a space of a few months at the start of [children's] first year at school' (86).
- There should be direct teaching of words that are not phonically regular (high-frequency words) (87).
- The chosen phonic programme must be 'well planned', 'incremental', followed with 'fidelity', 'consistently', 'daily' for short periods with a variety of related activities (56).
- The phonic sequence should be such that children rapidly acquire the necessary knowledge and skills (85).
- Children must learn about the alphabetic principle if they are to learn to read (34).
- Teaching sessions should be relatively short, daily, vigorous, briskly paced, engaging and multisensory, using stimulating resources (36).

Rose's recommendations about phonics have been implemented in the renewed PNS. In order to teach phonics sessions successfully, as envisaged by Rose, there is a body of subject knowledge which needs to be understood. We will start with some basic definitions and principles.

WHAT TEACHERS NEED TO KNOW

Phonics involves the use of a significant amount of technical terminology. As teachers, it is useful to have this terminology at our fingertips so that we can talk with precision about the teaching of reading. In this section we will examine some of this terminology and provide a glossary at the end of the section to assist you. However, you will want to consolidate this information to ensure a confident and clear approach in the classroom.

The roots of phonics lie in two branches of linguistics: phonology (the sound system of the language) and phonetics (the study of speech sounds). Knowledge from these two disciplines has been applied to reading, resulting in what we know as phonics. There are estimated to be approximately forty-four units of sound (phonemes) in the English language, represented by graphemes (written representations of sounds or phonemes). As there are forty-four phonemes but only twenty-six letters in the alphabet to represent them, this requires the alphabet to be accommodating. For this reason there are three key principles that we need to understand:

- *Phonemes can be represented by one or more letters.*
  The word 'man' is represented by three (graphemes) letters, one for each phoneme (m/a/n). A word like 'planet' is no different in this respect; six phonemes are represented by six letters (p/l/a/n/e/t). (Note that 'p' and 'l' are separate units of sound but are run together and known as a cluster – see glossary). However, take a word like 'thick' and count its phonemes. You should have noticed that it has three phonemes despite its five letters: 'th' and 'ck' are each one unit of sound (th/i/ck). They are called consonant digraphs. Now take a word like 'thief'; five letters, three

phonemes again, but this time the 'i' and the 'e' make one phoneme and are called a vowel digraph (th/ie/f).

- *The same phoneme can be represented/spelled in more than one way.*
  Look at these four words: 'pain', 'flake', 'sleigh' and 'day' and notice that they all share the same vowel phoneme but it is represented differently in each case ('p**ai**n', 'fl**a**k**e**', 'sl**eigh**' and 'd**ay**'). You will have noticed that 'ay' comes at the end of its word whilst 'ai' precedes a consonant. Test this out on other words and see if this generates a rule. You may also have noticed that the word 'flake' has what used to be described as a 'magic' or 'silent' 'e' at the end, where it has the power to make the previous vowel 'say its name'. Check out other words with this pattern and see if this rule holds. Words that end in 'silent e' are described as 'split digraphs' (DfEE, 1999b).

- *The same spelling may represent more than one phoneme (sound).*
  This principle can be illustrated by reading the following passage:

  > The man who boarded the train to Reading was reading the newspaper. He read that the Queen had flown to America on a state visit and forgotten to take her crown. He imagined himself making a bow to the Queen and noticing that she had a pretty bow in her hair.

  Words that look the same ('bow' and 'bow', 'Reading' and 'reading') but are pro-nounced differently and have different meanings are called homographs. As long as children do not lose sight of the fact that reading is about understanding the text, mis-pronunciations of such words are likely to be recognised as not making sense and will be reread and self-corrected.

Segmenting and blending

The NLS describes the key skills that are needed to decode (read) and encode (spell) successfully: 'Phonics consists of the skills of segmentation and blending, knowledge of the alphabetic code and understanding of the principles which underpin how the code is used in reading and spelling' (DfEE, 1999b:4).

We segment words in order to spell. When we segment words it is necessary to hear the individual phonemes within a word. In order to spell, a child must segment a word into its component phonemes and select a letter or letter combination to represent each phoneme. However, when we read we need to be able to blend. When we blend, we merge phonemes together in order to pronounce a word. To read an unfamiliar word phonemically, a child must attribute a phoneme to each letter or letter combination in the word and then merge the phonemes together to pronounce the word. Children need to be taught that the skills of blending and segmenting are reversible processes. In other words, when meeting a new word in his reading, a child must blend the phonemes to read the word; when the child is writing he has the word in his mind already and has to segment the phonemes in order to represent them in writing.

Analytic and synthetic phonics

There are several ways of approaching the teaching of phonics, but the two that have held centre stage in recent years are known as synthetic and analytic phonics. We start with a definition of analytic phonics:

Analytic phonics refers to an approach to the teaching of reading in which the phonemes associated with particular graphemes are not pronounced in isolation. Children identify (analyse) the common phoneme in a set of words in which each word contains the phoneme under study.

(Brooks, 2003:11–12)

An analytic approach invites children to problem-solve actively and bring their own ideas to the task in hand. The children may be operating with linguistic units that are larger than the phoneme. Children are encouraged to deduce and infer as they meet new words. They will actively detect patterns across words, as in this example of Tanya, aged five, who commented as she read a class list: 'You know, Miss, Katrina, Karmini and Kartik's names start with Ka'. Children may also use analogy as a way of getting at new words, so, 'cook' helps me to read 'book', which helps me to read 'took' if I change the first phoneme. However, critics warn that there is a risk that this approach is indirect and is unsystematic. MacMillan argues that 'this sort of instruction usually occurs after reading, where the reading material itself furnishes the words chosen for particular instructional focus. The teaching, therefore, tends not to follow any specific sequence' (MacMillan, 1997:41). There is an implied criticism in these comments and indeed, in recent times, analytic phonics has been cast as the villain of the piece in some quarters. Unhelpfully, the term 'analytic phonics' has been used as a convenient catch-all for anything that is not to do with synthetic phonics. It is not uncommon to find 'onset and rime' identified as an aspect of analytic phonics even though onset and rime's roots lie in phonological awareness. (For definitions of onset and rime and further discussion, see 'Phonological awareness'.)

Brooks also provides us with a definition of synthetic phonics: 'Synthetic phonics refers to an approach to the teaching of reading in which the phonemes associated with particular graphemes are pronounced in isolation and blended together (synthesised)' (Brooks, 2003:11–12).

With synthetic phonics, teaching starts at the level of the phoneme (a single unit of sound). The phonemes are introduced incrementally and systematically by the teacher. In many synthetic approaches the sequence is deliberately organised to facilitate the early, rapid synthesising of simple consonant–vowel–consonant words (CVC). An example of this would be the *Jolly Phonics* (2002) scheme's first set of phonemes, 's', 'a', 't', 'i', 'p', 'n', from which words such as 'i/t – it', 'p/i/n – pin' and 's/a/t – sat' can readily be made. Synthetic approaches always aim to have a clear progression for introducing the forty-four phonemes and emphasise 'all-through-the-word' reading. Central to synthetic phonics is that children should understand what is known as the 'alphabetic principle' (see below).

According to Rose, there are four very important elements which characterise a synthetic approach to teaching and learning phonics. He argues that these elements together add up to 'high quality phonic work' because they teach children directly what they need to know. Rose states that children starting out on reading need to be taught:

- grapheme–phoneme letter–sound correspondences (the alphabetic principle) in a clearly defined incremental sequence;
- to apply the highly important skill of blending (synthesising) phonemes in order, all through a word, to read it;

- to apply the skills of segmenting words into their constituent phonemes to spell;
- that blending and segmenting are reversible processes.

(DfES, 2006a:20)

These four points underpin the teaching and learning of phonics in the PNS. Prior to embarking on planning, teaching and assessing phonics, it will be necessary to become very familiar with them.

The alphabetic principle

In order to be able to decode print in English, children need to understand the alphabetic principle. Essentially, the connection needs to be made that speech can be turned into print and that print can be turned into speech. The concept that has to be grasped is that letters (graphemes) represent the sounds (phonemes) of the language. A key understanding is the reversibility of these two processes.

Phonological (phonemic) awareness

Phonological awareness is an umbrella term to describe sensitivity to speech at all levels. This complex area of research is about 'children's sensitivity to the speech sound structure of words' (Muter, 2003:5). Phonological awareness is very important as it provides a powerful predictor of early reading skill and achievement. Researchers have found out that there are differences in children's sensitivity to speech sounds, so by measuring children's phonological awareness it is possible to identify those who are likely to read easily and those who will find the task more difficult (see Chapter 9).

When thinking about phonological awareness we can consider it at different levels:

- awareness of syllables   Example: toybox = toy + box (2 syllables)
- onset and rime   Examples: t/oy   d/og
- phonemes   Examples: t/o/p   d/o/ll

It is generally agreed amongst researchers that the development of phonological skills starts with the larger units – syllables, onsets and rimes – and moves on to phonemes later (Liberman *et al.*, 1974; Treiman, 1985; Goswami and Bryant, 1990). This refining of phonological awareness is bound up with children's early language development and undergoes constant restructuring, particularly in early and middle childhood as children's spoken word vocabularies rapidly expand (Goswami, 2002). In order to distinguish subtle differences between words and units within words, children form phonological representations. These phonological representations are initially coarse-grained (syllables, onsets and rimes) but gradually become fine-grained as awareness of phonemes develops.

Phonemic awareness refers to sensitivity specifically to sounds at the phoneme level. Children have to learn how phonemes correspond to their written form, graphemes, and in order to do this successfully they need to develop the ability to hear and distinguish sounds in their heads. A single change of phoneme or grapheme can produce a quite different word with a very different meaning. If we say the words 'cat' and 'hat' we can hear that a phoneme has changed. If we now read the same words we notice that whilst the '-at' part of the word stays the same, the grapheme 'c' in 'cat' has changed to an 'h' to form 'hat'. This is how we differentiate the words one from the other. Once children start to learn to read and spell, and acquire the alphabetic principle, this knowledge has a further impact on phonological awareness. To quote Goswami, 'phonological aware-ness is never the same again' (Cook, 2002:42).

Research has shown us that children's awareness of the phonemic structure of spoken words is a strong indicator of future success in learning to read and progress in spelling. Well known longitudinal research (Bryant and Bradley 1985; Goswami and Bryant, 1990) looked at children's sensitivity to rhyme and alliteration as indicators of children's growing phonemic awareness. The findings revealed that children who had scored highly on an initial rhyming test progressed successfully in their reading and spelling. The tests were also given to a group of ten-year-old 'backward readers' (Bryant and Bradley's term). Significantly, the results of these tests indicated weaknesses in the children's sensitivity to rhyme. From this they argued that there is a clear link between the early development of sensitivity to rhyme and progress in reading.

However, more recently, Bradley, Bryant and Goswami's findings about the signifi-cance of rhyme have been challenged by other researchers. An interesting longitudinal study tracked thirty-eight pre-reading four-year-olds during their first two years of learning to read (Muter *et al.*, 1994; Muter *et al.*, 1997). Using a full range of phonolog-ical measures, which included rhyming and segmentation tasks, the children were tested at the ages of four, five and six. Their findings showed that 'segmentation was strongly correlated with attainment in both reading and spelling at the end of the first year of learning to read, whereas rhyming was not' (Muter, 2003:22). Thirty-four of the children were then followed up at nine years of age (Muter and Snowling, 1998). The researchers confirmed 'that rhyme and phoneme awareness are independent skills, and that phoneme, but not rhyme, awareness predicts independent variance in reading accuracy' (Muter and Snowling, 1998:332). In other words, the skill of being able to segment at the level of the phoneme, 'phonemic awareness', is a strong predictor of learning to read. Needless to say, these issues continue to be the subject of heated debate by researchers (see Goswami, 2002, and Muter, 2003).

It has been shown that children also develop phonemic awareness through their independent attempts at spelling ('invented' spellings). Marilyn Jager Adams (1990) has studied the relationship between children's hypotheses about spelling and their grow-ing understanding of phonics and suggests that the two areas are closely related. Her study points out that early attempts at spelling form a further crucial element in devel-oping children's phonemic awareness. It is through their spelling attempts, which involve the act of segmenting the word and trying to represent its phonemes, that the relationship between individual alphabet letters and individual sounds becomes self-evident to children. It is therefore important that children are encouraged to hypothesise how words might be spelled and are provided with opportunities to dis-cuss the construction of their 'invented' spellings. The child of six who writes that she fell down and 'hert her nee' is making good use of her phonemic awareness and her growing understanding of phonics.

What can we take from these arguments? Most importantly, all sides agree that phonological awareness is key to learning to read. What is also accepted is that direct instruction at the level of phoneme is needed for children to get to grips with the alpha-betic code. Phonemic knowledge will not progress without tuition.

Is there any point in working with rhyme if it does not have a direct impact on early achievement in reading and should we simply concentrate our efforts on the phoneme? Hulme *et al.* (2002) advise some prudence in going down the phoneme-only route. This is due to the developmental nature of phonological awareness, in children, from the larger to the smaller units. For this reason, we need to be aware of those children who have limited phonological awareness and make provision for them to develop rhyme awareness as a precursor to developing phonemic awareness. To read further on this, see Muter (2003).

We know that for many children awareness of rhyme develops informally through exposure to nursery rhymes and playground rhymes long before they go to school. In addition, children with good rhyming skills can make links between one word and another known as 'rime analogies'. For example, they are able to use the spelling–sound information in a word such as 'light' as a clue to help them read a new word that shares the same spelling pattern such as 'fight'. Goswami's (1995) rationale is that beginning readers find using rime analogies supportive because the correspondence between the spelling sequences that represent the rhymes and their sounds in spoken words is more consistent than the correspondence between single alphabet letters and individual phonemes. By analysing words in this way, it seems that children are distinguishing between onsets and rimes. The onset is the opening consonant or consonant cluster of a word or syllable and the rime is the vowel sound and any following consonants. So for the word 'sand', 's' is the onset with 'and' as the rime. In 'string', 'str' is the onset and 'ing' is the rime.

Where does this leave the all-important relationship between phonemes and graphemes? Goswami (1995) makes the connection for us in this way: she believes that children use their awareness of rhyme to make rime analogies that in turn help to draw their attention to phonemes. For example, you may have noticed the pleasure that children gain from playing with a rime such as 'at' and thinking of all the words that can be made by changing the initial sound, such as 'bat', 'cat' and 'rat'. Playing in this way isolates the individual phoneme that is changing each time. We also know that nursery rhymes can be used to help children deepen their understanding of phonemes and graphemes, as many have 'near miss' rhymes such as 'dame' and 'lane' or 'fourteen' and 'courtin'. By listening to these near miss rhymes and seeing them in print children learn about phonemic and graphemic contrasts.

As we shall see, phonological awareness is identified as Phase 1 in the PNS's six-phase progression. Rhyme is firmly there, along with a wide range of activities designed to enhance and further develop children's phonological skills. What does not appear to be in evidence in the documentation is the direct use of onset and rime. These are changing times for the teaching of early reading and, as we have discussed earlier, Rose's recommendations mark a significant shift of emphasis to teaching, from the outset, at the level of the phoneme. Onset and rime have no place on this agenda. Neglect of this area may prove to be mistaken.

Alphabetic knowledge

As we have seen, the ability to segment at the level of the phoneme is a key predictor for learning to read, but there is another key factor that needs to be considered, and that is alphabetic or letter knowledge. Byrne and Fielding-Barnsley (1989), for example, found that letter name knowledge made a stronger contribution to children's reading than did a test of their phonemic awareness. However, Muter (2003) and others have argued that although initially significant, letter name knowledge loses its salience at the end of the first year of schooling as by then children should have mastered this knowledge. On the other hand, phonological awareness, she argues, remains significant for predicting reading ability throughout the primary years. At a practical level, what matters for us is how children establish the links between their knowledge of letter names and the phonemes that they hear (see 'The alphabetic principle' and three key principles (the bullet list on p.33) above).

USING TERMINOLOGY WITH CHILDREN

As in all curriculum areas, there is an issue regarding when and whether it is appropriate to introduce children to specialist terminology, such as 'digraph' or 'phoneme' in the case of reading. The danger lies in assuming that because you have taught the label you have taught the concept; this is not always the case. Nevertheless, it is generally agreed that children need some metalanguage so that they can discuss and reflect upon their own language use, and teachers have to make considered decisions about when and how to introduce this. In fact, children positively enjoy having the labels. If they can relish labelling the parts of a flower or minibeast, why not the parts of language too? Since the NLS was introduced in 1998, teachers have been encouraged to use technical terminology with children. This has led to a healthy debate as it challenges preconceptions about notions of 'readiness' and brings into sharper focus our thinking about conceptual development. Perhaps the liveliest debate has centred around the use of the term 'phoneme'. To explore the thinking about this, it helps to consider the possible alternative word(s) that could be used. The most obvious choice is the word 'sound'. 'Sound', of course, is a word that has been used by teachers of reading for many years. However, consider what the word 'sound' is likely to mean to young children. It has many everyday applications in their lives in addition to the 'sounds' in words. On the other hand, 'phoneme' precisely describes the concept of the smallest unit of sound that can be spoken or heard. These days, when teaching even the youngest children, many teachers comfortably use the term 'phoneme' interchangeably with the word 'sound' but try gradually to shift frequency of use towards the technical term.

TEACHING PHONICS: PACE AND PROGRESSION

Traditional approaches to teaching phonics have sequenced the teaching of the forty-four phonemes into a systematic, structured, progressive order. However, in the lifetime of the NLS there were disagreements about not only the specific sequence in which phonemes have been introduced but the rate at which they were to be taught. The NLS made two attempts at addressing progression and pace in its teaching frameworks, the *Progression in Phonics* (DfEE, 1999b) and *Playing with Sounds* (DfES, 2004a) materials. These have now been superseded by the PNS document *Letters and Sounds* (DfES, 2007d), which is aligned with the renewed PNS Framework and EYFS Framework (DfES, 2007a). The *Letters and Sounds* programme is intended to provide an alternative to using a commercially produced synthetic scheme in order to deliver the daily, discrete phonics sessions which are now a requirement. PNS guidance (DfES, 2007b) builds on Rose's recommendations and informs the section that now follows.

The six phases of teaching phonics: outline of progression

If you look at strand 5 in the PNS, 'word recognition: decoding (reading) and encoding (spelling)', the emphasis in the EYFS and KS1 is on 'learning to read', with a firm focus on 'securing the alphabetic code'. The idea is that developing children's phonic knowledge and skills will be 'time limited' (complete by the end of KS1). The document provides the framework of the phonic knowledge, skills and understanding which children need to learn. The six-phase progression developed by the PNS provides much more detail and is intended to be used in conjunction with strand 5 of the Framework. Each phase in the guidance identifies the main purpose, outcomes and typical duration (an indication of the expected time children will be in each phase). Phonic knowledge and skills acquired are also identified, along with some information about activities to support each phase. It is only possible here to give a brief summary of the six phases and sample the content.

Phase 1

Main purpose: emphasis on speaking and listening and developing phonological awareness.
Outcome: explore and experiment with sounds; growing awareness of rhyme, rhythm and alliteration; speak clearly and audibly; begin to show awareness of differences between phonemes.
Typical duration: reflects developmental stages for communication, language and literacy in the EYFS. This paves the way for systematic phonic work to begin.

Phase 2

Main purpose: to introduce grapheme–phoneme (letter–sound) correspondences
Outcome: children know that words are constructed from phonemes and that phonemes are represented by graphemes. Using their knowledge of a small number of common vowels and consonants, e.g. 's', 'a', 't', 'p', 'i', 'n', they can blend them together in reading simple CVC words and segment them for spelling.
Typical duration: six weeks.

Phase 3

Main purpose: to teach children one grapheme for each of the forty-four phonemes in order to read and spell simple regular words.
Outcome: children link sounds to letters; recognise letter shapes and say a sound for each. They hear sounds in the order that they occur in words; read simple words by sounding out and blending phonemes all through the word from left to right; recognise common digraphs; read some high-frequency words.
Typical duration: up to twelve weeks.

Phase 4

Main purpose: to teach children to read and spell words containing adjacent consonants. *Outcome*: children can blend and segment adjacent consonants in words and apply this skill when reading unfamiliar texts and in spelling. Examples: CVCC words ('pots'), CCVC words ('spot'), CCVCC words ('spots') and in due course, CCCVC words ('split'). *Typical duration*: four to six weeks.

Phase 5

Main purpose: children are taught to recognise and use alternative ways of pronouncing the graphemes and spelling the phonemes already taught.
Outcome: alternative ways of pronouncing the graphemes and spelling the phonemes corresponding to long vowel phonemes; identification of constituent parts of two- and three-syllable words; able to read and spell phonically decodable two- and three-syllable words; increasing recognition of high-frequency words automatically; phonic knowledge/skills prime approach in reading unfamiliar and not completely decodable words. *Typical duration*: securing reading and spelling will extend through Year 1.

Phase 6

Main purpose: children to develop their skill and automaticity in reading and spelling; ever-increasing capacity to read for meaning.
Outcome: application of phonic skills and knowledge to recognise and spell an increasing number of complex words; an increasing number of high- and medium-frequency words read independently and automatically.
Typical duration: for most children this phase begins and continues in Year 2. In Year 3 emphasis will change from teaching word recognition to developing children's language comprehension.

Planning in the *Early Years Foundation Stage*

We need to be mindful about the role of assessment in helping us identify children's readiness for formal phonics instruction. This is especially important for the youngest children. Rose indicates that, for most children, this will be the age of five but argues that teachers 'need to be willing, and have the wherewithal, to test the boundaries of children's readiness for systematic phonic work' (DfES, 2006a:30). At this point, we need to remind ourselves that our phonics teaching must be embedded within a 'language-rich curriculum'. Within the EYFS framework, the 'communication, language and literacy' area of learning and development is designed in a grid format so that the 'linking sounds and letters' strand can readily be considered in relation to the other aspects of language and literacy, and, indeed, to the wider curriculum. Any phonics teaching needs to be saturated in high-quality spoken language, so linkage to the 'language for communication' strand is essential. The intentions of Phase 1 make this abundantly clear. The document is also finely tuned to reflect the stages of development of young children.

Early Years Foundation Stage: activities

In Phase 1, the emphasis is on speaking and listening and phonological awareness. At the same time, children's early graphic awareness will be developing. By making a special feature of the ideas below we can begin to sensitise children so that they listen out for sounds generally and begin to isolate and discriminate between phonemes. Phase 1 also places emphasis on helping children to develop their articulation of phonemes. Below are some suggestions and ideas for provision gathered from a range of sources over the years:

- Storytelling and reading aloud: repeated patterns and refrains, so that children can join in.
- Sound walks: take the children for a walk where they are asked to focus on the different sounds they hear in the inside and outside environments. These may vary from birdsong to gurgling radiator pipes. This can be done in the classroom as well, with the children closing their eyes. Invite children to imitate the sounds and play with their voices.
- Spot the instrument: put well known classroom instruments (e.g. tambourine, drum, triangle) in a bag and ask the children to guess which one you are playing. Be ingenious; add your own (the spoons maybe?). Use cassette tapes of different sound effects.
- Voice play: play with sounds that are part of our repertoire for expressing astonishment (oooooooh!) or the need for quiet (ssshhhh!) or being hurt (ow!). Note that these are all sounds that children will later learn more formally as phonemes.
- Rhythm and rhyme: let the children hear, sing, recite, and learn as many rhymes and songs as possible – daily! Use oral activities such as changing the rhyming words in nursery rhymes ('hickory, dickory, dock/The mouse ran up the watch') or leaving a gap in familiar rhymes so children are encouraged to predict a possible rhyme. Let the children use good-quality CD-ROMs such as *Nursery Rhyme Time* and *Ridiculous Rhymes*.
- Odd one out games: say (or sing) words that rhyme but throw in one that doesn't (clock, sock, lock, mock, tock, watch). The children should clap each time they hear the odd one out.
- Big books: use enlarged versions of rhymes so that children have the opportunities to look at rhyming words and begin to see their differences and to observe patterns.
- Syllable sensitivity: plan clapping activities (e.g. to the syllables of their names, place names, dinosaur names).
- Alliteration activities: read, recite and teach the children tongue twisters (Peter Piper; Red Leather, Yellow Leather; Betty Botter). By having enlarged versions of these available, children can begin to make phoneme–grapheme links. Compose together alliterative nonsense sentences such as 'Brave Betty bought beautiful bright blue bananas'.
- Games: play 'I Spy' using a set of familiar objects such as 'Things we use in the bathroom', 'Things we put in our lunch boxes'. Cards naming the items, with the opening phoneme highlighted, could be used later and put alongside the objects.
- Alphabetic knowledge: play with alphabet letters (in Play-Doh, sand and on a magnetic board); sing the alphabet and share many different alphabet books. Without a

thorough knowledge of the alphabet, children will find it very difficult to develop phonic knowledge and indeed to read and write. They need to know that there are twenty-six letters in the alphabet and how to name them (Rose has a balanced position on this but be aware that commercially produced schemes have strong views on the timing of the introduction of the alphabetic sequence. 'Fidelity' to a scheme might influence provision in some settings). Children need to be able to talk to their teachers about letters and in order to do this we should provide them with the relevant metalanguage. Children need knowledge of the letter names of the alphabet so that they are equipped with a way of referring to any letter in any situation. Letter names also have the advantage of remaining constant; the sounds they represent are not so obliging, as we have seen.

- Names: the child's name is a common starting point for developing both phonological and alphabetic knowledge. From a very early age children begin to notice names in their environment and quickly start to identify letters that are significant to their lives. The first word that most children learn to spell is their own name and after that they rapidly learn how to write the names of their family and friends. Learning to write their name is a key preoccupation for young children, so special books could be made for each child, e.g. 'David's All About "D" Book'. When they start school, they are surrounded by names in print, for example the label by their coat peg, on their tidy trays, place mats, paintings, on displays and books. They readily notice similarities and differences in their names, making comments such as 'Christopher's name starts the same way as Christine's', or 'There are three children whose names start with a T'. Through names, children naturally draw on their logographic knowledge but names can also be utilised to support and develop burgeoning phonological awareness: for example, playing 'I spy' but calling out the initial phoneme rather than letter name; playing games of the following type: 'Whose name rhymes with ball?' Answer: 'Paul'; 'Whose names have one clap? Two claps?'

Planning and teaching discrete phonics sessions

Having established the children's readiness for formal phonics instruction, the next consideration is to clarify the amount of phonics teaching which should be happening across the week. The PNS gives the following directive: there should be discrete daily teaching, based on assessment, with a balance of blending and segmenting each week (from Phase 3). In addition, there should be daily application in shared reading and writing, demonstrating how to apply new and existing phonic skills and knowledge so that the children can blend phonemes (reading) and segment phonemes (writing). There should be daily opportunities for cross-curricular application for children to engage independently in speaking, listening, reading and writing activities that allow them to explore and develop their growing skills. Guided reading and guided writing are also sites where knowledge should be applied and practised (at least once a week) (DfES, 2006c).

The balance between the discrete teaching and the all-important application of new knowledge through the key teaching routines needs to be maintained. The expected, cyclical, daily sequence of teaching discrete phonics sessions takes the structure shown in Figure 3.1.

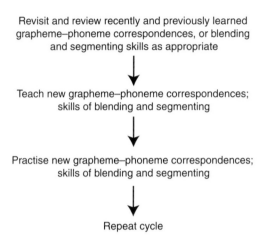

Revisit and review recently and previously learned
grapheme–phoneme correspondences, or blending
and segmenting skills as appropriate

↓

Teach new grapheme–phoneme correspondences;
skills of blending and segmenting

↓

Practise new grapheme–phoneme correspondences;
skills of blending and segmenting

↓

Repeat cycle

Figure 3.1 Daily sequence of teaching phonics sessions

At face value this sequence looks very arid, rigid and repetitive but there is a reason for this. The sequence is powered by the key features of high-quality phonics work as defined by Rose (see above). It should not be forgotten, however, that Rose demands interactive, multisensory teaching that engages all children's interests and which utilises stimulating resources. Typically, teachers will be following either a commercially produced phonics scheme during discrete sessions, such as *Jolly Phonics* (Lloyd, 2002) or *Big Cat Phonics* (Hiatt, 2006) or the PNS's *Letters and Sounds* (DfES, 2007d). There are also exemplar lessons on the DfES website.

Shared and guided work

As indicated in the remit for discrete teaching outlined above, shared and guided reading for the application of current phonic knowledge should be planned for on a daily basis. Guided reading is to be planned for twice a week and guided writing at least once a week (note the importance of the careful and well judged introduction of guided work for the youngest children). It is intended by the PNS that these sessions map onto the Phase that the whole class (shared work) and ability groups (guided work) are currently operating in. The knowledge and skills learnt in discrete phonics sessions are then applied promptly in these other reading and writing routines. It is important at this point to bear in mind the 'learning to read' emphasis of the 'simple' view of early reading as well as the distinction made between word recognition processes and language comprehension processes as we consider the shift in emphasis in relation to these routines. The purpose behind using the routines for phonics is very precise: to apply children's segmenting and blending skills. This is done firstly through demonstrations (shared work) and then through their independent attempts under adult guidance (guided work). The structure of guided reading sessions already lends itself well to the application of previously learnt skills but shared work in the past has always had room for children's spontaneous ideas whether or not they fitted precisely into a particular phase of development. Skilful teachers know how to filter children's suggestions and deftly manage those that are not relevant to the task in hand. Equally, the shared routines bring together children of all abilities and we need to remember that children can learn much from each other as well as from their teacher. There is tension here that sits around placing a 'ceiling' on what is to be learnt at any one time, in order to ensure progression and a systematic approach. The needs of the young fluent readers will need to be addressed carefully during whole-class shared sessions to ensure that they are not 'treading water' or becoming bored.

What about Key Stage 2?

By the time children reach KS2, there is an expectation that their phonic knowledge should be reasonably secure. Phonics teaching is 'time limited' in terms of learning to read and the 'limit' for most children should be the end of Year 2. According to the 'simple' view, there should be an increasing shift in Year 3 to a focus on comprehension. However, there will always be children who are still struggling and they may still need the kind of phonic teaching described above. Schools will provide Wave 2 interventions (see Chapter 8) for those who need more practice at phonics whilst for some children their individual needs will be more complex and will require specialised support (see Chapters 8 and 9). In KS2 children must begin to build on their phonic knowledge and skills by addressing more complex areas of spelling, including morphology and etymology. To find out more about this take a look at strand 6 in the PNS Framework, 'word structure and spelling'.

CONCLUSION

This chapter has shown that there has been a seismic shift in the landscape of teaching children to read. The PNS, through implementing Rose's recommendations, has delivered a prescription of content and pedagogy which necessitates teachers developing a secure understanding and knowledge of phonics in order to teach it well. However, we should not forget the children with their diverse needs in all this. We need to remember that in the EYFS, spoken language is still undergoing significant development, not least in the acquisition of speech sounds themselves. Children are also continuing to gain control over the articulation and pronunciation of these sounds. The PNS does recognise the importance of phonological awareness, speaking and listening and that phonics must be taught within a 'language rich' curriculum. This all adds up to a bold enterprise, and the proof of its success will be in the raising of standards, which has to be in everyone's interests, especially those of the children.

GLOSSARY OF TERMS

ALLITERATION: words in a phrase or sentence which begin with the same sound, e.g. 'Peter Piper picked a peck of pickled peppers'.

ANALYTIC PHONICS: an approach to the teaching of phonics which works by analysing chunks of words and encouraging pattern detection across words.

BLEND (verb): the process of merging phonemes together to decode a word. BLEND (noun) is sometimes used to refer to a 'cluster' of sounds which run together, e.g. 'br' ('bread') or 'spl' ('split'). See also SEGMENT.

CLUSTER: sounds that run together. See examples under BLEND (noun).

CONSONANTS: sounds which are produced when the speaker interrupts the air flow with lips, tongue or throat; the letters that usually occur at the beginnings and ends of syllables (all letters of the alphabet except for vowels; the letter 'y' can also function as a vowel as in 'ay', 'ey', 'oy').

CONSONANT DIGRAPH: two consonants which represent one phoneme, e.g. 'ch', 'gh', 'ph', 'sh', 'wh', 'gn'.

DIGRAPH: two letters representing one phoneme, e.g. 'ch', 'ai'. See CONSONANT DIGRAPH and VOWEL DIGRAPH.

DIPHTHONG: two vowel sounds which combine together to make a new sound within a syllable. The mouth changes position during the sounding process, e.g. 'cow', 'oil', 'they', 'toy', 'out', 'few' ('w' functions as a vowel).

DOUBLED CONSONANTS: two identical consonants which make the sound of one consonant, e.g. 'bb', 'dd'.

GRAPHEME: the smallest unit of sound represented as a written symbol. The twenty-six letters of the alphabet are graphemes and so are groups of letters which emerge as one sound, e.g. 'ow' as in 'hollow'.

GRAPHIC KNOWLEDGE: knowledge which draws from visual cues; relates to recognising whole words, common letter patterns and parts of words such as prefixes and suffixes.

LONG VOWEL SOUNDS: vowel sounds in the English language that are also the names of the alphabet letters, 'A', 'E', 'I', 'O', 'U'. Whilst there are other long vowel sounds, for instance the 'oo' in 'hoot', this definition is useful because it distinguishes long vowel sounds from short vowel sounds. (Note that vowel length can be influenced by dialect and stress within a word.)

MONOSYLLABIC: refers to a word consisting of one syllable, e.g. 'bun'.

ONSET AND RIME: 'onset' is the consonant or cluster of consonants at the beginning of a word or syllable which precede the vowel, e.g. str(-ing). 'Rime' is the rest of the word or syllable, including the vowel, which enables the word to rhyme with other words, e.g. (str-)ing.

PHONEME: the smallest unit of sound that can be spoken or heard, such as 'b' in 'bat'. Meaning changes with the replacement of the phoneme, e.g. 'cat' or 'bag'. Over forty-four vowel and consonant phonemes have been identified in English. PHONEMIC AWARENESS is the ability to detect such phoneme distinctions.

PHONETICS: the study of speech sounds, e.g. how they are produced in the mouth and how they are heard by the ear.

PHONIC KNOWLEDGE: 'the skills of segmentation and blending, knowledge of the alphabetic code and understanding of the principles which underpin how the code is used in reading and spelling' (DfEE, 1999b).

PHONOLOGICAL AWARENESS: the ability to hear and detect difference in sounds; may operate at the level of syllables, onset and rime or phoneme.

POLYSYLLABIC: refers to a word that has more than one syllable, e.g. 'caterpillar'.

PREFIX: an affix at the beginning of a word, e.g. '**dis**appear' or '**un**pleasant'.

REVERSIBLE PROCESSES: see SEGMENT

SEGMENT (verb): hearing and isolating the individual phonemes in a word. When a child spells a word she has to select the appropriate grapheme for each phoneme she detects. Note that when a child BLENDS she has the word in front of her and decodes it phoneme by phoneme whereas when she SEGMENTS, it is in her head and she represents it phoneme by phoneme. This is what is meant by reversible processes.

SHORT VOWEL SOUNDS: the sound qualities of the vowels in such words as 'bag', 'beg', 'big', 'bog', bug'. Where a word has a short vowel the final consonant needs to be doubled when you add suffixes such as '-ing,' '-er' and '-ed' as in the words 'begging', 'bigger' and 'bugged'. (Note that vowel length can be influenced by dialect and stress within a word.)

SILENT LETTERS: letters used in the spelling of a word which do not have a sound in the word; these can occur at the beginning, middle or end of words, e.g. 'thought', 'knock', 'thumb' and 'psalm'; 'e' is frequently silent at the end of words, e.g. 'rose', 'made', where it often signals a long vowel sound for the preceding vowel.

SPLIT DIGRAPH: a vowel digraph (e.g. 'ie', 'oe') when it is separated by a consonant and retains its sound ('ie' – 'tie'/'time'; 'pie'/'pile'; 'oe' – 'toe'/'tone'; 'hoe'/'home'). (This convention used to be described by the 'magic e' rule, where the children were told that the vowel at the end of the word made the preceding vowel 'say' its name.)

SUFFIX: an affix at the end of a word, e.g. 'count**ed**' and 'help**ful**'.

SYLLABLE: a rhythmic segment of a word, spoken or written, which is composed of a vowel alone (as in '**a**way'), or a combination of vowel(s) plus consonant(s) or of consonant(s) plus vowel(s).

SYNTHETIC PHONICS: an approach to the teaching of phonics which works by isolating the phonemes in a word. The phonemes are then blended together in sequence to decode the word.

VOWELS: sounds which are produced with no, or relatively little, interruption to the air flow from lips, tongue or throat movement; letters that usually occur in the middle of syllables ('a', 'e', 'i', 'o', 'u'. The letter 'y' can also function as a vowel, as in 'ay', 'ey', 'oy').

VOWEL DIGRAPH: a combination of two vowels that represent a single sound. Examples of vowel digraphs include 'ai', 'ay', 'ee', 'ie', 'oa', 'au'.

Further reading and website

Cook, M. (ed.) (2002) *Perspectives on the Teaching and Learning of Phonics.* Royston: UKRA.

Goswami, U. and Bryant, P. (1990) *Phonological Skills and Learning to Read.* Hove: Lawrence Erlbaum.

Johnston, R. and Watson, J. (2007) *Teaching Synthetic Phonics.* Exeter: Learning Matters.

Lewis, M. and Ellis, S. (eds) (2006) *Phonics: Practice, Research and Policy.* London: UKLA/PCP.

Muter, V. (2003) *Early Reading Development and Dyslexia.* London: Whurr.

www.whichphonics.co.uk

Chapter 4

The Reading Journey

Alison Kelly and Kimberly Safford

In this chapter we explore the reading journey that children make from their very earliest explorations into language and literacy through to becoming fluent and experienced readers. Because we know that children learn and develop in different ways, what we describe here are typical, but not exclusive, characteristics of children moving along the pathway. Some children will find this a more difficult journey than others and you will find much to help you about supporting these children in Chapters 8 and 9.

EARLY READING

Research about very young children's moves into reading and writing offers a complex picture of what it is to become a reader. Their early experiences of books, their talk and their play all lead children into understandings about both the big shapes and the smaller units of reading.

It is many years now since a New Zealand researcher, Don Holdaway (1979), looked carefully at the interplay between text, adult and child in bedtime story routines and revealed the ways in which these routines set the child up for literacy. His insights are still relevant today: as young children are read to, they learn about books, about their structure, their characters, their language, their emotional power and the way a story keeps going. Above all, they learn about the enjoyment and intimacy that come from the sharing of a book. Nearly thirty years later, the success of the government-funded *Bookstart* project is testimony to the seriousness with which such research has been taken. As the homepage of *Bookstart*'s website says, the intention of the project is to instil in every child 'a lifelong love of books'. To this end, packs of books are available for children at different ages (see Chapter 5 for more about *Bookstart*).

Another important contribution from Holdaway was based on his research into what he called 'reading-like behaviour' in very young children. He noted how children engaged physically with the act of reading: holding the book, turning the pages and putting on a special 'story' voice. His transcripts of retellings of favourite texts by children as young as two show how they are already grasping the big shapes of reading. These young readers confidently retell the stories using book language and they hold the overall shape of the narrative. They use the illustrations and their recall of earlier readings by adults to arrive at an approximation of the text. They may not be able to decode a single word and, in some cases, they may not even realise that the black marks tell the reader what to say, but some of the conditions for becoming a reader have been laid down.

With the rapid technological developments of the last decades children are experiencing what Millard describes as 'globalised, multimodal literacy encounters in the home' (Millard, 2006:234) and these add a new dimension to early forms of reading-like behaviour. Clare Kelly's work in a nursery school in east London provides revealing insights about the learning offered by computer games and videos. Her observations of the children at home and school showed how a deep interest in media technology played a very important role in their learning about literacy. She describes how four-year-old Jamie loves to sit at the home computer next to his grandmother while he expertly navigates his way round PlayStation games. She makes the point that 'These games involved Jamie in quite sophisticated manoeuvres as he makes predictions, hypothesises and interprets different symbolic systems, while engaged in reading both visual images and print' (Kelly, 2004:71). Kelly goes on to explain that these story-based games are teaching him about narrative and that the encouraging and supportive presence of his grandmother suggests that 'parallels can be drawn with the warmth, pleasure and security that can be experienced by young children when sharing books with adults' (in Gregory *et al.*, 2004:71).

Note how these experiences are rooted in children's play: children who have had good experience of play, particularly make-believe play, seem to find the entry into reading relatively straightforward (see Clark, 1976). In his fascinating chapter 'The prehistory of written language', Vygotsky (1978) illuminated ways in which children's play is a precursor of the kind of cognition needed in order to enter the world of print. Both reading and writing involve understanding the symbolic functions of written language – that the print represents a myriad of different meanings. Children have already embarked on this complex journey of understanding in their acquisition of language itself, the medium through which we represent experience. In their play, children characteristically make an object stand for something else; in Vygotsky's words, 'a piece of wood begins to be a doll and a stick becomes a horse' (1978:97). Such 'first order symbolism', as Vygotsky calls it, lays the foundations for the 'second order symbolism' that understanding written language involves: the written word 'doll' stands for the spoken word, which, in its turn, stands for the doll itself. So, thinking about all the different forms of children's symbolising, we can see that entering a pretend cave created by a sheet thrown over a table or sailing a make-believe boat manufactured from a cardboard box with a pillowcase sail is not very different from entering the imaginary world of *Can't You Sleep, Little Bear?* (Martin Waddell and Barbara Firth) or *Where the Wild Things Are* (Maurice Sendak).

There are other kinds of playfulness to be considered. Ferguson offers powerful evidence about play that she characterises as 'social reading play'. In this short extract, a group of children are delighting in their speculation about what the gingerbread man will get up to next:

Child 1: He'd slide down the swing!

Child 2: And he might push and when he goes fast he might get up and go fast … and then he might fall down [LAUGHS] and he'll bang himself like that [BANGING AND CRASHING SOUNDS]

Child 3: And then he [BANG] … like that and then he would turn into crumbs! [GENERAL LAUGHTER]

(Ferguson, 2002:30)

Ferguson's point is that these children are playing, both physically and cognitively, with the text in ways that are clearly hugely enjoyable but are also very sophisticated. They are, in effect, moving between two worlds – that of the story and beyond. The gingerbread man has a fictional reality but the actual reality is that he is only a biscuit. Ferguson's work is also a reminder of the centrality of children's talk in their early learning, something that the *Rose Report* also highlights.

Playfulness is also a feature of children's drawing, another milestone on the early reader's journey into reading. Tom, aged four, hugely enjoyed hearing the story *Traction Man is Here* (Grey) read to him over and over again. Figure 4.1 shows his action-packed drawing of one particularly eventful scene from the book where Traction Man (whose adventures have caused him to lose most of his outfit!) rescues some dolls who have been viciously buried by the evil Doctor Spade.

As he draws, Tom points to the figure in the top right of the picture, muttering to himself 'Traction man in his special knickers. He's going to save the dollies'. It is as if the 'pause' button has been pressed on the action. Tom is engaged in the discovery that he can draw 'not only objects but also action' (Barrs, 1988:115).

Young children also play with language itself. Here are Ella and Emily, who are not quite three years old, at the Play-Doh table. You need to read their dialogue out loud in order to appreciate the energy, pace and rhythm of the interchanges.

Ella:	My mummy says that I am her little princess
Emily:	My gran says that I'm her carrot top
Ella:	You can't wear a carrot, you have a stripey top on
Emily:	No, she calls me carrot top because my hair is red
Ella:	But your hair isn't red, it's not carrot either
Emily:	What colour is my hair then?
Ella:	I know, it's like a penny, isn't it?
Emily:	No, it's like a carrot
Emily:	OK, Ella bella wella
Ella:	OK, penny carrot
Emily:	OK, Ella bella wella
Ella:	OK, penny carrot silly billy
Emily:	Ella bella wella annabella
Ella:	Penny carrot silly billy Emily
Emily:	Ella bella wella silly billy princess annabella

(Robson, 2006:113)

Most importantly, this verbal play is triggered by their names. Young children are fascinated by their names and they provide a rich site for playfulness. Vellender (1989) reported what a potent force for learning four-year-old Katrina's name was: 'Gotrina, Matrina, Natrina' she chanted, over and over again. Language play like this sharpens children's phonological awareness and in Chapter 3 we elucidated the importance of this in relation to children's ability to use phonics. Vellender also observed the children making early visual (or graphic) connections: for example, Katrina spotted 'ice' in 'Alice'. This area of playfulness is priming children for the skills they need for later word recognition. Indeed, the phonic progression laid down by the *Primary National Strategy* (PNS) outlines a first phase that is rooted in children's speaking and listening. The expectation is that through their experiences of rhyme, role-play and song, children will develop the phonological awareness needed to underpin their learning about grapheme–phoneme (letter–sound) correspondences (DfES, 2007b).

Figure 4.1 Tom's Traction Man drawing

Children are also exploring reading through their early writing attempts. They see adults making marks on paper for all sorts of readers and purposes and will imitate these in their play. They will also make marks for pleasure and, from early on, we see a clear distinction in their efforts between drawing and writing. What these early marks show us is the attention young children pay to what written language looks like, to the letters and words, that are going to be all so important as they move to decoding in their own reading. Uta Frith (1985) shows us how intertwined early learning about decoding (for reading) and encoding (for writing) are. She shows children moving from an initial 'logographic' stage (in which whole words are recognised) to an 'alphabetic' stage where they attend to letters and sounds. What is interesting is that the logographic stage is powered by children's early reading attempts but it is early writing attempts that develop children's awareness of phonemes and this comes with alphabetic knowledge. Bringing logographic and alphabetic knowledge together contributes to the third stage (the orthographic), which is driven by reading again. Let us see what this looks like in practice. A two-year-old child has had a story read to her many times in which the characters play 'hide-and-seek'. She can say 'hide-and-seek' when it comes up on the page because its form is distinctive and she knows to look at the bottom of the page where it usually occurs. Eventually she can find it wherever it occurs on the page and even in other books. This is the logographic stage. Lots of paper and pencil play, singing of the alphabet and interest in the letters of her name eventually move our learner into first writing, and her attempt at writing 'hide-and-seek' shows how much she knows – 'hd ad sk'. This marks her moves into the alphabetic stage. Later, given a rich literacy environment that provides evidence about big shapes and smaller units, her writing will gradually approach conventional orthography and she will use this knowledge to help her decode unknown words in her reading. She is safely on the orthographic journey. Skilled reading needs orthographic processing for effective decoding and encoding and, as Svensson shows in Chapter 9, less skilled readers may find it difficult to progress beyond the first two stages, particularly the alphabetic one.

In the *Rose Report*, much is made of the importance of 'pre-reading activities' which ensure children are surrounded by print in many different forms. This print environment is just part of the 'broad and language-rich curriculum' (DfES, 2006a:29) that is expected for the *Early Years Foundation Stage* (EYFS). Such a curriculum also needs to include plentiful opportunities for play, listening to stories and non-fiction, songs and rhymes.

We have seen how children take hold of 'fragments of the complex literacy jigsaw' (Clay, 1998:2) and that their routes into literacy vary. Early reading and writing are about far more than just decoding and encoding; play, talk and drawing are all significant forms of symbolising that help to shape the young reader's route into reading. How does this understanding help you think about practice in the EYFS? What kinds of provision and opportunities for symbolising and for reading like-behaviour would you hope to see? How can teachers develop children's phonological awareness through song, role-play, rhyme and story? Subsequent chapters will help with your book choices and development of appropriate classroom routines.

We must also remember that, as the discussion of literacy in Chapter 1 explained, and as Malik's profile below shows, the journey into reading and writing is culturally specific. Researchers such as Eve Gregory (Gregory and Williams, 2000), Hilary Minns (1990) and

Shirley Brice Heath (1983) have shown us that literacy practices vary in different communities and cultures. For instance, in some communities, oral traditions are stronger than those of reading aloud. A child's 'approximation' of the text, which is what we see in reading-like behaviour, may cause anxiety in some families that the child is 'getting it wrong'. Perhaps there is an expectation that the child does not interrupt a reading or talk about how the book relates to her own life. In our classrooms, the way we go about the teaching of reading could thus seem very strange compared with home practices and you will need to take that into account, perhaps talking with parents (see sections on working with parents in Chapters 5 and 8).

FROM INEXPERIENCED TO EXPERIENCED READER

So far, our focus has been on early readers at the beginning of the reading journey. We will now take a look at what the next steps look like as children become competent and reflective readers and what you might expect to see at different stages in a child's reading development.

Let's start with a fluent and articulate reader: Malik. His reading profile (Figure 4.2) gives a fascinating self-portrait of a Year 6 pupil.

Other thought bubbles that Malik included in his profile said: 'My favourite classic is *Kidnapped* by Robert Louis Stevenson'; 'I like reading Russian folk tales', 'I read in two other languages beside English … Hebrew and Arabic' and 'I read to put me to sleep and to stop me getting bored'.

If you were Malik's teacher what would all of this reveal to you about:

- the range of reading he engages with;
- his pleasure in reading;
- his understanding of the purposes of reading;
- the role of his language and culture in relation to his reading;
- how he perceives himself as a reader and a learner?

What are the lessons to be learnt from studying such a profile? As an experienced reader, Malik is skilfully orchestrating a range of reading strategies and is able to reflect on his reading in critical and discerning ways. How did Malik become such a fluent and enthusiastic reader?

The Primary Language Record (Barrs *et al.*, 1988) offers a reading scale (Table 4.1) which charts how a child's experience develops across the years. Where would you place Malik on this scale?

You will see right away that the scale shows children moving from 'inexperience' to 'experience' as readers, and these terms are much more useful in evaluating children as readers than terms 'low ability' and 'high ability'. Children whom we label 'less able' may simply lack experiences of reading, and here your role as the teacher is significant: how will you organise and provide a range of experiences to enable children to practise and develop their reading skills at big shape and smaller unit levels?

The CLPE scale is useful in observing children's behaviour as readers and their attitudes to reading as well as their reading strategies, and it is important as a teacher to take note of all of these areas of development. These broad descriptors are not linear but are recursive. You may observe children sometimes showing behaviours typical of

**Figure 4.2 Profile of a fluent Key Stage 2 reader
(contributed by PGCE student on her final Block School Experience.
Idea taken from Boyd, in Bain *et al.*, 1992)**

more than one level of experience. Older readers may demonstrate the behaviours of inexperienced readers as they move to more demanding types of reading; younger children may demonstrate behaviours of experienced readers as they become confident, independent and reflective in their reading choices. Remember that children will take many different pathways to becoming readers, and that consistent access to enjoyable and powerful reading experiences will underpin their development.

Consider the factors that cause us to assess a child as being an 'able' or experienced reader. These may begin with observations that a child takes pleasure in reading and

Table 4.1 Experience as a reader across the curriculum (Barrs *et al.*, 1988:27)

INEXPERIENCED

Inexperienced reader	Experience as a reader has been limited. Generally chooses to read very easy and familiar text where illustrations play an important part. Has difficulty with any unfamiliar material and yet may be able to read own dictated text confidently. Needs a great deal of support with the reading demands of the classroom. Over-dependent on one strategy when reading aloud; often reads word by word. Rarely chooses to read for pleasure.
Less experienced reader	Developing fluency as a reader and reading certain kinds of materal with confidence. Usually chooses short books with simple narrative shapes and with illustrations and may read these silently; often rereads favourite books. Reading for pleasure often includes comics and magazines. Needs help with the reading demands of the classroom and especially with using reference and information books.
Moderately experienced reader	A confident reader who feels at home with books. Generally reads silently and is developing stamina as a reader. Is able to read for longer periods and cope with more demanding texts, including children's novels. Willing to reflect on reading and often uses reading in own learning. Selects books independently and can use information books and materials for straightforward reference purposes, but still needs help with unfamiliar material, particularly non-narrative prose.
Experienced reader	A self-motivated, confident and experienced reader who may be pursuing particular interests through reading. Capable of tackling some demanding texts and can cope well with the reading of the curriculum. Reads thoughtfully and appreciates shades of meaning. Capable of locating and drawing on a variety of sources in order to research a topic independently.
Exceptionally experienced reader	An enthusiastic and reflective reader who has strong established tastes in fiction and/or non-fiction. Enjoys pursuing own reading interests independently. Can handle a wide range and variety of texts, including some adult material. Recognises that different kinds of texts require different styles of reading. Able to evaluate evidence drawn from a variety of information sources. Is developing critical awareness as a reader.

EXPERIENCED

therefore feels confident in her or his reading choices. Confidence will develop a child's independence in choosing interesting and sometimes challenging texts. Through a wide variety of reading, a child develops a range of strategies involving word recognition, grammatical knowledge and language comprehension in order to decode unknown words and interpret the meaning of unfamiliar phrases or contexts. Wider reading also develops a child's stamina for reading and the ability to become a reflective, critical reader.

You will note that one of the characteristics of an inexperienced reader is an overdependence on one strategy, and as a teacher you will be able to observe what strategies children employ when they read, particularly when they tackle an unknown text. How does the child approach the text – from the 'bottom up' or from the 'top down'? How does she approach unknown words – decoding phoneme by phoneme or recognising larger chunks within words? Does she skip over unknown words, read ahead and read back, trying to make meaning of the whole sentence or phrase? What other cues is she using?

As inexperienced readers attend to phonemes and words, they may lose the overall meaning of what they read. Conversely, inexperienced readers may create meaning from picture and contextual cues but miss out on what is actually conveyed in print. Experienced readers learn to balance both of these approaches to reading by moving between big shapes and small units – but this skill takes time to develop. As a teacher, it is your role to model both big shape and smaller unit reading strategies to children, and to encourage children to use a range of reading strategies. For a more detailed exploration of how children approach texts, see Chapter 7 on miscue analysis.

At the beginning of the reading journey more attention is paid to word recognition processes, but as children become increasingly proficient in decoding, the emphasis shifts to language comprehension. However, we need to be cautious about the implication that for very young children teaching reading is just about decoding and word recognition. In their evaluation of the *Bookstart* project, Collins and Svensson (in press) found evidence of competent young readers whose responses to books had all the hallmarks of more experienced, critical reading – even though they were not yet decoding all the print accurately. For instance, the researchers read *Leon and Bob* (James), a multi-layered story about a boy and his imaginary friend, to five-year-olds. At no point in the story is the reader explicitly told that Bob is not real; this is left to be inferred. Children's responses to this challenge included: 'There are two Bobs. Maybe he's thinking he's next door. Maybe he has different hair but the same name,' and 'He's a little boy like him. He thinks he's with him.' The point is that both word recognition and language comprehension processes are important but the emphasis will shift with experience. We would expect to nourish children's responses to literature from an early age just as older, developing readers will continue to need support in orchestrating their reading strategies.

What is quite clear from research (e.g. Twist *et al.*, 2003) is that simply cracking the code does not necessarily guarantee the kind of secure progress that the CLPE reading scale suggests. As Safford showed in Chapter 2, many other factors may come into play which affect children's dispositions towards reading. So it is vitally important to keep children reading through lively and imaginative teaching which enables them to comprehend language. What do we mean by language comprehension? You may remember 'comprehension' exercises at school which required you to read a passage and answer questions. The reality of such exercises was that no comprehension (understanding) was required at all as all you had to do was retrieve the appropriate words from the passage that matched the wording of the question. With the *National Curriculum* came a richer view of comprehension: 'Pupils should be encouraged to respond to all forms of literature in ways which they find pleasurable, and hence which are likely to promote understanding. Their response should be stimulated through a range of active strategies' (Cox, 1991:84).

What was significant about Cox's recommendations for literature teaching was his emphasis on pleasurable, active engagements with texts. Drawing from more recent research, the PNS has focused even more closely on comprehension as an interactive, meaning-making process. It identifies the following reading strategies and behaviours that comprise the process:

- understanding the text;
- making connections with existing knowledge;
- reflecting upon responses;
- engaging with the text;
- critically evaluating the text;
- monitoring own understanding;
- making decisions about which strategies will help clarify understanding.

(DfES, 2005b:2)

In Chapter 5 you will find many examples of the kinds of active teaching strategies that can promote full and rich comprehension of texts.

Finally, there are important and mutually supportive connections to be made between children's reading and writing. Barrs and Cork (2001) have shown that there are clear links between what children read and how they write. Their research project *The Reader in the Writer* showed how extended work (including reading aloud, drama and writing in role), derived from high-quality literature, positively influenced children's writing development and their attainment. For instance, after a year of working extensively with carefully chosen texts, children developed a more sophisticated awareness of their reader's needs as they made more sustained use of complex writing structures in their own writing. This reminds us that reading and writing go hand in hand, through decoding and encoding but also through comprehension and composition.

Further reading and website

DfES (2005b) *Understanding Reading Comprehension* (Flyers 1–3). London: DfES.
Minns, H. (1999) 'Pathways into reading: Five young people and the development of the English curriculum', *Pedagogy, Culture and Society* (7) 3, 493–505.
OFSTED (2004) *Reading for Purpose and Pleasure*. London: OFSTED.
Whitehead, M. (2004) *Language and Literacy in the Early Years* (3rd edn). London: Sage.
Bookstart: http://www.bookstart.co.uk/

Chapter 5

Reading Routines

Anne Washtell

INTRODUCTION

In order to learn to read, children require instruction. This is best achieved through a set of recognisable and well understood routines. By 'routines', we mean the regular activities and organisational strategies that teachers employ to teach reading. Some routines, such as storytime in the *Early Years Foundation Stage* (EYFS), have stood the test of time. In contrast, other longstanding routines such as individual children reading aloud one-to-one with the teacher or other adults, although still clearly in evidence in the EYFS, have been reworked within newer routines, in this case as part of guided reading in Key Stages 1 and 2 (KS1 and KS2). As priorities have changed in terms of organisation and emphasis in the teaching of reading, some routines have become less in evidence, one of these being whole-class quiet reading.

Before the advent of the *National Literacy Strategy* (NLS) in 1998, these and other routines, such as group reading or paired reading, provided a way of structuring a programme for the teaching of reading, whatever the age range and whatever the particular constraints or possibilities of the classroom setting. Significantly, an inspection report on the teaching of reading in a number of inner-city primary schools noted that 'the best planning ensured that there were regular sessions for individual, group and whole-class work with clearly defined objectives and approaches' (OFSTED, 1996:23). The implementation of the NLS brought with it the notion of a dedicated, daily, objective-led literacy hour, which had within it specific timed phases. Although it was not statutory, many schools chose to adopt the structure of the literacy hour, which has at its core two key reading routines, shared and guided reading, which we will discuss later.

THE READING CURRICULUM

The routines included in this chapter take account of children's journeys from being dependent readers to independent ones. They recognise that learning to read is a developmental process which depends on being taught specific skills, strategies and knowledge. However, children also need to apply these in order to gain ownership and control over them. We start off by providing a great deal of demonstration and support (shared reading) whilst giving children regular practice at trying things out for themselves but with us still working closely with them (guided work). In addition, they must also have a chance to read independently, and this should happen regularly whatever their age. As we shall see, independent work can take place in different contexts such as individually, in a group or in pairs. Getting lots of practice is essential and, for this reason, we also want to involve parents and the wider community.

Underpinning all this will be a rich experience of being read to aloud by adults and also working with texts over time in order to deepen responses and understanding. The importance of spoken language, the use of questioning and setting our work within a language-rich curriculum are other expectations. Furthermore, with our early readers there will be a discrete part of each day dedicated to the systematic teaching and learning of phonics (see Chapter 3). The *Rose Report* (DfES, 2006a) has made very specific recommendations that are now part of the renewed *Primary National Strategy* (PNS, DfES, 2006b). Good planning will be essential, as we want children to read not just in timetabled English or literacy slots, but also across the curriculum. In this way we can help them become readers in the fullest sense of the word.

PLANNING AND ORGANISING FOR READING

At the time of writing, the original NLS has been replaced by the renewed PNS Framework (DfES, 2006b). Nearly ten years on, the close adherence to the literacy hour as originally conceived has become less rigid. For some time, KS2 teachers in particular have taken the elements of the hour and reassembled them across the week in order to organise and sustain work in a more coherent and appropriate way for the age group. In the PNS the need for flexibility is further articulated in order to maximise meeting the needs of both learners and practitioners. Six key principles are put forward to help achieve this flexibility (DfES, 2006b:9). It is important to familiarise yourself with these as they make important points about timing, planning for progression and communicating the purpose of planned activity to the pupils. You also need to think through how you will plan and manage the key reading routines within this more flexible structure.

In addition, you should decide which routines should feature in the wider weekly timetable beyond the designated daily literacy teaching slots. These might include the teacher reading aloud, paired reading, 'buddy' reading and independent reading, which could, on occasion, take the form of silent reading. Be mindful though that schools may have made decisions at policy level in relation to their targets in terms of which reading routines are prioritised, and may also have expectations in terms of the frequency of their use. Some of these routines such as buddy reading may be organised at a whole-school level and will occur at regular intervals. Consider, also, how these other routines can feed into, support and extend your core English teaching.

Alongside daily planning for literacy, planning for reading must also be undertaken in relation to other curriculum areas. The PNS explains that children need to be able to apply skills learnt in literacy lessons effectively in other subjects. In history, for instance, you might plan for children to spend time reading and extracting information from copies of census material and other primary sources; in science, you could plan for them to read the instructions that come with a battery. In both these examples, you would need to plan to demonstrate briefly or revisit the specific reading skills needed to complete the tasks successfully. This might be done through shared reading, using short extracts from the actual texts or from similar texts. In the history example, you might organise the children into reading pairs in order to hone further the skills of skimming and scanning.

As well as planning issues, you will also need to think about how best to organise the different reading routines, whether they are to be carried out in whole-class, group, pair or one-to-one settings. Consideration must also be given to the age phase in which you use them. We will start by discussing the two key routines of shared and guided reading. We will then go on to consider other important reading routines that may be planned for outside designated literacy time and which might have to jostle with other curriculum demands during the rest of the day. As we shall argue below, all of these routines can make significant contributions to the teaching of reading whether they are prioritised by the PNS or not.

SHARED READING

What is shared reading?

Shared reading is a whole-class, collaborative, teacher-led routine. Typically, the class and teacher will work with the same enlarged text, which may take the form of a big book or could be presented via the interactive whiteboard. Sometimes the text will be in A1 poster form; for example, a poetry or recipe card. The overhead projector can, on occasion, also provide flexibility. It is not uncommon in KS2 classrooms for children also to be sharing in pairs smaller copies of the enlarged text. This may be done so that they can highlight or annotate the text as the shared reading session proceeds.

When first devised, this routine was more commonly found in the early years of schooling, but is now well established throughout the primary age phase, as it forms a central plank of the literacy hour. The routine was developed in New Zealand in the 1970s by teachers working with Don Holdaway (1979). Holdaway had looked at the benefits of the bedtime story in setting children up for literacy, and wanted to reinvent this homely routine for the larger classroom context. This gave rise to the enlarged text, or big book, which allows a group of children to have the same intimate access to the book as is possible at home. Using enlarged texts that they had made themselves, the teachers working with Holdaway would spend initial sessions introducing and enjoying the story as a whole with the children. In this way, they developed what came to be known as 'shared book experience.' He talks, for instance, about the importance of pointing and describes masking devices that the teachers devised in order to focus attention on particular aspects of print.

What is the value of shared reading?

Shared reading provides children with experiences and activities that they cannot readily do alone but, through teacher modelling or demonstration and the collaboration of their peers, they can begin to move their understanding forward and gain increasing independence. Vygotsky's (1978) famous theory of the 'zone of proximal development' (zpd) provides a useful rationale to help us understand the underlying strength of shared reading as a teaching and learning tool. Not only does he draw attention to the collaborative and social nature of learning, but he also emphasises the role of the adult or more capable peers in enabling children to move out of their comfort zones as learners, so that they will try things that are currently beyond their stage of development. So, by placing children in their zpds, although not yet ready to take on a specific skill or task independently, learning will take place. This is summed up in Vygotsky's much quoted phrase 'what the child can do in cooperation today, he can do alone tomorrow' (1978:87).

The benefits of the shared reading routine are many. It ensures that children are listening to a model of fluent reading as well as being provided with regular reading practice. Because it is led by the adult, it can be used to make any aspect of the reading process explicit, be it word recognition processes or language comprehension processes. By using a direct pedagogic approach (DfES, 2006b:11), the teacher can enable children to acquire new knowledge and skills. This is done by the careful modelling of effective strategies. It is particularly helpful for less confident readers and children who are in the early stages of speaking English as an Additional Language (EAL) as they can have a strong sense of involvement in the reading without feeling personally pressured. Through demonstration in the form of unambiguous, sequential teaching, discussion and collaboration, the children are being supported as they are introduced to new material, skills and strategies. Equally, the most able children can also be challenged through the skilful use of teacher questioning.

Shared reading in action: *Early Years Foundation Stage*

Shared reading sessions with very young children are likely to be relatively short and highly interactive. If the text is being introduced for the first time, it is likely that the children will predict what the story might be about as the adult leafs through the pages; they will listen to the first read through and then join in. There are some obvious advantages in this shared experience for both the teacher and the pupils. The sharing of a common text means that all children have the opportunity to get drawn into the experience and participate at their own level. By making direct links to examples in the text, the teacher can demonstrate explicit teaching points about the meaning of the text, early concepts about print or early decoding strategies.

With the youngest readers the teacher might make explicit the early concepts about print by using a finger or pointer to indicate where she starts reading, left-to-right directionality, spaces between words, the use of capital letters as well as punctuation. Some early readers may not yet have understood the distinction between words and pictures. By talking about these features, children are being provided with prerequisite knowledge which needs to be in place prior to the commencement of formal instruction as envisaged in the 'simple' view of reading (DfES, 2006b).

Shared reading is a highly interactive open routine, and for this reason key objectives need to be clearly identified prior to sessions in order to maintain a clear focus. In the following example, in a Reception class, the focus is on rhyme. The class have been reading from a big book with their teacher and paused at the word 'hedgehog.'

Teacher	*(1):*	Hedgehog, look, it says 'hog'. 'Hog' and 'bog'; they sound the same.
Children	*(2):*	Hog and bog, hog and bog …
Teacher	*(3):*	What do we say when words sound the same?
Children	*(4):*	Hog, bog, rog, log … [said at same time as teacher's question].
Teacher	*(5):*	You say 'rhyme', don't you?
Child A	*(6):*	'Hedgehog' begins with 'h'.
Teacher	*(7):*	Well done, and 'h' and 'og' together spell 'hog'.
Child B	*(8):*	… [indistinct] rarren, gallen …
Teacher	*(9):*	That's right, they rhyme with my name [which is Allen].

Child B (10):   … randy, gandy …
        (11):   Patrick, ratrick [Child B is called Patrick].
Child C (12):   Ratrick, rucksack.
Teacher (13):   Words are fun, aren't they? You can do all sorts of things with them.

In this short extract, the teacher makes several significant teaching points, particularly in relation to her efforts to raise the children's phonological awareness. For instance, in the exchange about 'rhyme' (3–5) she is giving the children a piece of metalanguage (language about language) that they need for talking about their reading. She picks up on the child's spontaneous comment (6) and draws the class's attention to the way letters combine to make words, in this case dividing the word 'hog' into its onset ('h-') and rime ('-og') (7). She responds to the children's enjoyment of the sounds and rhymes and, importantly, links their word play with names (9). Her final comment (13) is one of the many messages she gives these young children about the enjoyment to be had from reading. Bearing in mind Rose's recent endorsement of synthetic phonics, the teacher could be criticised for blending 'hog' at the level of onset and rime rather than that of the phoneme 'h/o/g.' On the other hand, she recognises through her encouragement of word play the significant role that phonological awareness plays in laying the foundations for later formal phonic instruction. Saturating the whole experience in spoken language through high-quality interactions provides a telling example of Bruner's scaffolding (Wood *et al.*, 1976).

Shared reading in the *Primary National Strategy*

When first introduced as a key routine in the NLS, shared reading was recognised as a vehicle for focusing on several different levels of knowledge through planning at text, sentence and word level. In the PNS, when planning for shared reading in the teaching of early reading, account must be taken of the 'simple' view of reading. It is intended that there should be a much sharper distinction between planning for work that reinforces children's developing phonic knowledge and planning for the development of comprehension. Four specific functions of shared reading in the teaching of early reading are listed as follows:

- inducting children into the world of literature, meaning and response;
- providing rich opportunities for increasing children's stock of words and teaching early reading behaviours;
- serving as a vehicle for extending children's understanding of what is being read; that is, their language comprehension;
- providing opportunities to apply acquired decoding skills in context, reinforcing children's developing phonic knowledge and skills gained from discrete, daily phonic sessions.

(DfES, 2006c:58)

The implications of this are that before commencing a shared reading session, it is important to be clear about which dimension of reading is being addressed, so that relevant learning objectives are identified and an appropriate text selected to support effective teaching.

GUIDED READING

Guided reading is the counterpart to shared reading. It forms a link or bridge between the explicit teaching that characterises shared sessions and independent reading, which is the ultimate goal of reading instruction. When the routine was first introduced by the NLS, the intention was to replace the traditional routine of children reading individually to the teacher by 'carefully structured group activity' (DfEE, 1998:12). The idea behind this was to 'increase the time for sustained teaching'. In this routine, the children are organised by ability to be taught in small, rotating focus groups by the teacher or trained Teaching Assistant (TA), across the week. The length of sessions varies from school to school, but twenty minutes' duration is usual. In guided reading, there is a clear shift in emphasis towards independent work under-taken by the children, rather than the teacher modelling and demonstrating skills and processes for them. The teacher's role, as the name of the routine implies, shifts to that of being a very skilful guide: 'It gives a teacher and group of students the oppor-tunity to talk, read, and think their way purposefully through a text' (New Zealand Ministry of Education, 1997:89). Speaking and listening underpins a high-quality guided session as it provides the opportunity for children to articulate their growing knowledge and understanding about the reading process, as well as about the story or gist of the text.

Matching the book to the children's reading needs is very important in this routine, with texts being carefully selected in terms of levels of difficulty (see Chapter 6 for details on bookmatch and on choice of texts for guided reading). We should be aim-ing to choose texts at 'instructional level' (90 to 95 per cent accuracy rate when the children read them independently). The children in each ability group have individ-ual copies of the same graded text from which each child will read aloud, individually and independently, during each session. Planning and teaching in guided reading sessions will differ according to the Key Stage you are working in. It is worth remembering the emphases within the 'simple' view of reading: 'learning to read' in KS1 and the move to 'reading to learn' from Year 3 onwards. In other words, in KS1 there is likely to be a firm focus on the application of developing phonic knowledge, whereas in KS2 there will be an increasing shift to comprehension skills and knowl-edge. (For a more extended discussion on this point see 'Guided reading in the *Primary National Strategy*' on page 62.)

Structuring a guided reading session

Typically, a guided reading session follows this sequence:

Book introduction (adult led)

The adult leads this part of the session by stating the intended objectives and success criteria for the session, as well as introducing the text to be read. She will briefly dis-cuss significant features such as the title, the type of book and the illustrations in order to activate prior knowledge. New key words, names and unfamilar concepts will be identified and if necessary explained.

Strategy check (adult led)

Here the adult reviews specific reading strategies and skills that the children have been previously taught, perhaps in discrete phonics sessions (KS1). The children will be reminded to use these strategies when it is their turn to read aloud.

Independent reading (individual children)

In this part of the routine, the children individually and independently read all or part of the text at their own pace. This provides the teacher with the opportunity to monitor and assess the child's use of the previously identified and rehearsed reading strategies. The teacher will prompt where necessary and encourage a problem-solving approach, so that children's independence and stamina are fostered. Identification, encouragement and praise of the child's successful use of reading strategies should also be a feature during this part of the session.

Returning to text (adult led)

After having listened to all the children read, the teacher briefly discusses the text with the whole group to check for understanding. This may involve the teacher rereading sections of the book and engaging the children in discussion. She may then move on to praise successful problem-solving strategies. This praise will be accompanied by specific exemplification. Many teachers use phrases such as 'I liked the way you …'. In this way, they are making the mechanics of the skill explicit and thus furthering the children's metacognition (thinking about thinking). If necessary, the teacher will briefly reteach specific skills that were less successful or caused problems; for example, blending adjacent consonants in a word.

Response to the text (adult led)

In this phase, the children are encouraged to share their personal responses to the book, usually through a short discussion or some form of follow-up activity.

Next steps (adult led)

Finally, the teacher will return to the teaching objectives to recapitulate on what has been learnt as well as consolidate points or extend children's thinking. Next steps or targets are identified for the group, including those for independent reading and related tasks.

Guided reading in KS1 will have some discernible differences from guided reading sessions for older children. In KS1, it is common for a complete book to be read in a single lesson and, often, fresh texts will be introduced at each session. Children reading aloud will also be an important part of the guided session. Inevitably, the teacher will be focusing on the children's developing reading strategies and skills, particularly phonic knowledge. However, as we move up the age and/or ability range, longer texts will be introduced that may span several guided sessions. Indeed, at the top end of KS2, the children may well be working with novels over several weeks. We also have to bear in mind fluency: fluent readers read quickly and naturally want to read silently.

This may alter the character of a guided session for these children and for the teacher, who now has a different set of reading skills to consider. The children may come to a session having pre-prepared a chapter of a novel ready to discuss specific features. The discussion of new vocabulary and other language features, such as figurative language, will be significant with these more advanced groups of readers. An element of reading aloud will be maintained in order to work on phrasing and expression, as well as monitoring the decoding of more complex and unusual words. Sometimes, the title 'guided group' might be replaced by something that sounds a bit more sophisticated, such as 'literature circles', but the adult still has a clear role to play in these sessions.

Guided reading in the *Primary National Strategy*

The PNS (DfES, 2006c) reiterates the importance of children applying their recently learned skills in context. It also suggests some caution when judging the most appropriate point at which to introduce younger children to guided work: 'Children gain most from guided reading when they have already developed a sound understanding about how texts work, about the alphabetic code, and when they have considerable experience of listening to and talking about texts' (2006c:59). In relation to phonics, teachers need to be knowledgeable 'about the exact state of the child's phonic learning' (2006c:60). The role of robust assessment is emphasised in order to maximise the purpose and quality of teaching within guided sessions. It is recommended that when planning for guided sessions, teachers consider the four types of reader identified in the 'simple' view of reading:

- those who have good comprehension but poor word recognition skills;
- those who have good word recognition skills but poor comprehension;
- those who are weak in both of the above;
- those who are strong in both of the above.

(DfES, 2006a:60)

This pushes us to consider carefully the grouping and differing needs of children who fall into these four categories and the adjustments that we have to make to our planning prior to embarking on guided sessions in order to meet these needs. The idea is that children who have good comprehension but weak word recognition skills require phonic work to be strengthened through its application in guided sessions. Conversely, those with strength in word recognition skills but weakness in comprehension will need a focus on meaning. With the current emphasis, since the *Rose Report*, on early reading development, the very able and talented children, who fall into the fourth category of the above list, should not be overlooked. We need to consider what a guided session might be like for these children who need to be stretched and intellectually challenged. The following section on questioning will help you; see also Chapter 8 for more information about these gifted and talented children.

The role of talk and questioning

The teacher is responsible for developing children's thinking and understanding during guided reading, and talk is at the heart of this enterprise. However, the quality and type of talk that occurs are crucial, as is the balance between teacher and pupil talk during discussion. Alexander (2006) has identified several kinds of talk that teachers use in the classroom. These are rote, recitation, exposition, discussion and dialogue. Two of these, discussion and dialogue, are particularly useful in developing and advancing children's thinking. In discussion, children have a chance to try out ideas, shape them, alter them and pose their own questions. The role of teachers is to enable this to take place by positioning themselves within the discussion rather than overtly controlling it. Dialogue is characterised by working towards a shared understanding by using questions that build one upon another, cumulatively. It involves the teacher engaging in several exchanges with individuals, listening to their responses and then building on these with further questions in order to develop the child's thinking. Hobsbaum *et al.* (2006) define 'dialogic' talk as 'conversation with cognitive challenge' (2006:49). They argue that dialogic talk occurs only 'if there is evidence of a change in children's understanding' (2006:49). Changes in understanding happen when thinking is challenged. This kind of talk is powered by the skilled use of open-ended questions, with the children expected to justify or explain their views. Skilled questioning clearly contributes to children's developing comprehension. Some of Chambers' (1990) questions are designed to elicit children's reactions and understanding of what they have been reading. For instance, they can be questioned on what puzzled them in the book or on things that they really did not like. Were there any words or phrases that pleased them? Which character did they find most interesting? Do they know other children who would really like this book and what would they tell them about it to whet their appetites? The teacher will monitor the content of the child's responses, for example by seeking further clarification or justification and by asking supplementary, searching and challenging questions. We now need to turn to what is meant by comprehension.

Comprehension

As we saw in Chapter 4, comprehension is a multilayered and multifaceted business: it is about the relationship between the writer, the text and the reader. It is highly interactive and reciprocal in nature. The writer is working hard to influence the way we read, so that we get at the intended meaning of the text whilst we are bringing our own experiences and prior knowledge to the task in order to interpret the text. The PNS states that 'in formal terms, successful reading comprehension depends on the construction of a rich and elaborate mental model of the text that is read' (DfES, 2006c:66).

Bielby (1999) explains that we can think about reading in terms of 'learning to read' (the domain of KS1) and 'reading to learn' (KS2). However, he warns of the possible danger of an over-literal or rigid interpretation of this distinction: 'This over-simple distinction ignores the fact that children are still developing their processing skills throughout KS2, and that children at KS1 are not learning to read properly if they aren't at the same time understanding and learning from what they read' (Bielby, 1999:50–51). The implication here is that comprehension, meaning-making, is important at every stage of learning to read, but certainly as children move into KS2 the emphasis shifts even more strongly towards it. The diagrammatic representation of the 'simple' view of reading could at face value imply a sense of 'cut-off' and false separation between the key processes of reading: word recognition skills and comprehension. In fact, the PNS sees it like this: 'According to this view of reading,

reading comprehension is the product of word recognition skills and listening comprehension skills' (DfES, 2006c:61).

In reading comprehension, we draw on a complex range of linguistic knowledge. For example, we bring into play our knowledge of syntax, of lexical and grammatical cohesion as well as our word recognition skills and our growing word stock or vocabulary. The PNS (2006c:61–72) offers a complex and intricate explanation which stresses the role of listening comprehension (comprehending what you hear) and its relationship with reading comprehension. The paper emphasises that 'practitioners and teachers must encourage the development of oral language skills in order to safeguard children's reading comprehension' (2006c:61).

To engage in comprehension, then, we need to use our oral language resources as well as our general knowledge and prior knowledge and experiences of a wide range of texts. We also need to be able to use two skills: inference and deduction. Put very simply, inferences are made continuously as we read; in fact we may almost be unaware of the extent to which we use inference. Inference is often referred to as 'reading between the lines', which, although based on the text currently being read, will go beyond what is actually stated. On the other hand, deduction is about reasoning our way through the evidence presented in the text in order to reach a logical conclusion or viewpoint.

What kinds of questions might we use then in guided sessions (or indeed, in other reading routines)? We could use literal questions, one of whose main functions is to recall information and key content at a basic level. Teachers tend to use these at the opening of sessions to activate prior knowledge about texts and to check a basic level of understanding. They will be much more in evidence when working with less experienced readers. Typically, they will be closed, tightly focused and be used to recall precise details about content. For example, you might ask the children what Eric Carle's hungry caterpillar had to eat on Monday. However, in order to develop children's comprehension we need to draw on a much wider repertoire of questions as well.

Deductive questions

These require the reader to draw conclusions from the information and evidence provided in the text as a whole. For example: in Michael Morpurgo's *Wreck of the Zanzibar*, how is it that Laura eventually gets to row in the gig? How do you know this? Can you provide some evidence to back up your views?

Inferential questions

These will seek to get the reader to make the implicit explicit. In order to do this, readers need to draw on background knowledge and prior experience of similar texts. Whilst taking account of the information conveyed in the text, the reader needs to go beyond the text itself (read between the lines). For example: Laura's passionate and long-held desire to row in the gig gets sidelined eventually. Why do you think this is?

Evaluative questions

These ask the reader to be critical and to make judgements about the text under discussion. They may also require the reader to consider qualities of the authorship itself.

For example: how well did Morpurgo manage the 'diary within a diary' format of the novel?

Whilst working with the more challenging types of questions, children will be expected to provide justification in their responses. This demands that they seek evidence from the text itself and beyond. In this way, their ideas will be informed as well as leaving room for personal response, empathy and interpretation. They will learn to tolerate uncertainties, to value the opinions and viewpoints of others, as well as to develop the skill to reconsider and modify their 'reading' of characters, events and facts as a text unfolds. They will also discover that there can be multiple 'readings' of fictional and poetic texts.

Strategies to support and develop comprehension

The following strategies are summarised from a series of three PNS leaflets *Understanding Reading Comprehension* (DfES, 2005b). Some of the strategies are similar to those recommended for the first *National Curriculum* (NC) and reported on in Cox's book (Cox, 1991). Others owe their existence to the work of Lunzer *et al.* (1984) in the 1980s, who devised Directed Activities Related to Texts (DARTS). The list is quite extensive, so needs to be used selectively. The strategies also can be used in conjunction with any of the reading routines: shared and guided reading, reading aloud, working with the class reader (picture books or novels) and independent reading. They will also spill over into key writing routines, i.e. shared, guided and independent writing. It is recommended that the strategies should be demonstrated first, via shared work. Not only will these strategies help children remain engaged with the task in hand and deepen their understanding but they will also tap into a wide range of learning styles.

ACTIVATING PRIOR KNOWLEDGE

Help children make links between the known and the new. Work with the title, front cover, the chapter heading or even use a related resource, e.g. a photograph or object. Make a simple record to refer back to, e.g. a concept or mind map to establish links between ideas. Alternatively, use Post-its for children to record briefly their own existing knowledge. These can be stuck on the wall for future reference.

PREDICTION

This can be done at different points in the process of reading a complete text and before any of the text is read. Note predictions and retain these, as they can be referred back to at later readings when information is revealed. The children are then able to evaluate, revise and review their opinions. This works well with characters and twists of the plot. Children may find keeping a reading journal is another point of reference.

CONSTRUCTING IMAGES

VISUALISATION

This can be modelled in shared reading by reading a text aloud and then talking about the ideas that you had whilst reading. Compare these to the children's. Some children may find it hard to describe the pictures in their head.

DRAWING

Character 'mug shots' or 'thumbnail' sketches can help lift a character off the page. These can be referred back to as the story unfolds to be reviewed. Children could write key words and phrases around the drawing as a record to be returned to. Perhaps, as the story progresses, some words and phrases no longer apply and new ones need to be added.

DRAMA

Working with key sentences or images from the text children can create a still photograph or 'freeze frame'. These can be recorded on the digital camera for future use. Thought and speech bubbles take these captured moments a step further. (For a more extended discussion of drama see below.)

MAPS, CHARTS AND TIMELINES

These can be constructed for the duration of reading a text and are especially useful in more complex novels, so that the structure, e.g. embedded plots and time changes, is made explicit. These can also be used with non-fiction texts in the form of grids.

SEQUENCING

By asking children to reorder chunks of text their attention is drawn to cohesive devices, particularly connectives that are used to hold narrative and non-narrative texts together. In poetry they may be drawn to rhyme schemes or the use of repetition.

SUMMARISING

Through shared reading, we can demonstrate the art of skimming a text in order to identify the key idea and locate the key words and phrases that sum up that idea. Using highlighting pens, we can pinpoint the most useful information and then model, initially through spoken language, how the material can be transformed into a useful summary to be followed by written representation, e.g. a chart or labelled picture.

SEMANTIC STRATEGIES

These are designed to help children get at the meaning of words and phrases.

PREVIEWING VOCABULARY

Identify/list unfamiliar words prior to shared/guided sessions and discuss these with the children.

BUILDING WORD BANKS

Demonstrate to children how we get the meaning of words through their roots and morphology. The idea is that this approach to discussing and analysing word structure can then be applied in guided sessions.

WORD TRACKER AND ORAL THESAURUS

Focus on a word or groups of words, e.g. synonyms for adjectives such as 'nice'. Discuss with the children how words hold subtle differences of meaning, e.g. 'hot' and 'scalding'.

CLASS DICTIONARIES AND GLOSSARIES

Dictionary skills need to be modelled for children. Compiling 'topic' dictionaries or glossaries is one way of applying this knowledge.

INTERPRETIVE STRATEGIES

CHARACTER DEVELOPMENT (SUITABLE FOR ALL AGES)

This could include journals, media interviews, character sketches, relationship charts and character emotion registers (rating characters on a five-point scale in terms of how they are feeling at any particular time).

MULTIPLE MEANINGS (HELPING CHILDREN UNDERSTAND THAT WE CAN RESPOND TO TEXTS IN DIFFERENT WAYS)

This could include ranking characters (e.g. good/evil), noting different roles played by characters in the course of a story, the role of illustrations, focusing on minor characters, considering dilemmas facing characters.

PERSONAL RESPONSE

Encourage children to make their own personal responses, e.g. in a reading journal, comparing books by the same author or books on similar themes by different authors (DfES, 2005b).

INDEPENDENT READING

For children to read independently is the ultimate goal of the reading curriculum. When reading independently, children are operating unaided by the adult and, by this stage, they should be automatically applying the skills and strategies that have been practised in the shared and guided routines. The application of knowledge from guided reading is particularly important in supporting the move into successful independent work. Experience gained from such routines as listening to stories read aloud, responding to class novels, reading at home and outside school, will all feed into the child's growing repertoire of skills. The child now has the time to read at length and build up reading stamina and fluency. She also has the opportunity not only to refine her skills, but also to develop choices and preferences as a reader and, most importantly, get lost in a book.

It is never too young to start participating in independent reading, as has been shown in the *Bookstart* evaluation. As part of their research, Collins *et al.* (2005) interviewed reception children and found out that they enjoyed reading on their own. One child, Lizzie, told them that 'every day I get a book for myself and read to myself'. The mother of a child called Jane reports that, after reading their three bedtime stories every night, 'Jane would sit in her bed and read stories to herself' (2005:51). A chance to read independently clearly will be a need for a group of children known as 'young fluent readers' (Clark, 1976). These children start to read before receiving formal instruction and it is not uncommon for their parents to be puzzled or even apologetic as to how this came about. Children such as Lizzie and Jane serve as reminders of the importance of partnership with parents in order to provide continuity and celebrate the achievements of this group of children. (See the section below on parental involvement.) Lizzie was identified by her mother as being advanced in her reading and, at school, observations recorded that she read regularly to herself. A child such as Lizzie would benefit from discussions with an adult to establish the level of her enjoyment of the books that are available in the classroom and to identify preferences or interests that could be met.

Whole-class sessions

During whole-class literacy sessions, independent reading may be planned for the time that the teacher and other adults work with guided groups. Reading-related activities may be set up briefly for a whole class and then the majority of children will be required to undertake these independently. This can prove challenging for both adults and children unless the tasks are achievable and the children are clear about self-help strategies. Independent reading could mean tasks that involve reading from the screen, for example using a CD-ROM which has interactive stories requiring the child to read in order to make choices about possible outcomes. Alternatively, the child might be using the computer to research the meanings of a list of key vocabulary required for work in another area of the curriculum. In KS2, children may be reading the next chapter of a novel and making notes in response to key questions in preparation for a guided reading session.

Finding time for children to engage in private reading is vital. The time can be found, for example, if children are encouraged to see it as a worthwhile option when other work is complete. The value of private reading time becomes very obvious when a long-awaited children's book is newly published. The Harry Potter series is a case in point; teachers reported hordes of children appearing the day after publication clutching their copies and secretly reading under their tables. It is surely worth tapping into the reading climate that this kind of success story brings in its wake.

Visiting the library

Equally importantly, children should be given the space to browse and sample books and this is well catered for in visits to the library. This could be the class library but should include regular slots in the school library and if possible the public library. Collins *et al.* (2005) found in the schools that they visited when evaluating *Bookstart* that the arrival of the literacy hour had taken a toll on public library use by schools. Hopefully, the more flexible nature of the renewed PNS will redress this trend so that meeting librarians and benefiting from their advice and information will become a strong link between school and community. The value of joining a public library goes without saying as, in so doing, children not only borrow books but also become members of the wider reading community. To use a library, certain skills have to be learnt and the choice at first may be overwhelming for some children. However, the chance to sit, relax and read several books at one sitting and independently is a luxury for many children.

Everyone reading in class

This routine sits outside the dedicated PNS daily literacy time and is much less strongly in evidence than it was fifteen to twenty years ago. Various acronyms are used to describe periods of quiet reading undertaken by the whole class, and in some cases by the whole school, including teachers and support staff. Amongst the more common are USSR: uninterrupted sustained silent reading; ERIC: everyone reading in class, and SQUIRT: sustained quiet uninterrupted reading time.

A quiet reading routine, properly implemented, can provide opportunities for children individually to get lost in a book and is another context for developing personal preferences, as well as the sheer enjoyment that books can bring. Because the children are required to read quietly and with concentration for a specific and sustained period of time, this reading routine can foster reading stamina. When the whole class (or in some cases the whole school) stops for the sole purpose of reading, then important messages are conveyed about its status. This routine can allow all children to read independently, at their own pace, to get a taste of what it is like to 'read in their head'. Some children seem to make the transition from reading out loud to silent reading very easily, whilst others will benefit from the time that this routine offers to practise such a skill.

Of all the routines that we describe in this chapter, quiet reading is the most vulnerable to misuse. Just like any other reading routine, it requires careful planning, and, when first introduced, some discussion with the children will be needed in order to instil key principles and expectations for behaviour. The teacher's role in quiet reading sessions needs clear definition. It is an opportunity to model what experienced readers do, so it is a time when she can be seen to be reading too. With careful attention to the organisational details and purpose of these sessions it is possible to convey to children the important part that reading plays in your daily life and theirs.

Independent group reading

This may sound a contradiction in terms but children benefit from opportunities to enjoy independent group reading without an adult. This is particularly the case in KS2. The following example demonstrates the value of this routine for promoting independence in reading, as well as fostering wider social skills.

Group reading: poetry, KS1/2

This group activity (which could also be organised with the whole class) helps develop children's active response to literature. A suitable poem should be chosen, preferably one with a clear pattern and rhythm, and one with content that will engage the children.

1 Before reading

Divide the class into four groups. Give each group a version of the poem prepared in one of the following ways:

   a without the title;
   b with the last two lines missing;
   c with words/phrases blanked out (this procedure is known as 'cloze' and the words you choose to remove will add to or lessen the difficulty of this version);
   d cut up for reassembling. This 'sequencing' activity is based on the coherence and logical ordering that is found in all texts (large chunks will be easier to work with than lines or half lines so prepare according to the competence of the group).

2 The reading

The children work in groups with their version. It is important to emphasise that the activity is not about guessing what was in the poet's head but about the ideas that the children have. It is best to take feedback in this order: title, cloze, last two lines, cut-up sections. Use the children's ideas as a springboard for discussing issues such as what makes a good title, or why the poet made particular vocabulary choices.

3 After reading

An extension of this activity is to ask the children to make a couple of statements about the poem (e.g. 'It is sad', 'I like the description of the old man's house'). Then help the children to turn these into questions ('Why is it sad?', 'What is good about the description?'). They can either answer these themselves or pass them on to another group. This version of 'traditional' comprehension-type questions has the advantage of starting with the children's reading and understanding of the poem. The whole activity invites close scrutiny of the text itself with children referring closely and confidently to it.

4 Rereading

A final activity is to ask each group to prepare a group reading of the poem. By this time they know it well and will have explored aspects such as voice, audience and hidden meanings. Close knowledge of this kind informs and gives resonance to such group readings.

Reading across the curriculum and ICT

Much of children's independent reading will occur in other curriculum areas and will also involve reading off the screen. Children's reading skills are tested to their limits as they meet new and varied genres and forms. They have to adjust to differences in the use and density of new vocabulary (for example, when researching an historical period or a specific scientific process), as well as linguistic structures (such as the passive mood of verbs in some information texts). In addition, contents, indexes and glossaries will need to be navigated. When using the computer, children are faced with icons and layouts that have to be interpreted in order to access programs and other material. It is a very different kind of reading that has to be done. However, if they have appropriate demonstrations in shared work, for example skimming and scanning with non-fiction texts or navigating a website on the interactive whiteboard, then they are far better placed to meet the reading challenges of the wider curriculum independently.

READING ALOUD TO CHILDREN

Reading aloud to children is one of the most enduring and well loved activities to take place in the primary classroom. Teachers have always read aloud daily to children and many of these children as adults remember storytime with great clarity and pleasure. Daniel Pennac describes a teacher who read aloud to his class as one who 'developed the photograph for his pupils as cleanly as possible'. His voice spared them 'the slog of code-breaking, made situations clear, established settings, stressed themes, accentuated nuances'. In short, this teacher

> opened eyes. He lit lanterns. He set people off on the road to books, a pilgrimage without end or certainty, the path of human towards fellow human … From the word go, he trusted

in the listener's desire to understand ... When someone reads aloud, they raise you to the level of the book. They give you reading as a gift.

(Pennac, 2006:95, 121)

At the heart of this routine is children's active listening. This is a chance for the ears and brains to be engaged and for the eyes to take a rest – unless looking at the pictures.

The lasting appeal of this routine lies in the fact that for a few minutes a day, the physical act of reading has itself been taken over by a more experienced reader, and the learner is placed most enjoyably in Vygotsky's 'zone of proximal development' (1978). The experience may be enjoyable but there is, of course, serious intent behind this routine, as the children are also being shown the promise and potential of their own futures as readers. Reading aloud to children is all about allowing them to give their imaginations free rein through creating worlds and images to which they will enjoy returning for the rest of their lives. It opens the door to the world of books and entices children into becoming lifelong readers.

Reading aloud regularly to the class is clearly about fostering positive attitudes to reading. OFSTED's report *Reading for Purpose and Pleasure* (2004) looked at the reasons behind variation in attainment in reading in forty-five schools. One aspect that is of interest to us here is that of developing positive attitudes in pupils towards reading. Unsurprisingly, the report found that children who were not progressing successfully in their reading tended to have negative attitudes. But, more surprisingly, few of the schools that *were* raising attainment in reading and producing competent readers succeeded in getting these children to read for pleasure. However, in an example of a high-achieving school, a love of literature was actively promoted and given a high profile throughout the school as a whole. As the report says, 'teachers' influence in introducing pupils to new texts and authors was significant. Pupils enjoyed being read to and responded very positively to the regular reading of class novels' (OFSTED, 2004:12). Reading aloud must have a strong place in the reading curriculum and it must be actively maintained throughout the primary school age range.

Reading aloud is a central means for introducing children to texts of all sorts, as it exposes them to each genre's distinctive language. Children with EAL, and indeed all children, need to hear the complex sentence structures and vocabulary of non-fiction texts in order to become independent readers of these eventually. As children meet an ever-widening range of books and authors, so their own potential for developing personal choice is enhanced. In early years settings teachers have traditionally shared picture books with their children whilst those working with older children will also read aloud from longer texts which may or may not be illustrated. It is quite a responsibility, then, to select the highest-quality books from the multitude that are currently available. You need to be knowledgeable about children's books and Chapter 6 provides a helpful starting point.

Reading aloud provides a vital and very special element within the 'language rich' curriculum recommended by Rose and the PNS. For some very young children, the language they hear read aloud may be their first sustained exposure to written English, which is different from spoken English in many significant ways. Take the classic story opening, 'Once upon a time there was ...' and you immediately know that this is not how people talk. The patterns and tunes of book language have to be learnt and reading aloud is when they are taught. For children learning EAL, listening to fluent reading provides essential information about how their new language works. In addition, as texts are usually written in Standard English, this is when children can appreciate and operate the distinctive structures for themselves. This is also true for other key elements in stories, such as twists of plot and subtle characterisation, which are more likely to be taken on board when listening to an enthusiastic, expressive and skilful reader.

We should not underestimate our youngest children's capacity to respond to seemingly more advanced texts. OFSTED (2004) found a school where teachers successfully used classic children's books with children from an early age. The following extract from a read aloud session in a Reception class shows young children being empowered to make meanings from a complex text. For half an hour the teacher read aloud to the children from an original version of *Alice's Adventures in Wonderland*. She sustained their interest and ensured their engagement through her questioning, through the space she gave for the children's own ideas and by relating difficult concepts in the book to their current understanding. The children were working on 'flight' in science and had just made parachutes; when the teacher asked the children about the story so far, one child gave the following succinct summary:

> She saw a bunny with a watch in his pocket and then ... and then she saw it and she was bored with that sister telling stories with no pictures in, and the bunny went down the hole and he went quick cos he didn't have a dress cos he's a boy and ... and Alice went down with her dress like a parachute.

The teacher read lengthy passages of text, stopping to discuss points she considered needed clarifying for the children. For instance, at the point where Alice shrinks she asked:

Teacher: Can you answer this important question? If you were very, very, very small what would everything look like?
Child: ... things would look bigger than you.
Teacher: If you were small what would I look like?
Child: Big giant.
Child: I got the video of *Honey, I Shrunk the Kids*.
Teacher: What did the grass look like?
Child: Thorns.

This fragment clearly signals the children's understanding and involvement with a text more challenging than any they could tackle single-handedly. The teacher helps them make the necessary conceptual links, encouraging them to draw from both story experience ('big giant') and the influences of media (*Honey, I Shrunk the Kids*).

Older children also benefit from hearing more demanding texts being read aloud. These induct children into more challenging forms of language (fiction and non-fiction alike) and indeed they will be able to enjoy and accommodate far more complex language than they can manage on their own. A Year 4 teacher was reading *A Fairy Tale* (Tony Ross) and was particularly keen that the image found within 'a yellowy light tickled the black clouds' should not be lost on the children. He made sure that he included it verbatim in his summary of the story which he gave at the start of the next session and children started to comment on the use of language in the book as a whole.

In these ways reading aloud shows children what lies ahead for them in books. This is especially important for inexperienced readers who may be able to tackle only quite limited texts, but who badly need the enrichment this routine can provide. It can give them a sense of fluency with sustained text that they may not be able to achieve on their own.

Finally, the way we read aloud to children can offer them a model for developing their own read-aloud style. We can demonstrate how to bring the story to life through, for instance, our use of intonation or the way we read dialogue. Dropping your voice to a whisper increases suspense, as do prolonged pauses at key moments. Try to keep eye contact with the children as much as possible and use your face and gesture to underline meaning. Detailed analysis of a teacher reading aloud to a child with reading difficulties revealed that the child's retelling of the story was structured entirely around such things as the teacher's exaggerated intonation, facial expressions and gesture. For this reason – and for many others – storytelling, where you tell a story from memory, is very supportive and you should do your utmost to build up a repertoire of told stories.

Managing reading aloud

Finding time to accommodate the routine in amongst countless other curriculum demands can be a challenge and for this reason it needs to be included and ringfenced within weekly planning. First of all think about timing: is storytime always at the end of the day? Are there other times that would be more appropriate? One teacher tells of the dramatic effect that reading an enormously popular class novel from nine o'clock every morning had on her class's lateness! It is not uncommon in early years settings to have several short reading-aloud slots in the course of a day. With older children read-aloud sessions may be less frequent (perhaps two or three times a week), though if a teacher knows that the pace of a novel needs to be sustained then she will plan more frequent sessions accordingly. Collins' (2005) study of forty-five student teachers found that more than a fifth had not seen a KS2 class teacher reading a novel aloud to their class. Although a small-scale piece of research, it serves as a reminder for the need to protect this routine in KS2.

High-quality reading-aloud sessions are the result of careful planning. Whether a picture book or novel, a preliminary read through first will help anticipate any potential difficulties, for example with complex or specialist vocabulary or where dialects are used. It is tempting to simplify difficult words for children, but children can manage more complex language when it is being read aloud, and very often the embedding context of the overall narrative gives the difficult words meaning. Similarly, when abridging lengthy novels, the cutting process needs careful consideration. If you find you are cutting out too much then you have probably made an inappropriate choice and the children will need wider reading experiences before they are ready to take on a text of this type.

When reading aloud, we also need to remember that children are active 'meaning makers' (Wells, 1987) and they will make personal responses to texts as they connect the reading both with their own experiences and with other texts they know. A reading of *This is the Bear* (Hayes and Craig) may call up the children's own stories about their teddy bears or about being lost, but may also lead them to think of other stories by Sarah Hayes or to remember *Dogger* (Hughes). Typically, very young children will want to make these connections straight away, leading to the lively and interactive sessions you will see in many early years classrooms. As children become more experienced readers, they will be able to internalise and hold on to such links and you will find it easier to sustain the reading. Anticipating points which invite response can help here. For instance, children are always desperate to contribute their own plans for trapping the Iron Man (in Ted Hughes' powerful book of the same name), so much so that one teacher reports an eleven-year-old rushing up to draw his suggested trap on the board. However, when appropriate, teachers of all age ranges may wish to invoke a 'no interruptions' rule, and there may be times when, feeling the momentum of the story is at risk, you will want to insist on this.

So far, we have focused on the teacher or adult reading aloud but there are other possibilities. For instance, older children can read aloud to younger classes, and this is where the earlier point about the teacher offering a good model of reading aloud is salient. In one class there was a 'Read Aloud Request Board' to which the children pinned their requests for a particular poem, short story or picture book that they wanted to hear. They also nominated a reader. We conclude this section by offering you a checklist that students have found helpful in planning for this routine.

Reading aloud to children: a checklist

SELECT – PLAN – PRACTISE – DELIVER!

1 SELECT your book (don't leave it till the last moment!). Aim for a quality text by a reputable author. Think about the children's interests, cultural backgrounds and ongoing work.
2 Write a PLAN for the session. This should include:

- resources needed to accompany your reading, e.g. cut-outs, puppets, objects, photographs;
- an indication of how much you intend to read (if a novel);
- identifying any conceptual or vocabulary difficulties;
- how you intend to introduce the book, e.g. a discussion of other books by the same author that the class may have read;
- list discussion points/key questions;
- how the session will conclude, e.g. predicting what might happen next in a novel;
- back-up material in case of an early finish (e.g. finger rhymes for younger children; some poems for older children).

3 PRACTISE reading the book aloud. If it is a picture book, you will need to try reading *and* showing the pictures – not as easy as it sounds!
4 DELIVER your plan! Enjoy your session.

THE CLASS READER

A class reader is typically a children's novel that you select for reading with the whole class. Normally, it will be read aloud to them within the traditional storytime slot. Although it is possible and even desirable that books are read aloud to children unaccompanied by written and other activities, in this section the assumption is made that the class reader will have been chosen because of qualities and depths which can profitably be explored through related activities, some of which may take place in other literacy slots.

Children's literature plays a very important role in children's lives and it is well understood that it develops and extends their imaginative faculties. It allows them to enter 'secondary worlds' (Tolkien, 1964) where they will encounter other situations, places and times and where they can empathise with characters. A class reader can be a powerful medium for developing children's experiences of and responses to literature. It provides a point of shared culture in the class through the communal experience of listening, discussing and responding to the same text.

One criticism of the literacy hour's original structure was that it offered children only fragments of text and denied them the experience of the whole book. Thankfully, the renewed PNS acknowledges the need for more flexibility and encourages working with more extended units of planning, spanning several weeks. Working with a class reader will fit in well with this more flexible approach and can go some way to restoring the balance towards the sustained study and enjoyment of an extended text in its entirety.

A class reader ensures children of all abilities and languages have access to books that provide appropriate challenge. As is explained in 'Reading aloud to children' on page 70, you can read books to children that they may not be able to tackle for themselves; for struggling readers, this access to books, with rich language and plots that meets their interest level, is crucial.

The class reader is also another context for developing children's reading repertoires and their competence in choosing books for themselves. For example, you might decide to read Dick King-Smith's *The Sheep Pig*, which is about a pig who believes he is a sheepdog. You could then lead the class to other books by the same author such as *The Fox Busters* or to other anthropomorphic stories such as *Charlotte's Web* (E.B. White). The book could also be an incentive to read information books about sheepdogs and pigs. Reading a short novel such as *The Firework Maker's Daughter* (Philip Pullman) may act as a launch pad for some children to start reading his more demanding *Northern Lights* (the first part of the *His Dark Materials* trilogy). In the same way, shorter novels by Anne Fine such as *The Angel of Nitshill Road* could inspire individuals to move on to her *Goggle Eyes*.

This routine can be a powerful context for promoting children's active comprehension. As you will remember from discussion earlier in this chapter, the teacher's role in developing children's comprehension strategies is crucial, with direct and explicit teaching and careful questioning being recognised as key. For instance, as described in the section on 'Constructing images' on page 65, children could draw their own maps of the farm in *Charlotte's Web*, adding details as the story unfolds. In *The Firework Maker's Daughter*, Lalchand (Lila's father) is thrown into prison: the children could create a 'freeze frame' of the moment that Lila is given this news. Digital photos could be taken and the children could add thought and word bubbles later.

Managing the class novel

First choose your book. You will need to try reading some of it out loud to hear how well written it is. Look for a good balance of dialogue and narrative, rhythmic language, varied sentence length, recognisable characters who are credible and consistent and a well paced plot that will sustain the children's interest. Your own commitment to the book also matters; your enthusiasm will help to motivate the children but will also motivate you in terms of the effort you put into presenting and mediating it to the class.

What should you do if the children do not like the book? You can use the opportunity to demonstrate that readers can make choices; that they do not have to read everything! You can discuss with the children why it is not working and use the opportunity to develop their critical awareness, maybe getting the children to write reviews saying why they would not recommend it. However, you may have planned a unit of work around the novel, which means it is not practical to abandon it. If this is the case, you could still discuss the difficulties with the class, bearing in mind it would be most unusual for everyone to dislike it; critical reviews could still be made, as could a class search for other books with similar themes. But you could also inspect the way in which you are working with the book and ask yourself some questions. Are you reading for too long or too short a time? Are you leaving too long a gap between the readings? Are you ending the reading at sufficiently interesting points that will encourage the children to want to know more? How enthusiastic is your reading aloud? Are you killing the book through overuse of related activities? Would some judicious abridging prevent dragging the book out? Reading a text aloud deserves the same attention as you would give to any other area of the curriculum so remember why you are using a class reader and, as with any planning, keep monitoring and reviewing.

There are different ways of organising how the book is read with the class. The most usual model is of the teacher reading aloud to the children. If resources allow, the children can read from their own copies at the same time (although this practice is more often found in secondary schools). Sometimes children and teacher share the reading aloud in reading round the class. This is a long-standing practice but the pressure of reading aloud for struggling readers can be detrimental to their self-esteem and progress. The tension for these children of waiting for their turn, often trying to anticipate their passage in order to practise it, can completely detract from the benefits that are claimed for this routine. One student told us of a memory she has from school of a rather more benign version where the class all sat together on the carpet with their readers and chose whether or not to read aloud.

With many demands bearing down on the curriculum, it might seem expedient to choose only shorter novels in order to avoid leaving longer ones unfinished. This would be a mistake, as it would preclude the selection of many books that children want to hear. One way round this is to use multiple copies and taped versions which can be rotated amongst groups who are asked to read prescribed sections during independent reading time or for homework. For those children who could manage it, the book could also be read in group sessions, whilst those who cannot read it for themselves could listen to the same section on tape.

When teachers plan activities to accompany class readers they are guided by a wish to enhance children's responses to literature, to provide opportunities for contextualised

English work and sometimes to draw out cross-curricular links. There are two important caveats about activities: firstly, do not kill the book with a surfeit of activities; secondly, do not try to make every book connect with ongoing work in other curriculum areas. Literature can teach many lessons on its own. Make sure you have literature there for literature's sake.

These activities also provide the teacher with opportunities to assess children's literary development in speaking and listening, reading and writing. Here are two examples: *The Owl who was Afraid of the Dark* (Jill Tomlinson), which has been planned in this example to be used with a Year 2 Class, and Michael Morpurgo's *The Dancing Bear*, which has been planned for use with a Year 5 class.

Working with a class reader: KS1: *The Owl who was Afraid of the Dark*

This old favourite is written in short chapters and lends itself to a range of activities. It links to strand 8 in the PNS, 'Engaging and responding to texts' – 'explain reaction to texts, commenting on important aspects'. Below is a brief indication of some starting points for planning across eight short sessions.

Before reading the book

Set up a display of owls, information books and other picture storybooks about owls, and photographs of night-time. Provide a selection of other books written by Jill Tomlinson, including the picture book version of the story. At a future point, once they have been read some of the story, the children could add to the display by making silhouettes of the owl family perched in their tree, in order to extend the display and use it as a reference point.

Session 1: first impressions

Show the children a copy of the image of the owl on the front cover of the book (minus the title, etc). Ask the children to talk in pairs and then tell you what they see. Possible responses might be: 'It's an owl'; 'It's falling'; 'It's night-time'; 'I can see the moon'. Now ask the children if they have any questions about the picture. Responses might include 'What is the owl doing?' 'Is he happy?' 'Is he jumping?' 'Where's he going?' If the children are unforthcoming, then model some questions of your own, or use some prompt questions such as 'How do you think the owl is feeling?'. Using shared writing, list their ideas on a poster for future reference.

Session 2: introducing the book

Introduce the story by reading the title and naming the author. Now they know the title, ask the children to brainstorm what they think the story will be about (prediction). Activate prior knowledge by asking what they already know about owls and their lifestyles and whether they have read any books about owls. Record some facts; for example, owls are generally thought to be nocturnal.

Read aloud 'Dark is Exciting'.

Activity: Talk partners: Do you like the dark? What does Plop's mother teach him about the dark?

Session 3

Read aloud 'Dark is Kind'.

Activity: What words describe Plop at this point? Make a list and then transfer the words and phrases to surround a portrait of Plop. Add to the display.

Session 4

Read aloud 'Dark is Fun'.

Activity: Write to Plop describing all the things you like to do at night.

Session 5

Read aloud 'Dark is Necessary'.

Activity: What do you think Plop might be dreaming about? Ask how the little girl helps him understand why dark is necessary. Role-play in pairs a short conversation between the girl and Plop.

Session 6

Read aloud 'Dark is Fascinating'.

Activity: What sort of character is Plop now? How he is changing? List the differences. Compare with Chapter 2's findings (session 3).

Session 7

Read aloud 'Dark is Wonderful'.

Activity: Draw and label all the different things you can see at night.

Session 8

Read aloud 'Dark is Beautiful'.

Activity: What made Plop so afraid of the dark? Chart his fears and how he overcame them.

Working with a class reader: KS2: *The Dancing Bear*

In this example, a Year 5 class were read Michael Morpurgo's *The Dancing Bear*, a short but complex novel. The teacher's planning maps on to the PNS requirements for strand 8, 'Engaging with and responding to texts' – 'compare the usefulness of techniques such as visualisation, prediction and empathy in exploring the meaning of texts'. Some of the activities below are designed to be worked on flexibly within the English timetable across the week.

Before reading the book

Before embarking on reading the book, the teacher planned two separate activities. First, he set up a display about the author, including some of Morpurgo's many other books, which a number of the children knew already. Second, because the film crew in the novel arrive to make a film of *The Pied Piper of Hamelin*, the teacher read the class extracts from Browning's poem in a version illustrated by André Amstutz.

Introducing the book

Then the teacher introduced the class to the book by focusing on the front and back covers. The children were asked in pairs to speculate about the front cover and the relationship between the girl and the bear who appear together in the foreground. They then turned to the back cover where the blurb confirmed some of their speculations and added new detail which made them want to read the book (e.g. 'arrival of glamorous film crew'!).

Reading the book

When he was ready to begin reading, the teacher alerted the children to the fact that this book is written in the first-person narrative voice of a middle-aged schoolmaster. The reading of the book was carried out to the whole class over three sessions with the sections to be read chosen as follows: the first was about the main character, Roxanne, and her early life in the village with the bear; the second was the arrival of and early rehearsals with the film crew, which included a young and handsome pop star; the last section was where Roxanne is seduced away from the village by the pop star and the bear dies.

First section: activity

The teacher's aim for the activity connected to the first section was to emphasise the peaceful, rural simplicity of the mountain community, and how the novel sets up the lull before the storm. In a whole-class session, the children talked about and then listed individually what was different in Roxanne's life from their own lives; for example, the making of cheese, being cut off by the snow, making honey and having a bear in their midst. They then formed groups and made two predictions about what they thought would happen next. When they reported back to the whole class, the most popular predictions were, firstly, that the bear would have to die soon and that Roxanne would be heartbroken; and secondly, that as a young woman Roxanne would lose interest in the bear.

Second section: activity

In the second activity the teacher's purpose was to explore the extent of the disruption to the community as experienced by the characters. The class as a whole, with the teacher as scribe, listed the differences between the community and the visitors, such as the high-tech equipment, their outrageously gaudy clothes and, particularly, the presence in their midst of the glamorous Niki. Role-play in fours where each child was a character in the story talking about the day's filming led to individuals writing an entry in a diary which their character might have kept during the filming. Then they made two more predictions: most popular was that Roxanne does not agree to appear with her bear in the video in the major role envisaged for her; and second was that she does and that the bear wrecks the whole film.

Third section: activity

By this stage the children's involvement in the story was so great that they could hardly wait to see which of their predictions would come true. The teacher's aim for the third activity was to ensure that the children could see that the ending was appropriate even though sudden and tragic. Immediately after the reading the whole class talked about Roxanne's departure and the bear's death and how it made them feel. The teacher hoped that through this discussion the children might appreciate that the bear's death was the price the village, personified by Roxanne, had to pay because it had sold out to the commercial world. If this sounds a tall order, remember that the activities for sections one and two were leading up to this. The final written activity required the children to compose individual letters to Niki in the role of Roxanne on her return to the village many years later.

DRAMA

As indicated above, there is a wide range of strategies that can be utilised when working on developing children's comprehension. One of these strategies, drama, will be looked at more closely here in order to consider its potential to develop children's response to texts.

Dramatising a text or parts of a text is something many teachers do spontaneously. If they know that the book they have chosen is rather challenging they may want to give more help with lifting the voice off the page. Drama and role-play can be planned for, before, during and after reading. Drama gives us the opportunity to work in a creative, exciting medium which is part and parcel of the 'broad and rich curriculum' envisaged in *Excellence and Enjoyment* (DfES, 2003a).

As you start to read a story, images – of a forest, perhaps, a ramshackle cottage, two waif-like children – are supplied by the brain. Certain expectations are aroused and these depend not only upon our reading of other stories, but also on our personal life experiences. The reader is active in recreating the story and moving into a secondary world. However, for some children the words remain black marks on the page and imagined characters, settings, movements, emotions, dialogue, tension and anticipated endings are not part of reading for them. These children are the ones for whom reading may remain difficult. Drama, whether spontaneous or planned, has a valuable role in enabling children to reach the deeper levels of meaning in literature.

Managing drama activities

The ways into dramatic exploration of text with a class can be brief and controlled and need not place any of the participants, including the teacher, under stress. The following points can help you think about using drama in the classroom to help children develop a closer relationship with texts:

- Think about situations in the story where the characters have a problem to solve and thus where there is dramatic tension.
- Get the children to see parallels with their own lives. Even the simplest picture book such as Pat Hutchins' *Titch* has themes (sibling rivalry, growth) of great significance to all children.

• Extend the story backwards, before the story began, or forwards, after it is finished.
• Develop a scene only glossed over in the original story.
• Develop a minor character from the story and his or her reactions to events. You can add characters not in the original story.
• Present the class with new problems that could have arisen in the story.
• Think about how a character from the text could be 'hot-seated', i.e. asked questions by the rest of the class about their actions, feelings and thoughts. Children can 'be' the character and answer in role.
• Use other specific drama strategies such as freeze-framing or thought-tracking to help understand fictional relationships and motivations.
• Think of how your role in the drama can be minor but facilitating (for example, a visitor, a traveller or a reporter). Often if you take a questioning, worried or sceptical line, you will find the class providing you with information and opening the situation out.

READING PARTNERS/BUDDIES

In this section we look at the routine of pairing younger and older classes so that a child reads regularly with a reading partner from another class. This is also sometimes known as 'buddy reading'.

This routine addresses aspects of the *Every Child Matters* (DfES, 2004b) agenda. For both parties, this should be an enjoyable routine that will provide each child with reading practice which will support them in their journey towards achieving their full potential. The one-to-one attention from an older peer can be highly motivating for the younger child as well as flattering. Being the more experienced reading partner can have a very positive impact on the older child's self-esteem as he is gaining valuable experience of life skills, such as taking responsibility, as well as discovering for himself the value of listening to children read, which will be a good preparation for his own adulthood.

In effect, the older child is being placed into the role of teacher or mentor, which will require him to think hard about the learning processes involved. This means standing back from the learning and trying to make what is involved in the act of reading clear for the less experienced learner. So a powerful element of this routine is that it offers a meaningful context for children to consider the different aspects of the reading process. In addition, the older child may have to think about the books he will share with the younger partner. This means considering the content, illustrations and language that make a book an appropriate choice. The child will realise that choosing a book for someone else also means that he will have to find out a bit about the reader's interests and needs.

When it comes to the actual reading session itself, the children will be using metacognition. As they read with readers less experienced than themselves, they are pushed to make explicit the things that readers do. They may not have needed to think about or articulate these skills and processes before. Vygotsky's zpd has already figured prominently in this chapter and this is yet another instance of its relevance. For the younger child the partnership allows for development within the zpd, while for the older child the routine itself is empowering as it moves his thinking on.

All this makes reading partnerships a particularly powerful routine for struggling older readers. Confidence and motivation are typically very low for these children and the opportunity to work with easier texts in a setting that genuinely requires them is a valuable one. And of course the opportunity to stand back from the reading process in the way described above is equally important for this group of readers. The benefits for boys are especially noticeable. When younger boys see older role models enthusiastically involved in reading, their own views of reading are likely to be positively affected.

Managing reading partners

To succeed, the routine needs to be carefully structured so that the children can talk about their reading in a non-threatening context. Reading partnerships work best as part of a whole-school policy where classes are systematically paired and there are regular timetabled slots for the routine. However, it can be organised between two classes, for instance with a mentor and another pupil in the school. In some schools, it runs across the whole academic year; others prefer to use it across just one term. Some form of training or preparation may need to be undertaken, particularly with the more experienced partners, prior to embarking on being reading partners. This is so that they learn how to structure a session, ask good questions and support the younger reader. Teachers will need to make decisions in the first instance on identifying partners, bearing in mind reading experience, personality, interests and also gender considerations. Some schools that have operated reading partnerships successfully have prepared the older partners by working with them first, to think through:

- what they want out of a reading partnership;
- how they can make sure that the experience is enjoyable and relaxed;
- selecting texts;
- how a session might be structured;
- useful questions that they might ask their partner;
- short activities that they might do linked to the book;
- how reading or sharing a book differs with (a) very young children, and (b) slightly older children;
- what prompts they might use if a child gets stuck;
- how they can evaluate themselves as reading partners.

One school used techniques such as role-play in pairs to help the experienced partners practise their skills first. Circle times were built in at regular intervals during the year to provide the children with opportunities to share the things they found easy and difficult. The children were keen to compile a short booklet to help new reading partners. We move on now to consider how this routine might work in practice.

The older class

1 Introduction: getting started

This could be done as a whole class and would need to include:

- introducing the routine;
- looking at a range of picture books for younger children and using these as the basis for a discussion about the kinds of books younger children enjoy. This list could be brainstormed in groups of two or three and then fed back to the whole class, who could come up with an initial shortlist of books they might take to the first session;
- shaping a mini-conference that the older child could carry out with the younger one. Again children could think about questions they might ask the younger child (favourite books, authors, topics, etc.), which could be collated to construct a shared prompt sheet;
- deciding on a structure for the session. Obviously this will vary but a typical structure might be:

5 minutes	Older child reads to younger child
5 minutes	Mini-conference
5 minutes	Younger child reads
2/3 minutes	Praise, review, and looking forward to the next session.

2 Pairing up

The first step will be to plan the actual pairing up session itself with the other teacher and decide how to organise the children physically (for instance, half going to each class or both classes meeting in the hall). It is probably best to keep early sessions quite short and build up towards the kind of structure described above.

This introductory, pairing up session will introduce the two classes. The partners should then be put together for a few minutes during which time the older child shares a pre-chosen book with the younger one. The following week's slot could be a little longer to include the conference.

As with other routines, time will need to be spent at the outset establishing ground rules and clear expectations about behaviour. This is time well spent as once these are all in place the experienced child can get on with the important job of reading with her partner.

So what is the teacher's role in these sessions? First, it is an invaluable opportunity for observing the children. Second, it may be necessary to intervene from time to time to keep the children focused or to make suggestions. For instance, a teacher might suggest encouraging the more experienced partner to prompt the other child to use initial sounds. It might be necessary to advise children on how to respond sensitively and not punitively to persistent miscues. Some strategies might need to be demonstrated when the session is reviewed. Advice might be needed on what to do if the text is too challenging. The way the session is introduced and concluded is important too; it is yet another opportunity to talk about books and reading with children.

Some teachers have found it helpful to construct a brief sheet that the children jointly fill in at the end of the session; one such example included the titles of the books the children had shared and was signed by both children. It is a very simple idea but one that gives the children ownership of the routine and gives the teacher a record. The teacher also might want to offer brief comments, for example on particular book choices the children have made, saying why they were so appropriate. A teacher commented on a child's choice of *Handa's Surprise*, saying, 'I liked your choice of this book; it's a wonderful story *and* it's got lots of the different fruits that we are learning about in our food project'.

3 Following up

Some time needs to be spent after the session asking the children how it went (what went well? any difficulties?), what they learnt, what they might do differently next time, and what book they are going to choose. This engages children in self-evaluation, which could be done at a whole-class level. The children could form pairs to discuss specific questions before reporting back to the class.

The younger class

There will be many points in common with those made above. In particular, the section on pairing up applies to both classes.

1 Introduction: getting started

Again, a brief whole-class introduction to the routine would be appropriate. After telling the children that they will be reading regularly with an older partner, it could be suggested that they think about choosing a favourite book ready to show their partner. Suggestions could then be made and written up and displayed on a large sheet of paper in the book area. Later, the teacher or the children could collect the books and put them in a specially labelled box ready for the first session.

2 Following up

A focused follow-up session with the younger children might include asking them what they enjoyed about the session, what books their partners brought for them, and what they would like to take next week.

READING ONE-TO-ONE

Introduction

For many years the one-to-one reading session between teacher and child was the only reading routine that really 'counted'. Confined almost entirely to the early years and KS1, it typically consisted of the child reading a short extract from her current teacher-chosen 'reading book', with the teacher recording the pages read and words to be learnt. The 'ideal' teacher heard her children read every day. Such practice was based on a partial view of what comprises reading; it is one where decoding can easily be privileged above aspects such as understanding, response, personal involvement and strategies for choosing books.

In 1981, Southgate and Arnold's research cast a different light on this practice. They revealed that short spurts of reading practice were not as productive as fewer but longer sessions. From their work came the idea of developing the session into one which included some discussion with the child about his reading. Through such discussion the child's response to literature was developed as well as his decoding skills. As this practice developed, teachers began carrying out what has come to be known as a 'reading conference', pioneered in Britain by the Centre for Literacy in Primary Education (CLPE). These shifts denote a broadening of the view of what might go on when teacher and child meet on a one-to-one basis.

As we know from our earlier discussion, this routine was criticised by OFSTED as being both ineffective and time-consuming, and guided reading has now become established as a well embedded alternative. Despite this major shift, teachers may feel that one-to-one reading still has a significant, albeit reduced, role as a teaching routine for certain children. This is true especially for beginners and those children struggling with their reading who, because of other more complex needs, may find participating in guided groups problematic.

It is quite likely that adults other than the class teacher (TAs or volunteer parents) will be undertaking reading with individual children. It is not uncommon for schools to provide some basic training to help these adults manage the sessions effectively. For example, in the case of struggling readers who require one-to-one support, the adults might need to be aware in advance of specific strategies or targets that are to be addressed.

The struggling reader

For some struggling readers, a 'paired reading' session might be appropriate. The paired reading technique was developed by Keith Topping (Topping and Wolfendale, 1985) from a procedure devised by Roger Morgan (1976). In this procedure an experienced and a less experienced reader work together. The idea is that both read in unison with the aim of keeping up the momentum of the reading and avoiding an overemphasis on mistakes. If the child wants to read alone or pass the reading entirely over to the adult, she indicates this and there is no price to pay either way. The bare bones of a session might look something like this:

1 'warming up' and previewing the text;
2 identifying key vocabulary and reminders about strategies for decoding words;
3 reading out loud:
   a paired reading (both adult and child together for agreed stretch or until child gives signal);
   b child alone (but if agreed signal given, adult joins in again);
   c discussing strategies that worked/need to be developed further/setting targets;
4 reviewing the book;
5 concluding the session (including brief self-evaluation by child).

For very unconfident struggling readers who do not see themselves as readers, paired reading might provide a starting point for rebuilding confidence and self-esteem. As can be seen from the outline structure above, the child is carefully supported throughout. The crucial element in the session is the actual reading aloud part where the child is given a strong start by reading in unison. During this period, the child has a chance to tune in to the tone and style of the book but when she feels ready she can give the agreed signal (e.g. a nudge) and continue reading solo. If she begins to lose confidence or falter, then the signal can be used again and the adult joins in. This technique can be used throughout the reading aloud part of the session, which will help provide the child with stamina, an opportunity to use her decoding skills successfully, and also raise levels of confidence. When reviewing the session, the adult can pick up on the extent to which the child managed independently and carefully negotiate how this might be extended in the next session. Key to the success of the session will be the effective matching of the selected text to the child's needs and interests.

The youngest reader

Reading one-to-one will have a special place for children in the earliest stages of reading. Typically, these children will have enjoyed being read to by adults, have established some favourite books and will have been introduced to the early concepts about print (Clay, 1979) via short 'bursts' of shared reading and writing. They may also be displaying what Holdaway (1979) describes as reading-like behaviour. In other words, they may engage in 're-enactments' of stories that have been read to them, i.e. showing awareness of print and drawing closely on the textual structures and language of the text. Evidence may also be shown of growing phonological awareness; for example, an enjoyment of rhyming activities. These children are likely to be operating within Phase 1 of the PNS phonic progression. However, as the PNS acknowledges, teachers need to use professional judgement about these children's social readiness to participate in guided reading groups. For those children who are not yet at that point, reading individually with an adult will be a very secure, rewarding and appropriate experience. Indeed, very young children may well initiate this routine themselves with the familiar request, 'Miss, can I read to you?' Reading may take the form of simply sharing short books together or, for those who are ready, could take the following structure:

1 preview of the book (briefly discussing content, pictures, title);
2 adult reads text aloud, encouraging child to turn pages, showing her where to start reading, i.e. exploring aspects of concepts about print;
3 adult invites the child to join in on a rereading (child may 'echo'-read);
4 child takes turn to read (adult drawing attention to print, where to start reading, pointing to the words, use of early phonic knowledge, as appropriate). With children who are ready, adult may use 'pause', 'prompt', 'praise' strategy;
5 together respond to content – short discussion;
6 adult gives feedback on child's reading using statements of the type 'I like the way ...'
7 adult concludes session by encouraging child to try to reflect on her achievements.

As we have discussed, reading individually to the teacher is now expected to happen within guided reading. However, one-to-one reading outside a group setting still has its place for certain children. Although much less prominent than it was prior to the arrival of the NLS, this routine fulfils a very specific and useful role and therefore should remain part of our armoury of reading routines.

PARENTAL INVOLVEMENT

Introduction

This reading routine is slightly different as it involves parents or those who are in *loco parentis* (guardians and other carers), and can happen both inside and outside the school setting. It relies on good will and an understanding of the important role that families can play in their children's development as successful readers. It requires hard work on the part of schools in the form of regular maintenance to keep this routine running smoothly and effectively. In the following discussion, the word 'parents' will be used but account should be taken of the opening sentence above.

Historically, parents have not always been regarded as a resource. Many schools in the past kept them at arm's length and certainly believed that parental attempts to help with reading were likely to do more harm than good. *Children and their Primary Schools* (the Plowden Report, DES, 1967), *A Language for Life* (the Bullock Report, DES, 1975) and numerous research projects set up in the 1970s and 1980s (details below) changed our perceptions of the role of parents, showing that children made more literacy progress where parents were involved and encouraged their children's reading. In fact, parents have always cared about their children's literacy and there are few schools nowadays that do not realise how important it is to work in cooperation with parents. Many schools now have PACT schemes and the evidence is that they improve attitudes and attainment.

PACT is the acronym commonly used to describe arrangements made between Parents and Children and Teachers, all working together to promote literacy. The term is used to describe schemes, set up by the school, in which parents are involved in helping their own child at home with reading. Typically, the child takes a book home; the parent is encouraged to read to the child and to listen to the child reading and then to enter comments on a reading record card or in a booklet.

Why do we involve parents?

Parents are their children's first teachers and many would say that they are their children's most natural teachers. They know more about their children than teachers will ever know, and their investment in their children is greater and more personal. They spend more time with their children than teachers do and the time they give can frequently be one-to-one.

In school, the individual attention and ample time which are critical in the process of becoming literate are harder to reproduce. Parents give their children 'differentiated' reading lessons; they respond to the child's comments and questions as they arise; they tolerate interruptions; they judge when to allow the child to take over the reading; they allow the child to have her own choice of text; they encourage and understand the personal or private connections that the child makes and they sense when the child is tired. Parents are potentially in the very best position to make reading a personally rich and rewarding experience. However, not every parent will model and encourage reading in exactly the way described above. Literacy practices vary tremendously in different communities, as Shirley Brice Heath (1983), Hilary Minns (1990) and Eve Gregory (1996) have shown. In some families there may be more storytelling or there may be more recounting of happenings or TV stories. There will, in nearly all families, be models of reading and writing in situations where the purposes become clear for children. Checking TV programmes or recipes, or writing a note for the milkman or a shopping list, are examples of meaningful literacy events. In addition, most parents will respond to children's interest in the environmental print around them and in turn will draw children's attention to print, sharing speculations and observations.

But even if there were to be little of this shared family literacy (and we should be very careful in the assumptions we make that some homes are not literate places – see Chapter 1), the evidence is very clear that school–home liaison is of great benefit to children's literacy. Through home visits prior to the child starting school, we can find out about how much children have already learnt about literacy practices and then build on and from these ourselves. We need to be mindful of different literate traditions as we induct children into the school curriculum, and plan our provision to support the necessary transitions. In other words, for some children starting out in school, schooled literacy practices and routines will be more familiar than they are for others. In addition, if men can be encouraged to take a full role in the partnership, home–school liaison can provide an important context for developing boys' views of themselves as readers. (See also 'The Family Reading Campaign' on page 91.) Finally, if children feel that their parents and their teachers are talking to each other about them, keeping tabs on their progress and seeing eye-to-eye about their needs, they will feel far more secure and positive about their learning.

How do we involve parents?

Schools these days have policies for parental involvement. These will include aims and express the school's philosophy for working in partnership with parents. Staff, perhaps the EYFS Coordinator and/or the English Coordinator, will typically meet with parents of new entrants and provide an introductory workshop where their vision for the home–school reading partnership will be shared. Parents' own experience will be valued and questions will be invited. It is more than likely that they will be given a short guidance brochure. This will contain tips and 'dos' and 'don'ts' on sharing books or reading with their children. The guidance brochure may well change as the child moves through the different phases of their schooling and effective schools will run workshops periodically to support parents in moving along with their children's development as readers.

It is not possible here to give a full recipe for setting up successful PACT schemes and it would be misleading to suggest that once up and running they will be trouble-free. What must be discussed with parents is the need for reading encounters at home to be enjoyable. This is not as easy to ensure as it is to state, and it would be a mistake to believe that there is never any conflict in the parent–child reading encounters. Reading raises anxiety levels in parents and often this worry cannot be hidden from children. Parents understandably want progress to be rapid and may be concerned if their child does not appear to be moving rapidly enough through the school's scheme. Perhaps the child wants to bring home the same book again and again, and appears to be reciting by heart rather than reading the words, or the child may be having difficulty sounding out the words, or loses interest quickly. In some cases, parents may believe that their own literacy levels are inadequate (and the comments card may present terrors in this respect) and that they cannot keep up with the school's high expectations of them to spend time with their child. For some parents for whom English is a second language, the problems may be to do with feeling that they cannot make judgements on their children's reading in English. In this respect, it is important that schools encourage reading in the home languages too. So, the encounter may not always be easy but enjoyment and pleasure must be the result or the activity will be counterproductive. It may help parents who themselves are new to English to be provided with copies of the guidance brochure in their community language (translation software packages are readily available). Where schools have taken trouble to guide parents, to listen to them and are open to their concerns, parents learn to trust the school's approach.

It is helpful if parents can spend time in the classroom to see the teacher's approach in practice; equally, the teacher should learn from parents of their successful practices and activities. The following points may be useful to consider when setting up formal PACT schemes at a whole-school level.

- PACT schemes need to be set up with the full support and shared understandings of the school staff. Without the preparation and agreement of everybody, they are difficult to start or to operate successfully and even harder to sustain.
- The PACT scheme needs to be introduced in detail to the parents, probably at parents' evenings or workshops. Reading jargon needs to be avoided. Many schools have successfully used DVDs or demonstrated the process of reading with a child as part of their workshops. Many schools produce a booklet for parents, attractively illustrated and translated into other languages where necessary. Interactive sessions, with perhaps small groups working together, are useful.
- All efforts have to be sustained. Subsequent meetings are needed to keep the issues and the parents' interest alive.
- The books that are taken home from school need to be quality books so that the child and the parent can remain interested in the text. The child should always be involved in choosing.
- Reading sessions at home should be kept short; perhaps ten minutes for the youngest children, unless the child requests longer.
- Encourage parents to use 'pause, prompt, praise' when listening to the child.
- Parents should be encouraged to make comments on a reading card or in a little booklet, noting what has been done and adding comments. As the record of books read grows, so does the child's confidence and competence. (Sensitivity should be shown towards parents who may not feel confident in their own writing skills. Word of mouth is just as valuable.)
- Ideally, the teacher should respond and enter her own comments, often guiding the parent towards a deeper understanding of the reading process. Depending on the setting, TAs may take on this role, although it is the teacher's responsibility to maintain an overview.
- Continued renewing of efforts and of contacts must be part of the scheme, otherwise the benefits may start to subside.

- Where the link with the home is successful, there may be opportunities to extend the scheme into other curriculum areas. Maths and science schemes have been introduced with success in some schools.

It is important for student teachers going into schools with parental involvement schemes up and running to find out some key information:

- how many times books are taken home each week;
- whether there is a timetabled slot for choosing books to take home;
- how the books are sent home (in book bags, folders);
- what additional documentation goes with the books (e.g. book/card for parent and teacher to write on; different-coloured bookmarks, perhaps labelled 'Please read this book to your child' or 'Your child can read this book to you').

Family literacy

In the final part of our discussion on parental involvement we will look briefly at recent initiatives which recognise the importance of involving parents in their child's reading in the home.

Bookstart

Bookstart is an initiative (see Chapter 4) that recognises that it is never too young for parents and children to get involved with books and reading. The first pilot project was set up in Birmingham in 1992 and the scheme has now been rolled out nationwide. The project was based on the importance of reading with very young children and set out to:

- provide free resources that encourage parents to share books with their children;
- support and encourage them to make book sharing a habit;
- empower parents to help build the foundations of literacy;
- enable parents and children to share the pleasures and satisfaction that books offer.

(Wade and Moore, 1993)

Children currently entering EYFS and in KS1 will be '*Bookstart* babies'. That is to say that their parents will have received at the child's seven- to nine-month health check a free *Bookstart* bag containing a selection of board books, an information leaflet and also an invitation to join the local library. Children then go on to receive a *Bookstart Plus* pack between eighteen and thirty months and *My Bookstart Treasure Box* between the ages of three and four years. Collins *et al.* (2005), in their evaluation of the *Bookstart* programme, studied two cohorts of *Bookstart* children entering nursery and reception classes in September 2003, and monitored their development as readers through the first year of their formal schooling. They arrived at many important findings, some of which are listed here, as they underline the invaluable influence that parents can have on their children's early literacy development:

- Regular and consistent reading to and with babies and young children had a positive effect on young children's literacy development.
- Parents of highest-performing readers engaged in a diverse range of reading-related activities.

- Home-based literacy routines and the value parents placed on books had a positive impact on children's reading.
- The presence of wide-ranging reading material in the home was a feature of children who were progressing well in their literacy development.
- The average and highest-performing readers chose to read voluntarily in their leisure time.

(Collins *et al.*, 2005:2–3)

These findings further underline how essential it is for schools to aim to draw all parents into reading partnerships in order to give their children the very best opportunity to become fluent and avid readers.

The Family Reading Campaign

Partnership and involvement with parents is reaching out even more widely into the community. In recent years there have been initiatives to heighten the profile of family literacy and to do this by encouraging a wide range of services within communities to get involved and promote reading. Currently, the *National Literacy Trust* (NLT) is supporting this through the Family Reading Campaign. The aim is to involve services in encouraging reading in the home. Educational establishments and libraries are obvious groups but there are initiatives with employers, sport, health, housing, parent support organisations and prisons. The NLT website disseminates a wide range of information about the campaign, including family reading case studies, which are well worth taking time to look at. In addition, the *Reading Connects* initiative, which is aimed at primary and secondary schools, provides a 'family engagement toolkit' to help schools encourage families to make their homes 'reading homes'. These are exciting initiatives which recognise that reading should be a way of life and that the home is at the heart of children becoming readers for life.

Further reading and website

Bickler, S., Baker, S. and Hobsbaum, A. (2003) *Book Bands for Guided Reading*. London: Institute of Education.

Chambers, A. (1990) *Booktalk*. Stroud: Thimble.

Gamble, N. and Yates, S. (2002) *Exploring Children's Literature*. London: Paul Chapman Publishing.

Goodwin, P. (2005) *The Literate Classroom*. London: David Fulton.

Literacy Trust: http://www.literacytrust.org.uk

Chapter 6

Reading Resources

Fiona M. Collins

In this chapter we start by looking at why we need a range of reading material and genres and how to select these for the different reading routines discussed in Chapter 5.

WHAT DO CHILDREN NEED TO READ?

It should go without saying that we want to introduce children to as much and as wide a range of reading as possible. We want children to know that through reading, they will learn about the world and about people whose feelings and experiences will teach them more about themselves. We want children to know of the joys of entering the 'secondary world' of the book and we want them to experience the tunes of poetry. Not all children will respond to every item in the range of texts available but it is their right to meet them in their early lives. There are children who love poetry and those who are indifferent to it, but none should be deprived of the chance to experience it. And this applies to all other genres. That is not to say that the youngest children are to struggle through newspaper editorials or Shakespeare's soliloquies but there are plenty of texts, from comics to letters to instructions to songs, that children want to read and which widen their understanding of the functions of literacy and prepare them for the wealth of text types that they will meet as they grow older.

The *National Curriculum* (NC) has always acknowledged the importance of offering range and the *Primary National Strategy* (PNS) bases its planning framework on three genres: narrative (including plays), non-fiction and poetry. In addition, the *Rose Report's* (DfES, 2006a) endorsement of a 'language-rich curriculum' includes the need to choose quality texts. Most schools will have criteria for book selection, possibly written into their language policies, and of course the more people who can read, discuss and comment on the suitability of books the better. If you feel confident that your books have been chosen with care, you will have gone some way towards meeting your responsibility as a teacher of reading and you will feel that everything is more under control.

As well as the necessity for a wide range of genres, as government documentation prescribes, here are some additional pointers to support you when thinking about children and their reading material.

- Children develop favourite authors and favourite illustrators and these authors and illustrators seem to develop children as readers. Teachers need to provide as many titles by popular authors as possible. Enid Blyton, Roald Dahl and J.K. Rowling convince children that they are readers; on completion of one book, children cannot wait to find the next or indeed to reread.

- Children's feelings are involved when reading. Teachers should be seeking out affecting texts at all levels. The predicaments, sometimes terrifying, that characters in traditional tales fall into, make for real stories and real involvement on a scale that whets the appetite for more. Suspense, making the heart beat faster, is a quality lacking in some older reading scheme stories.
- The role of the story on the screen or audio cassette should not be underestimated. Children demand and need more retellings of stories than we can ever give them.
- If all the children we teach are to believe that books speak to them, we need to give much more thought to the range and quality of what we offer. For instance, sensitive representation of black people is now more the norm; there is no excuse for giving space to books with negative or token characters or stereotypical illustrations. Similarly, there is a need to check that the books we share show girls who can be strong and brave and clever and that boys, equally, can be liberated from conforming to the expectation to show these qualities at all times.
- Humour, comics, graphic novels and novelty books have a role to play in a child's becoming a reader. There is no doubt that the interactive nature of some novelty books forms an ideal transition from the toy to the book for the youngest readers and that all children return to books that make them laugh and to comics that are part of the group culture of the classroom. Teachers should welcome these ways into reading.

The purpose and place of fiction

All art imposes order on human behaviour and feelings. We take some aspects of life, give them a shaping that they never have in the hurly-burly of real life and produce an artefact, pleasing and satisfying to contemplate. In doing so, we feel less adrift; art (story, painting, music) makes the world less confusing and more beautiful. How true this is for even the youngest child is obvious; start telling an anecdote, an account of an incident, a little story about a family member (particularly perhaps a story about your listener) or a traditional tale and you can see rapt attention and delight personified in a two-year-old's face. If you want to get over a moral or ethical point, embed it in a story and you can probably make an impact. (This has been known since time immemorial – think of Aesop's fables, written down in the third or fourth century.)

If we can accept that story is significant to all of us but particularly to children, for whom it is a basic way of appreciating and supporting understanding of the world (Wells, 1987), we have to satisfy this hunger, and thus the best texts for reading aloud to young children are usually narrative texts. We are all interested in human behaviour (or in animals who behave in recognisably human ways) and the satisfaction of seeing a story develop is the strongest incentive to go on listening or reading. In addition, narrative texts usually rely on clear story lines, including, for instance, characters who have changed by the end of the story, a suspense-filled denouement and a resolution that brings the story reassuringly full circle. These story shapes are quickly recognised by children and give them a feeling of familiarity and competence as well as developing comprehension.

Learning about story shape takes place most powerfully when children read and hear traditional tales. Because these stories were handed down orally they have memorable and robust structures which have survived generations of retelling. These stories have universal shapes so it is important that you find stories from across the world. The fact that Disney has made films of the more well known European traditional tales means that a story such as *The Sleeping Beauty* is better known than the powerful stories of Anansi or ancient tales from China, India or North America. A recognition that there is a rich worldwide store of tales needs to be evident in your classroom.

Often it is traditional tales that present girls and women in passive roles with boys and men being brave and having all the adventures. The move now is rather away from the 1970s initiative to rewrite these stories, having Red Riding Hood for instance kill the wolf herself, and more towards unearthing the 'forgotten' traditional tales that were ignored in the nineteenth century by such collectors as the Brothers Grimm. James Riordan and Alison Lurie have made good collections of such tales.

In addition, there is a rich seam of 'new' tales where traditional expectations are upset to amusing effect. Tony Ross and Babette Cole create books of this type that are very popular with children. Children will enjoy rewriting traditional tales themselves once they have had exposure to enough examples of the genre and of course the full enjoyment of Allan and Janet Ahlberg's books or those of Jon Scieszka and Lane Smith and of Lauren Child depends upon a grasp of the traditional stories that are quoted or subverted.

As well as choosing a range of stories you also need to consider their language. Most writers are very careful with the language of their books, especially in picture books, where each word counts and is going to be read by teacher, parent or child scores of times. Some of the best stories have been reworked so that the language is simple but very telling. However, you must also ensure that you have included books that offer rich images, simile, metaphor, personification and alliteration. Texts by authors such as Joan Aiken, Kevin Crossley-Holland, Geraldine McCaughrean and Jill Paton Walsh are rewarding in these respects.

When selecting books for your classroom you will also want to take a careful look at content as well as structure and language. Stories that focus more on domestic themes need to be interspersed with something more fantastical, so a Jacqueline Wilson title could be followed by one by Philip Pullman. Across a year children need to have met stories with boy and girl main characters, set in Britain and abroad, in real and fantasy worlds, in present and past times and so on. The key is balance.

The purpose and place of poetry

Children's natural affinity with and pleasure in rhyme and rhythm predisposes them to like poetry. Poetry could be said to be similar to music in that it has a tune and the tune can remain in the head long after the actual reading has passed. In addition, there are a succinctness and directness to many jingles, rhymes and poems which please children. Access to poetry has improved over the last thirty years with a more informal and child-friendly strain of poetry that has been published and frequently performed. Poets such as Michael Rosen, Gareth Owen, Kit Wright, Allan Ahlberg, Jackie Kay, John Agard, Grace Nichols, Roger McGough and Brian Patten have opened up the world of poetry for a new generation of children and made the genre attractive to boys for perhaps the first time. Teachers have been able to explore this varied output and then to approach the work of other, perhaps more demanding, contemporary poets such as Charles Causley, Ted Hughes, Seamus Heaney and James Berry. It is likely that classical poetry has always found followers amongst certain teachers and pupils but the net is probably cast much more widely now that familiarity with newer poets has created confidence and enthusiasm.

The following list suggests what kinds of verse to look out for in terms of range:

- nursery rhymes;
- finger rhymes;
- contemporary and classical poetry;
- poetry from around the world;
- long and short poems;
- some for declamation, others for quiet individual reading;
- some rhyming and some unrhyming;
- a variety of forms, e.g. haiku, sonnets, rhyming couplets, four-line verses;
- poetry by children.

The purpose and place of plays

Reading a play together is one of the most interdependent forms of reading aloud. Experiencing how a story can come alive in a group reading or, if the play reading develops, in a performance, is likely to benefit all involved, bringing a class together in a collaborative and purposeful way. There are also lessons to be learnt about intonation and characterisation that are scaffolded by sharing a play script together. Teachers concerned about boys' attitudes and progress have found that play readings can be one successful way of providing motivating contexts.

When looking for play scripts, the quality of the narrative is the first priority and if you know the story in its original format, you will probably find the play scripts to be of equal quality. There are many plays within reading schemes and programmes; make sure you think they are written well enough to be worth having multiple copies.

Children need a lot of help in the early stages of reading from play scripts regarding the conventions to be observed (e.g. not reading the stage directions aloud, following the story rather than looking ahead to see where your lines come in again). With your support, the activity can become extremely popular and makes a clear contribution to literacy levels.

The purpose and place of non-narrative texts

We know that story is important for young children and that most early texts are stories and that even non-narrative texts for the young tend to include narrative elements. Nevertheless, we also all know many children who have an equal hunger to possess information texts and, in truth, neither narrative nor non-narrative should be neglected. With the emphasis on writing in a range of non-narrative genres it is even more important that children are experiencing the shapes and conventions of the language of non-fiction.

There is a specific role for the teacher in teaching children how to use non-fiction texts. Children need to hear you read aloud from information texts so that their different 'tune' is heard. There are also some important factors to take into account when choosing non-fiction:

- Does the contents page help children find the section they want?
- Does the index work in terms of full coverage, useful categorisation, etc.?
- Is the glossary written in language that children can understand?
- Is the page layout balanced between image and text, so that one extends and supports the other?
- Is the general design attractive to the child reader? Is it colourful and up to date? Does it make use of subheadings to break up the text?
- Are the facts accurate as far as can be determined? Are they presented without undue bias?
- Are new words clearly explained in context as well as in the glossary and are they repeated frequently?
- Are readers helped with words which have one common and one specialised meaning?
- Is it recognised that, because there is no supportive narrative structure, vocabulary might need to be simpler than in narrative texts?
- Is it recognised that long sentences are not necessarily harder than a string of shorter ones?
- Is there variety in the prose, perhaps supplied by dialogue or case studies or perhaps through alliteration, simile and metaphor, and rhythmic prose?

TEXTS WITHIN THE ROUTINES

Shared reading

Big books (texts enlarged by the publishers up to as much as 50 × 36 cm) provide a major resource for shared reading, which, you will remember from Chapter 5, is when teachers demonstrate reading for children and encourage them to join in the reading. In Don Holdaway's days, there were no published big books and all his examples are of books made by the teachers themselves. However, publishing companies were quick to see a gap in the market and Scholastic Publications (which was Holdaway's original publisher), Arnold Wheaton (original publishers of the reading scheme *Story Chest*) and Oliver & Boyd (*Storytime Giants*) all produced large-scale texts. Sometimes the big books were originals, such as *Hairy Bear, The Hungry Giant* and *Mrs Wishy-Washy* (*Story Chest*), and sometimes a text that appeared in conventional size first proved extremely popular and was then reissued in large size. *Not Now Bernard* (David McKee), *Oscar Got the Blame* (Tony Ross), *Each Peach Pear Plum* (Janet and Allan Ahlberg) and *The Lighthouse Keeper's Lunch* (Rhonda and David Armitage) all fall into this latter category. Probably the success of these enlarged texts has influenced the size of all children's picture books, which are now appreciably larger than they used to be and so very useful for shared reading (and reading aloud to the class).

Today big books cover the range of genres required by the PNS: fiction, non-fiction, plays and poetry. Stories are often traditional, rhythmic, predictable and include patterned language and intrinsic repetition with which children quickly join in. Many books make a great effort to vary and play with the print size to make it distinctive and indeed there is evidence that children are attentive to print which grOWS or Shrinks or changes in some way. Books that rely on a complex interplay between text and illustration, such as *Handa's Surprise* (Eileen Browne), obviously lend themselves to enlarged text format as the whole class can then see the game that author and illustrator are playing.

As previously discussed, shared reading occurs across the primary age phase and teachers working with Year 1 children will build on work carried out in the *Early Years Foundation Stage* (EYFS). Stories with patterned, predictable and rhythmic language are essential for this age group as children delight in the telling of the story and in making up their own rhymes. (This features in the PNS Framework, Year 1, Unit 2. For subsequent PNS links, we will give the Year and Unit.) Although there is a vast range of titles available today in big book form it is not always necessary to use these: sometimes you may wish to share for a specific reason a particular book which is only published in a conventional format. If so, you will need either to seat the children close to you or project pages from the book on the interactive whiteboard or use your school's projecting equipment (e.g. a 'docu-cam'). *Where's My Teddy?* and *It's the Bear!* (Jez Alborough) are two examples of amusing rhyming books neither of which is in big book form and it is perfectly possible to use them effectively in shared reading so that their compelling stories, rhyme and rhythm can be enjoyed.

> He sat on the hamper and tried not to cry, then …
> "I CAN SMELL FOOD!" yelled a voice from nearby.
> "IT'S THE BEAR!" cried Eddy. "WHERE CAN I HIDE?"
> Then he opened the hamper and clambered inside.
>
> (*It's the Bear!*, Jez Alborough)

Handa's Surprise (Browne) is another example of a book which holds exciting potential in terms of its narrative and linguistic qualities. Handa sets off from her village, basket on head, to make a present of fruits to her friend Akeyo. Each fruit is stolen by an animal but Handa is blissfully unaware and so it would seem is the narrator. But we, the readers of the book, can see the drama unfolding in the illustrations and anticipate Handa's approaching surprise. Browne uses extended noun phrases to describe the fruit that Handa is carrying:

> Will she like the round juicy orange …
> or the ripe red mango?
> Will she like the spikey-leaved pineapple …
> The creamy green avocado
> Or the tangy purple passion-fruit?

It's the Bear! and *Handa's Surprise* and similar books can stimulate children's own oral and written language.

Traditional tales play an important part of literacy teaching in Key Stage 1 (KS1, Year 2, Unit 2) and contribute to a child's literacy development as discussed earlier. Numerous traditional tales are published in big book form. Some tales reinvent or change traditional tales such as *The Three Little Wolves and the Big Bad Pig* (Eugene Trivizas and Helen Oxenbury) and *Once Upon a Time* (John Prater). Both stories use intertextuality to alter and rearrange traditional tales. *Once Upon a Time* is a told story with short rhythmic lines which encourage children to join in with the reading. The detailed illustrations add humour to the storyline and extend the narrative beyond the printed word. In contrast, *The Three Little Wolves and the Big Bad Pig*, which is for older Key Stage 1 (and Key Stage 2) readers, changes a well known story completely by giving the story a modern spin. The story can promote lively discussion about why the pig mellows at the end (Year 2, strand 7). Big books of traditional stories are also published as play scripts which allow KS1 children to take different parts and act these with the rest of the class as the audience. Using play scripts in this way allows the teacher to discuss the metalanguage of acting, for instance 'scene', 'actor', 'part' and 'offstage'. One series by Vivian French (e.g. *The Gingerbread Boy, The Three Billy Goats Gruff*) is particularly useful for KS1 as the parts are colour-coded for ease of reading and differentiation.

Teachers also use non-fiction texts in shared reading, and an ever-growing selection of non-fiction big book titles is published today, for both KS1 and KS2. Teresa Heapy's *Korky Paul: Biography of an Illustrator* provides a lively mixture of graphics, photographs and accessible text. It comes complete with contents page and index and its non-patronising tone, as well as the use of Paul's own distinctive illustrations, mean that it could be used with older KS1 children as well as in KS2. Shared reading of non-narrative texts and information books in KS2 can be linked clearly to other curriculum areas. Within the daily literacy lesson children will learn about the linguistic and structural features of texts such as non-chronological reports, explanation or diaries. Big books are published which cover each of the six non-narrative genres. Children learn how such texts are organised and discover the way connectives and tenses that characterise non-fiction are used. Using texts linked to other curriculum areas will also help children to understand the relevance of such texts as well as helping them with their own writing.

Poetry anthologies are also published in big book form for children in the EYFS, KS1 and KS2. Such anthologies are ideal for shared readings, performance and class discussions about the stories held in narrative poems, the emotional impact of certain poems as well as how rhyme, language patterns and form contribute to the overall effect. John Foster, the poet and writer, has put together several poetry collections for sharing that are published in big book form for KS1 children. For KS2, anthologies of classic poetry are also available; for example, *A Collection of Classic Poems* selected by Wendy Body includes poems by Christina Rossetti, John Keats, Walter de la Mare and Robert Louis Stevenson. This type of collection will give KS2 children a taste of different poets before moving on to study one or two in more depth as a class project (Year 5, Unit 2).

Many teachers use texts or extracts projected onto the interactive whiteboard. It is important to note that if an extract is studied children do need to read or be told the complete story or article before, during or after the shared reading. It is important to link reading aloud, outside the daily literacy lesson, to shared reading. An example of this would be to read, over a period of time to a Year 4 class (Year 4, Unit 2), the short story *The Fog Hounds* (Joan Aiken), a mysterious and multi-layered tale that leaves many gaps for the reader to fill. During the shared reading, questions of who characters really are, whether they are good or evil or a mixture, the role that magic played in the story and what happened before the story began and after it ends, can be raised and discussed. With such an enigmatic story, the children themselves will ask many questions that you may not be able to predict. A story like this opens up many possibilities for enhancing children's comprehension (e.g. media interviews with the villagers, who, at the beginning of the story, appear to be terrorised by the nightly visits of the fog hounds).

Another rich text to use with a KS2 class would be *The Pied Piper of Hamelin*, of which there are several picture book versions in print. This story would encourage a range of drama events to develop after shared reading, such as hot-seating different characters, holding a press conference with the parents of the missing children, writing a newspaper report about the loss and dramatising the whole story (OFSTED, 2004).

Teaching phonics

The *Rose Report* (DfES, 2006a) states that synthetic phonics should be taught in short, discrete daily sessions. The report recommends that these sessions should draw on a range of stimulating resources and be multisensory. This has implications for the type of resources that teachers use in such sessions. In the past there has been an over-reliance on dull worksheets to teach phonics but Rose is against such dependency. To implement his recommendations, teachers need to find activities that are enjoyable and engaging.

The PNS, in its guidance to head teachers and chairs of governors, gives specific criteria for selecting commercially produced phonic schemes for the whole school. These include the need for the phonic scheme to:

* be systematic;
* have clearly defined progression;
* be delivered in discrete sessions on a daily basis;
* be underpinned by a synthetic approach;
* be multisensory and linked to speaking and listening;
* have clear guidance on assessment;
* contain guidance for use with individual needs.

(DfES, 2006c)

Examples of schemes that claim to address these criteria include *Jolly Phonics*, *THRASS*, *Collins Big Cat Phonics* and *Read Write Inc.* Another option is for schools to use the PNS's own phonic scheme – *Letters and Sounds* (DfES, 2007a).

Along with these programmes, EYFS settings and KS1 classrooms should be resourced with a range of materials for further practical work on phonics. Such materials could include:

* magnetic or wooden letters to blend and segment individual words;
* interactive games which utilise reading rods and cubes to engage children in using digraphs and blends to make words;
* pictorial card activities which support children in relation to the initial, medial and final phonemes in words;
* phonic fans and wheels to encourage children to manipulate individual letters to make words;
* board and card games for group work on phonics and words;
* flash cards for teaching and learning high-frequency words;
* small whiteboards and marker pens for segmenting activities;
* TV programmes, CD-ROMs and computer programs for learning phonemes.

Although children benefit from working with such materials independently, they do need to be carefully planned for within the discrete phonics lesson for both whole-class and group work.

With the publication of the *Rose Report* publishers have developed their production of 'decodable readers'. These contain staged vocabulary which gradually introduces the forty-four phonemes. Such books put emphasis on decoding skills and as a result the content of the books can sometimes be weak, particularly in the early stages, where the narrative structure suffers. However, Rose clearly states that 'there is no doubt, too, that the simple texts in some recognised favourite children's books can ful-fil much the same function as that of decodable books' (DfES, 2006a:27). He goes on to argue strongly that children should never be denied access to higher-quality texts and favourite stories. So take heart – there is no compulsion to use dull stories.

Guided reading

In most schools, guided reading (see Chapter 5) is taught on a regular basis outside the daily literacy lesson at both KS1 and KS2. In some schools it is still organised within the literacy lesson and can be closely linked to the content of shared reading. Guided read-ing is seen as an efficient way of regularly hearing all children read and an important element of the routine is the choice of texts for the differentiated groups. Texts chosen for a guided reading group should match the children's level of reading proficiency, as they should be able to read the text with 90 per cent to 94 per cent accuracy (Hobsbaum *et al.*, 2006; OFSTED, 2004).

Key Stage 1

Hobsbaum suggests you consider the following when choosing KS1 texts:

- amount of print on the page;
- size of the font and spacing between words;
- range and familiarity of vocabulary;
- extent to which the language follows spoken or literary conventions;
- extent of repetition in various forms including vocabulary and story structure;
- extent to which illustrations support the text;
- variety and complexity of sentence structure;
- predictability of storyline;
- length and complexity of the book or story;
- formality of language and layout used;
- extent to which the text genre is familiar to children.

(Hobsbaum, 2000:12)

Preferably the texts used in guided reading should link to the texts used in shared read-ing and also to the requirements of the PNS. A story such as *Alfie Gets in First* (Shirley Hughes) is an ideal choice for Year 1. It is emotionally engaging and holds the chil-dren's attention, and its 'familiar setting' (Year 1, Unit 1) means children can easily bring personal meaning to it. After shared reading, differentiated guided reading groups might go on to read *This is the Bear* (Sarah Hayes and Helen Craig), *Dogger* (Shirley Hughes), *Ginger* (Charlotte Voake) or *Leon and Bob* (Simon James).

As well as reading picture books at KS1 many class teachers use the graded structure of a reading scheme in guided reading. Schemes such as *Oxford Reading Tree* are extremely popular. Teachers of early reading choose reading schemes because they are levelled and use controlled vocabulary; they also cover a range of narrative and non-narrative texts and some are written and illustrated by well known authors and illustrators. For instance, *Oxford Reading Tree* publishes a series of stories which are phonic-based written by the well known author Julia Donaldson (*The Gruffalo*). Some children may need the support of such texts in the early stages of learning to read but it is important that this type of decodable book is one aspect only of children's reading diet and that they regularly share a range of picture books and texts with experienced adults. In this way, young readers will be immersed in a range of text types and their reading experience broadened.

An alternative to reading schemes is Book Bands. This method of organising and grading books has become more popular as guided reading is integrated into schools' literacy routines. Originating from Cliff Moon's 'individualised reading' (see Chapter 1), which categorised books into colour-coded levels, Book Bands have developed with guided reading specifically in mind. *Book Bands for Guided Reading* (Hobsbaum, 2000) is one such publication. In this scheme, each gradient of difficulty is linked to both NC levels and to individual years. The books identified for each year cover a range of genres. Its authors state that schools do need, however, to be aware of the needs of individual children and 'to make special provision for children falling above and below the ranges indicated, if necessary on an individual basis' (Hobsbaum, 2000). The Institute of Education, London University, also publishes *Guiding Reading: A Handbook for Teaching Guided Reading at KS2* (Hobsbaum *et al.*, 2006). This publication contains annotated lists of trade books, categorised into the four different years of KS2.

Available currently are series of books which are graded into bands; an example of such a scheme is Collins' *Big Cat*. The books in the *Collins Big Cat* scheme are specifically written for each band and are sold in packs by Collins Education. The series covers guided readers for both KS1 and KS2 and is a mixture of a reading scheme and *Individualised Reading*. In fact, Cliff Moon is the series editor and each of the teachers' manuals is introduced by Moon. Once again the books are organised into colour-coded levels. They cover a range of genres – fiction, non-fiction, poetry and play scripts – and some are written by known authors and poets. For each band, there is an accompanying teachers' resource book which gives useful activities and guidance on the assessment of reading. Such publications seem to do the selecting for us. But, in practice, the potential of such material can only be realised in the skilful hands of a knowledgeable and effective teacher and inevitably, in such a large scheme, the quality of the stories is somewhat uneven.

Key Stage 2

Guided reading at KS2 should reflect the diversity of readers within an individual class. For the majority of readers, guided reading will give KS2 readers a chance to develop their skills in using inference and deduction, widen their responses to different types of texts and extend their reading diet. As Hobsbaum *et al.* argue,

> Texts for guided reading should be selected for the quality of their content, language and attractive presentation. A principal aim in teaching reading is to develop independent readers,

capable of dealing with sophisticated texts for a range of purposes, including study and recreation. To achieve this, they need to encounter engaging, well-written and well presented books and other resources, reflecting the full range of fiction and non-fiction types.

(2006:39)

Guided reading can enrich children's reading repertoire by introducing them to new authors. A focus on a particular author is an excellent way to introduce children to new books and to stimulate class discussions on a variety of texts (Year 3, Unit 4). Award-winning writer and former Children's Laureate Michael Morpurgo has written over 200 short stories, novels and picture books. He demonstrates in all his books a concern for the environment, the horrors of war and questions of time, generations and freedom. His books include historical fiction (*The Wreck of the Zanzibar*), mysteries (*The Butterfly Lion*), football stories (*Billy the Kid*) and autobiography (*Farm Boy*). Experienced readers (indeed all readers) need books that take them vicariously into situations which extend their thinking socially, culturally, politically and emotionally. Children's classics such as *Tom's Midnight Garden* (Philippa Pearce) take the reader into another time through entering a parallel world. *Skellig* (David Almond) will allow children to discuss what the creature Skellig is, the reader's changing response to Skellig and the link between reality and fantasy. *The Other Side of Truth* (Beverley Naidoo) is about the reality of migration for two children from Nigeria to Great Britain. Texts chosen with care and thought deepen a child's knowledge and understanding of the world.

Poetry in guided reading can be from single-author collections (e.g. *Daft as a Doughnut*, Adrian Mitchell), themed anthologies (e.g. *Sensational! Poems Inspired by the Five Senses*, chosen by Roger McGough), multi-author collections (e.g. *From Mouth to Mouth: Oral Poems from Around the World*, selected by John Agard and Grace Nicholls) or poetry might come in the form of poetic narratives (e.g. *Love that Dog*, Sharon Creech).

Children should also read non-fiction material in guided reading sessions. As well as using published scheme books and information books, material such as newspaper articles, travel brochures and publicity leaflets will broaden a child's reading range. Biography and autobiography also feature in the PNS (Year 6, Unit 1), and a book such as Jacqueline Wilson's memoirs, *Jacky Daydream*, which is specifically written for child readers, is ideal for a guided reading session. As Safford states in Chapter 2, whilst there is concern about boys and reading, equally some girls are reluctant to read non-fiction texts and a book such as *Jacky Daydream* might encourage them to do so.

Those KS2 children who might be called reluctant readers can be stimulated and engaged with texts through interaction and the support of their teacher or Teaching Assistant. Books need to be chosen so that the content is applicable to age, gender and interests as well as matching reading level. Books in reading schemes are regularly used with struggling readers at KS2 but for several reasons, such as their contrived stories and the stigma attached to being seen reading them, they are not always popular. Paul Jennings and Gary Paulsen are two authors whose books are short and action-packed and the reader is gripped throughout. If reading is difficult, the struggle has to be worthwhile.

Reading aloud

The act of listening to a story read aloud expressively by a teacher is all-involving for a child, whether the child is three or eleven years of age. Stories that are read aloud can stand alone or be linked to other literacy activities, such as shared reading, role-play or other curriculum areas. Books that are read aloud introduce children to new texts, new genres and new authors. As OFSTED found in schools which taught literacy effectively, 'teachers' influence in introducing pupils to new texts and authors was significant. Pupils enjoyed being read to and responded very positively to the regular reading of class novels' (2004:12). This routine will also develop a community of readers within the class, in that the shared text gives children the same point of reference for discussion and this is a very powerful tool for a teacher to use. However, it is important that texts are chosen carefully and thoughtfully so that they generate rich and insightful discussions between the children and their teacher.

Over time, we build up our repertoire of tried and trusted books to read aloud to children. When asking an experienced teacher which books work best for our youngest children, she immediately identified the following: *Where's Spot?* (Eric Hill), *Each Peach Pear Plum* (Allan and Janet Ahlberg), *Not Now Bernard* (David McKee), *The Very Hungry Caterpillar* (Eric Carle), *A Dark Dark Tale* (Ruth Brown), *The Enormous Turnip* (Ian Beck), *Mr Gumpy's Outing* (John Burningham), *Where's My Teddy?* (Jez Alborough) and *Handa's Surprise* (Eileen Browne). 'I could go on', she laughed. 'There are at least fifty more titles where these came from!' When asked about their appeal, she picked up on their repetitive structure, strongly patterned language, the underlying messages, the importance of humour and the quality of their illustrations. Books such as *Scarface Claw* get young and old giggling at the alliterative language – 'jittery jot', 'lollop and leap' – as well as drawing them into the rough and tumble of the story through the use of rhythm and rhyme. The author, Lynley Dodd, also makes superb use of names, 'Bottomley Potts', 'Hercules Morse' and, of course, 'Hairy Maclary', as well as the amusing illustrations. This reliable stock of favourites provides a positive starting point but we should aim to be on the look-out for new titles to add to our collection. Books such as *Tadpole's Promise* (Jeanne Willis and Tony Ross), *Traction Man is Here* (Mini Grey), *Rumble in the Jungle* (Giles Andreae and David Wojtowycz) and *Giraffes Can't Dance* (Giles Andreae and Guy Parker-Rees) are relative newcomers, but their chances of entering 'the hall of fame' depend entirely on the response of their sternest critics – the children.

Reading aloud needs to be planned for all ages. The readings may be chosen because they cover a particular theme, link to another curriculum area or are relevant to the PNS strands for that particular year. The PNS states:

> A planned read-aloud programme is one key to the development of early readers, providing them with the essential tunes, rhythms and structures of language. It offers an ever-increasing store of vocabulary on which children can draw in speech and writing. Teachers promote pleasure in reading through reading aloud a wide range of stories, poems, rhymes and information texts.
>
> (DfES, 2006c:107)

For example, in the EYFS you might plan your role-play area using a book from the Happy Family series as your context. This series includes *Mrs Wobble the Waitress* – an ideal vehicle for setting up Mrs Wobble's café – or *Miss Dose the Doctor's Daughter* – the ideal opportunity for a doctor's surgery. There are many information texts for this age which will complement work going on in the classroom. Penelope Arlon's 'eye know' books are fact books about nature with flaps, fold-outs, activities, recipes and are suitable for children in the EYFS and KS1.

In KS1, a planned reading aloud programme could develop around a theme such as 'home', a topic of relevance for all children. For children in Year 2, books such as *The Colour of Home* (Mary Hoffman and Karin Littlewood), *Home Now* (Lesley Beake and Karin Littlewood) and *Grace and Family* (Mary Hoffman and Caroline Binch) address what home actually means to a child, and the issues of migration, loss and separation. Linking picture books through common themes allows for fruitful and extended class discussions that may help some children who are dealing with these issues themselves.

A planned reading aloud programme can also link texts together for a particular purpose. An example of this might be to widen KS1 children's repertoire from listening only to picture books to listening to a novel. Here is one teacher's way of allowing for a smooth transition for her Year 2 class:

> I wanted to read short novels to my Year 2 class but I was concerned as they had only been used to listening to me read picture books to them. I decided that after Christmas I would read them the classic *The Owl who was Afraid of the Dark* (Jill Tomlinson). In the autumn term, I read them a selection of picture books, fiction and non-fiction about owls and others that reflected the recurrent themes of the novel: feeling lonely and lost, being afraid of the dark, growing up. Two books I read were *Owl Babies* (Martin Waddell and Patrick Benson) and *The Park in the Dark* (Martin Waddell and Barbara Firth). In January I read a chapter of *The Owl who was Afraid of the Dark* to the children every day. I made the reading corner into a tree and I sat, on my chair, in the tree with the children at my feet. Initially, when we started to read the story, I asked them to close their eyes as I read and after the reading we would discuss what they had visualised. As the reading progressed we started to make comparisons between the novel and the books we had read in the autumn term. This worked out very well as the children learnt how to visualise for themselves as well as discussing their own personal responses to the story.

Reading aloud is a routine that has been neglected at KS2. However, it remains as important for older children as it is for the very youngest children. Picture books can still be read to children in Years 3 and 4 but it is also the time to strengthen their repertoire of novels. Bear in mind how Charles Dickens left the end of each chapter on a cliff-hanger so the reader would want to know what was going to happen next and see if you can plan where you will stop in your novel reading to keep children wanting to know more.

In choosing novels you need to consider their texture: if the prose is too dense, children may lose concentration, especially if the book is not read daily. On the other hand, books need more substance than just dialogue and action. Try to find books that engage the children in the class from the beginning of the reading such as *Charlotte's Web* (E.B. White), for example:

> '"Where's Papa going with that axe?" said Fern to her mother as they were setting the table for breakfast.'

But a teacher can 'warm up' a story so that the class will respond positively to the opening and want to continue listening to the serial reading. As a trainee teacher once told me, after reading *The Midnight Fox* (Betsy Byars) to a class of Year 5 children:

They all listen to me while I'm reading and the mother of a boy who can't read has bought him a copy so he can follow when I'm reading and another boy who can read, but doesn't, asked me to recommend another Betsy Byars novel because he enjoyed the story so much.

The main character of *The Midnight Fox* is a boy, and boys unquestionably respond well to books where the main character is male. However, your planning needs to ensure that a balance of male and female main characters is maintained. In boys' *private* reading (see below), this is less of an issue.

Reading aloud can also be linked to other curriculum areas. Books such as *Goodnight Mister Tom* (Michelle Magorian), planned in conjunction with studying the history of World War II evacuation, can help bring children closer to the heart of the events. A Year 4 class, having worked with the novel, went through the simulated experience of being evacuees for themselves. The teacher planned an extended drama and went so far as to arrange for them to arrive at their own village hall where they were duly billeted in the school overnight, with staff and parents in role! This creative approach to the curriculum did much to deepen their understanding and whetted their appetite to learn more. There are many other novels set in World War II that can be read aloud to children. *Friend or Foe* (Michael Morpurgo), *Friedrich* (Hans Richter), *Blitzcat* (Robert Westall) and *When Hitler Stole Pink Rabbit* (Judith Kerr) are just four which cover different perspectives of the war. Also suitable for this age range is the picture book *Rose Blanche* (Roberto Innocenti and Ian McEwan), which leaves no reader unmoved.

Private and independent reading

Children learn to become independent and critical readers through reading a range of texts both privately and in school. An international comparison (PIRLS) of children's reading achievement carried out in 2001 in thirty-five countries (Twist *et al.*, 2003) showed that England ranked third behind Sweden and the Netherlands in children's reading achievements. Sadly, however, the gap between our highest and lowest achievers was greater than in other countries. Equally worrying was the finding that pupils in England had more negative attitudes to reading and read very little for pleasure compared with their counterparts in other countries. So, whilst we are teaching children the mechanics of reading, it seems that we do not make them into readers. A further point emerged after OFSTED's report *Reading for Purpose and Pleasure*:

> Many children read at home, either on the computer or in magazines and information books. However, they seldom pursue their personal reading interests at school. We need to ask whether schools are doing enough to capture children's enthusiasm and to explore their own interests.

> (Bell, press conference, 2004)

Bell went on to say that schools needed to entice children into reading through having a broad range of texts available for them to read in school and to take home, so that pupils had access to good-quality books both at school and at home. In the EYFS and KS1, books are often sent home for parents to share with their children (see Chapter 5) but at KS2 such links are less common, so generally children at KS2 will depend on books in the home and library books for their personal reading. This situation clearly disadvantages many children.

OFSTED also found that in the most effective schools, teachers monitored children's reading choices and suggested new and varied texts and authors so that the children's reading horizons expanded. However, in a recent national survey of children and their reading (Maynard *et al.*, 2007), it was found that only 13.3 per cent of KS2 children said that their teacher helped them choose books and only 8.8 per cent of KS2 pupils said the recommendations that their teacher gave them were acted upon. This compared with 48.7 per cent of pupils who stated that their mothers recommended books to them. The urge to read privately and independently is enormously significant in children's reading development, which is acknowledged in the PNS in strand 8, 'engaging and responding to texts'. Below is a selection of statements from strand 8 which clearly reflects the significance of children's personal reading in their literacy development:

Year 1: Select books for personal reading and give reasons for choices
Year 3: Share and compare reasons for reading preferences, extending the range of books read
Year 4: Read extensively favourite authors or genres and experiment with other types of texts
Year 6: Read extensively and discuss personal reading with others, including in reading groups.

Strand 8 has significant implications for all primary teachers, literacy coordinators, school libraries and public libraries. A thorough, up-to-date knowledge of children's literature is required by all those involved in teaching children to read in order to help children choose relevant books and move from one genre to another, thus widening their reading repertoire. A teacher's knowledge is required not only of book titles but also of the content of the books so that they can talk meaningfully with children.

It may be that in an early years setting, practitioners will send specific picture books home which read aloud well, are multi-layered and will engage the interest of the child. Picture books such as *How to Catch a Star* (Oliver Jeffers) or *Baby Brains* (Simon James) have big, clear and uncluttered pictures, rhythmic texts, and pleasing, predictable storylines – and parents will enjoy them as well. Books for children at this young age (such as *Hello Twins*, Charlotte Voake; *Whatever*, William Bee; *Silly Billy*, Anthony Browne; *Seahorse: The Shyest Fish in the Sea*, Chris Butterworth and John Lawrence) can help them come to terms with problems or fears in their young lives. Others, such as the Ahlbergs' *Starting School*, anticipate future issues: 'A child just before starting full or part-time education, for example, will be very interested indeed in hearing stories about schools or various other experiences in the future that also tend to crop up in story-books for this age' (Tucker, 1981:52).

For a developing reader at KS1, picture books, poetry, books in series and simple novels can all be recommended. Lauren Child's zany picture books have a sophistication and allure for this age range and are particularly suited to private reading; any volume of poetry by Michael Rosen will be received with great excitement (two of his very popular titles have been combined in a new edition, *Mustard, Custard, Grumble Belly and Gravy*, whose title says it all!); Kes Gray has a series about Daisy who, in the latest book, *006 and a Bit*, plays one of her imaginative games; Jan Mark's title *Road Closed* is a short novel exploring friendship ideally pitched for this age range.

Newly fluent readers at KS2 will continue to need picture books, short stories and poetry. The children's book magazine *Books for Keeps* includes in its reviews a short section on picture books relevant for older readers (e.g. *Fly Pigeon Fly*, John Henderson, Julie Donaldson and Thomas Docherty), which will be very useful to you, as children at this age do not want to be seen reading 'babyish' picture books. Many traditional tales are collected into anthologies and give children chances to revisit stories that you may have read aloud to the class. There are sophisticated retellings in collections such as *Dragons: Truth, Myth and Legend* (David Passes) which combine rich language, fascinating facts and robust stories. Short story collections abound but you will never go wrong with old favourites such as *The Julian Stories* (Ann Cameron) and *The Winter Sleepwalker* (Joan Aiken). You can use anthologies for poetry as well. *The Puffin Book of Utterly Brilliant Poetry*, and others like it, can be your starting points for widening children's experience of poetry.

Books in series such as the *Horrid Henry* series and the Lemony Snicket books offer an important scaffold for children who are developing reading fluency. These books are so popular because of the familiarity of the characters and the repetitive and formulaic plots, which mean that the child knows what to expect. It is easier to enter a secondary world when you have been there before, and when you come out of it you have the confidence to want to enter it again in the follow-up books. By reading and rereading such stories, children build their stamina for reading and come to understand narrative structure. The formulaic nature of series books, however, means that we also need to help children move on when they are ready. For a child hooked on the fantasy world of Lemony Snicket, you could recommend Robert Swindells' *The Ice Palace* or Beverly Cleary's *Dear Mr Henshaw*. A child who is constantly reading and rereading the Harry Potter series might be offered the *The Wind on Fire* series by William Nicholson or the *Artemis Fowl* series by Eoin Colfer. Alternatively, the teacher might feel the child needs to move on to another genre altogether in order to broaden his reading diet. Joan Aiken's James III series, which starts with *The Wolves of Willoughby Chase*, is a mixture of fantasy and historical fiction. The Aiken books might then interest the reader in pure historical fiction (such as *Children of Winter*, Berlie Doherty, and *Coram Boy*, Jamila Gavin).

Children's personal reading choices are often varied, eclectic and much influenced by popular culture. Young children enjoy the books and artefacts that accompany Disney tales, Barbie, Bob the Builder and Angelina Ballerina. These texts, which go in and out of fashion, are an important part of children's reading development as children make these reading choices for themselves and have ownership of them. Older children and more sophisticated readers may move on to books such as the *Alex Rider* series (Anthony Horowitz), the *Young James Bond* series (Charlie Higson), Jacqueline Wilson or *Point Horror* books. Such texts are often gender-specific and are aimed at boy or girl readers. The National Centre for Research in Children's Literature (Maynard *et al.*, 2007) survey also found that 71 per cent of KS1 and 70 per cent of KS2 children read comics. A range of titles was mentioned by KS1 children mainly linked to popular fiction and television programmes, while the *Beano* and the *Simpsons* comics were the two most popular for KS2. One of the main findings of OFSTED's *Reading for Purpose and Pleasure* was that 'schools seldom built on pupils' own reading interests and the range of material they read outside school' (2004:4). The class reading corner and the school library should be stocked with books, magazines and comics which appeal to a range of interests for both boys and girls.

It is also important that children are given the opportunity to share their personal reading in school, in literature circles or reading groups. In both of these activities they will be introduced to the reading choices of other children as well as having a chance to articulate why they read particular texts.

We also know that the attitudes of boys to reading are less positive than those of girls (e.g. OFSTED, 2004; Twist *et al.*, 2003; and see Chapter 2 of this book). Teachers need to respond to boys' interests and to recognise the importance of peer culture if boys are to develop positive and personal reading preferences. A currently popular series of titles is that purportedly written by Dylan Douglas (age 13), which has titles such as *Itching for a Fight, Going Out with a Bang* and *They Think it's All Over!* If a boy is interested in football he may read about football at home in magazines such as *Match!* and *Shoot Monthly*. In school, teachers can suggest novels which focus on football, or biographies of football stars. Some boys are reluctant to read books which have main characters who are female, so perhaps books such as *Hacker* (Malorie Blackman), *Holes* (Louis Sachar) or *Millions* (Frank Cottrell Boyce) will appeal.

The last area to be explored is the ever-growing area of finding information from the Internet. Chapter 2 raised many points about technology in children's reading lives and we know that the majority of children have access to the Internet in school, in the public library and (for some, but not all) in their homes. They surf the Net for information about their personal interests, their school work and purely for pleasure and, as they do this, they read the print, icons and images on the screen. Wikipedia is one website that is growing in popularity with children. It is an easy online encyclopedia to use but children need to understand that the information on Wikipedia cannot always be trusted and thus they need to be critically literate and compare the information with other material. The Web also offers children the opportunity to develop their imaginary secondary worlds through, for instance, joining the Alex Rider fan club, listening to Anthony Horowitz's podcast or just joining an online children's reading group. As David Bell (press conference, 2004) stated, this aspect of children's reading needs to be included in the literary diet of a primary classroom and the PNS inclusion of reading from paper and the screen should ensure this.

MATCHING THE CHILD TO THE BOOK

There are no short-cuts to the art of putting the right book into the child's hands at the right time. A child who does not want to read will reject everything, and we know how difficult it is when a child insists on choosing a long 'chapter' book which she really cannot tackle but wants to be seen reading. Then there is the child who is unwilling to take any risks and wants to keep returning to the same books. An equally painful scenario is where children who do not want to be 'shown up' race through books from a reading scheme to keep up with their friends.

There are three things to disentangle here: range, personal interest and motivation, and an appropriate available text choice for the reading stamina of the child. In order to help, you need to keep records of what the child has read before, to have read a great deal yourself and to have found some way of remembering what you have read so that you can access it usefully. A database or card index will help you here. Also (see below), you need to have organised your book collection so that the books are easily accessible.

The planning that you do across different routines (see Chapter 5) can ensure that children are meeting as full a range as possible across the school year. As we saw above, this has to be balanced alongside the child's personal interests, particularly when the child is reluctant to read. Children's interests may or may not coincide with ours but if we ignore them totally we are in danger of jeopardising a potential site of reading growth and this may affect boys more than girls. You might want to negotiate with the children as to where, when and how a place is provided for magazines, comics and books that they bring in. Individual time spent with children is an excellent context for finding out about the child's out-of-school interests and reading habits. You may well discover that the most reluctant reader in school turns out to be an avid consumer of anything he finds written about pigeons – on screen, in his monthly pigeon fanciers' magazine or in the information books he regularly borrows from the public library.

Then there is motivation: the motivation to choose, which only works if you know how to choose a book. Shared reading is an excellent context for demonstrating how you chose the book you are currently sharing and how you will choose subsequent titles. In addition, teachers can get children to start reading again by offering a book that:

- is new so the child will be the very first one to read it;
- you are very informed and enthusiastic about;
- you think has a main character rather like the child in front of you;
- is by an author or illustrator whom you know the child likes;
- is considerably shorter than the book the child read last;
- is in the area of the child's known interests;
- is 'more for older children but I think you're probably ready for it';
- other children are enthusiastic about;
- you found frightening but which you think the child will be brave enough to read;
- is going to appear (or has appeared) as a film;
- you are considering for reading to the whole class or to a younger/older child.

Possibly hardest of all is ensuring that a book matches the reading stamina of the child, that the text is one that he or she can realistically tackle. This is not to say that children should never be allowed to choose books that appear either too easy or too hard for them; on the contrary, returning to old favourites and browsing through more challenging books is to be encouraged. The former confirms children as readers and the latter shows them what lies ahead. But they also need to be tackling texts that will push them forward and this is particularly tricky. It may be that the challenge lies in the length of the book or the complexity of the plot, or, with a younger reader, it may lie in the need to ensure ever more accurate decoding. If you are working with a reading scheme or colour-coded system you will have a ready-made structure and a sense of progression that may seem reassuring. However, you will need to inspect this structure closely so that you are sure that it is appropriate for the children's needs and that it is predicated upon a sufficiently broad view of reading to allow for both individual learning styles and NC requirements. The danger here can be that you are lulled into a false sense of security as the child moves up the ladder and that you lose sight of the individual needs of the child so that his or her capacities for choice are stifled. This is where careful monitoring of the child's reading strategies and choices will help (see Chapter 7).

However, there is no doubt that structure is important and that there are significant points in children's reading development where you will need to choose books for them with enormous care. If you are using 'decodable books' (DfES, 2006a), it is all the more important that these are complemented by carefully chosen books with supportive, predictable and meaningful language. In the final analysis, if your classroom is one where the initial selection has been made with care, children's interests and choices are reflected and respected, children's progress is attentively monitored, access is easy and discussion of books takes place frequently, then you should have the time and incentive to match child with book and you should have great pleasure when your pupil says, 'It was really good, Miss'.

MANAGING AND ORGANISING RESOURCES

This section of the chapter is about controlling all the resources we have mentioned, making them manageable for you and the children and giving you a rationale for doing that. It is a section that must be read in conjunction with the rest of the book. You can have the best-organised resources in the world but they will only help in the teaching of reading if they are properly and efficiently mediated by you. Their organisation and manageability are an important part of the structure that you give to the teaching of reading and of your feeling of being in control.

Start by making a detached survey of the classroom in which you are working and consider the messages it gives about the status and desirability of reading. Try reviewing both the provision itself and the children's use of the resources. Look, for instance, at the book area and consider not only the range of books on offer but also how inviting the area is for all the children and to what extent they actually use it.

If we are concerned to promote children's skills in choosing books then their accessibility is hugely significant. Children may go to libraries and meet classification systems there, but it is important that the foundations for using these systems are laid in the classroom. Organising and categorising the book corner can be an extremely productive exercise and one that is most usefully done with the children. (Incidentally, it can provide useful information about the children's understandings: in one Reception class a group of children classified the books according to shape and size so all the square ones went together!) Do not feel you have to pigeonhole every book; some broad categories will be enough. You can define some of these and ask the children for theirs too. One Year 3 class used the following teacher categories: information books, specific information books around the class topic, poetry, short stories, novels. Then the children looked at the picture books and suggested their categories: books that make us laugh, favourite books, books in Urdu, and animal stories. These were displayed in inexpensive plastic baskets from a supermarket and labelled by the children.

You will need to think about where you keep non-fiction books and maybe having a permanent section for these. More difficult is managing ephemeral non-fiction material such as newspapers, fliers, brochures and current advertisements. Some teachers find a separate box, tray or even noticeboard useful for these.

In some schools, all reading scheme books are integrated with children's literature. You may prefer to keep these separately. You may also wish to keep your sets of books for guided reading separately; your school may have a central storage point for these so they can be shared between year groups.

The example that follows shows how teachers in one primary school organised their book corners. Unless the category was obvious (e.g. hardbacked books), the books were marked with a shape, letter or coloured sticker to help the children find and put them back in the right baskets or shelves.

Early Years Foundation Stage

- rhyming story books;
- nursery rhyme collections (including finger rhymes);
- enlarged poetry cards;
- alphabet books;
- counting books;
- picture books (including wordless);
- information books;
- favourite books;
- traditional tales;
- poetry;
- box of big books, both published and teacher/children made (along with easel and pointer for class and group shared reading sessions);
- small versions of big books;
- books written by children.

Key Stage 1

- favourite books;
- alphabet books;
- rhymes/poetry;
- picture books (which children may organise into subcategories);
- short stories;
- traditional tales;
- non-fiction;
- longer/harder-to-tackle paperback picture books;
- hardback picture books;
- short novels;
- sets of books for group reading;
- box of big books, both published and teacher/children made (along with easel and pointer for class and group shared reading sessions);
- small versions of big books;
- books written by children.

Key Stage 2

- picture books;
- traditional tales;
- collections of short stories;
- short novels;
- longer novels;
- poetry (individual authors and anthologies);
- sets of books for group reading (including plays);
- non-fiction books;
- books written by children;
- animals;*
- funny;*
- adventure;
- transport;*
- magic/ghosts.*

* categories chosen by the children

Kinder boxes, plastic baskets and sloping shelving will all help with the presentation of these categories and you will need to work hard initially to ensure that the children understand and maintain the categories. You might find it useful to devise a set of class rules with the children for the book area. All this is about more than a tidy book corner; it is also about demonstrating the range of authors and genres, developing children's understanding of these and helping the children to make informed choices. Nigel Hall's suggestion (in conversation, 1992) of a collection of 'books that wolves would like to read' demonstrates how one can take categorising on to even more subtle levels. In organising this collection, the children had to respond critically to the text, reading the books from a predatory wolf's point of view. A book such as *The Cultivated Wolf* (Pascal Biet and Becky Bloom) might well involve the children, as they try to categorise the book, in animated talk on how the wolf changes from a predatory loner at the start of the book to a cultivated member of the reading community at the end! So organising books is not just about range and accessibility; it can include teaching and learning about such things as evaluation and narrative viewpoint.

You can draw attention to specific themes, books, authors, poets or illustrators by setting up special displays. If these are to be effective and more than just window dressing they need to be brought alive for the children through their involvement but also through your planning.

Children in one nursery had been reading books about bears and the resulting display was not only of all their teddy bears but also of at least two dozen books about bears. The children had particularly liked *Can't you Sleep, Little Bear?* (Martin Waddell and Barbara Firth) and it was not long before a dark cave appeared in the corner of the classroom with a little bear within. At the entrance to the cave was a notice 'Please take the torch and a bear book and read to little bear'. Lots of reading went on.

A KS1 class was learning about pulleys and the teacher read them *The Lighthouse Keeper's Lunch* (Ronda and David Armitage) in which the keeper's wife devises an ingenious pulley system to get her husband's lunch to him, avoiding the greedy seagulls. The class constructed a lighthouse and pulley and this became the focus of a display of books about sea creatures.

In a KS2 class the children were asked to nominate their favourite author, giving reasons for their choice. Then they voted. Some of the authors they chose included Charles Keeping, Dick King-Smith and Anne Fine. A special display was set up with books begged and borrowed from other teachers and libraries and also biographical information about the author (*Books for Keeps* authorgraphs proved a useful source). The children researched the author and made a poster or flier for their display. They also redesigned the cover of their favourite book. The teacher's planning for her read-aloud programme included books and extracts from the display. This did not include all the books but enough to whet the children's appetites and invite them into reading other texts by the author.

In another school children took it in turns to nominate their 'top ten' books; you can extend this to include books from home as well as school since this can give you useful insights into your children's reading choices.

Highlighting poetry is usefully done through a 'poet's corner'; in one class this included a 'poetry request board' where the children used Post-its to request both a poem they wanted read aloud and its reader. Carefully worded notices can also convey useful messages.

We have at least five anthologies in our book corner and lots of picture books that are written in verse. Come and browse! We've got:

Title	Editors
A Caribbean Dozen	John Agard and Grace Nicholls
Classic Poems to Read Aloud	James Berry
Talking to the Sun	Kenneth Koch and Kate Farell

(This has got paintings in as well from the Metropolitan Museum of Art.)

A World of Poetry	Michael Rosen
The Utterly Brilliant Book of Poetry	Brian Patten

(Read it – it really is brilliant!)

The books need to be accessible to the children and to be displayed in a context that is attractive and inviting. The idea is that children will want to go and browse, share a book with a friend, get lost in a book on their own or listen to a book being read aloud. You might find it useful to ask yourself if you would want to sit and read in the book area. Try it sometime. Cushions, a carpet, a lamp and comfortable chairs all contribute to an inviting environment, although you might find that you need to set up a rota for which group gets to sit there! PCET publishes posters of author profiles for classroom use accompanied by useful teachers' notes or you can sometimes get free publicity posters from publishers and could also start to make your own collection of pictures of readers, images from books, or maybe information about films of children's books. This is an ideal opportunity to make sure that you are including representations of readers that challenge stereotypes; we know that boys' interest and motivation in reading are more vulnerable than those of girls so the more images they can see of boys and men reading the better. We have seen posters of the English football team reading displayed in one classroom. In one nursery book area pictures from publishers' catalogues were effectively displayed at eye level. You may be constrained by space and money but even the smallest collection of books can be invitingly displayed in a limited space.

Finally, you need to think about the actual access the children have to the books. All too often the very realistic constraints on space mean that book areas are used for a great deal more than reading: taking the register, class sharing times, shared writing, construction activities, whole-class ticking off … the list is endless. What is important is that you take stock of all this and make sure that reading is firmly built into your planning for use of this area so that it is not just a place to go and read 'when you've finished your work'. You might, for instance, devise a rota with the class whereby groups take it in turns to be in the book corner. This can be very effective, especially when combined with that group having access to the 'favourite books' collection. The trouble with favourites is that everyone wants to read them!

USEFUL TEACHING RESOURCES

This section gives information about a range of organisations and websites that will be useful for both students and newly qualified teachers. The information was relevant at the time of publication but websites are liable to go offline at any time. You need to keep yourself updated.

Literacy organisations

The Centre for Literacy in Primary Education (CLPE)

Webber Row, London, SE1 8QZ
http://www.clpe.co.uk
> CLPE is a centre for language and literacy (which includes an extremely good children's library), a publisher of books on literacy education and a training centre. In recent years, CLPE's significant research projects have included:
> BookPower
> The Power of Reading Project
> The Reader in the Writer
> The CLPE website covers the range of its activities, initiatives and current information on courses.

National Association for Language Development in the Curriculum (NALDIC)

http://www.naldic.org.uk
> The NALDIC site contains a great deal of information on bilingualism and EAL learning which is relevant to primary education. The ITTSEAL (Initial Teacher Training Subject English as an Additional Language) website (which you can access through NALDIC) is particularly useful for students and includes articles such as the following: *Language and Literacy in EAL Learning, Developing Reading in EAL, English and EAL: Subjects and Language across the Curriculum.*

National Association for the Teaching of English (NATE)

http://www.nate.org.uk

NATE is the UK subject association for both primary and secondary teachers of English. It organises both national and regional conferences covering both age phases and publishes several journals as well as useful materials for primary teaching, e.g. *Cracking Good Books* and *Cracking Good Picture Books* (Judith Graham). The website contains some useful background information on the association.

National Centre for Language and Literacy (NCLL)

http://www.ncll.org.uk

NCLL publishes a range of booklets and resources for the teaching of language and literacy. Its website is very useful and gives clear guidance about the centre's publications and courses that are run at the centre in Reading, Berkshire.

The National Literacy Trust

http://www.literacytrust.org.uk

The *National Literacy Trust* is an independent charity dedicated to building a literate nation. The site contains a wealth of information including useful downloads (PDFs) on different aspects of reading. The charity runs various initiatives such as the Family Reading Campaign, Reading Champions: Reading the Game, and Talk to your Baby.

United Kingdom Literacy Association (UKLA)

http://www.UKLA.org.uk

The UKLA publishes the journal *Literacy* and has a valuable academic website. The full website can only be accessed through membership; however, there is some useful information on literacy on the general site.

Reading Connects

http://www.literacytrust.org.uk/readingconnects/

Reading Connects is part of the *National Literacy Trust* and is a DfES-funded initiative that supports schools in developing a reading culture. The site includes case studies, advice, relevant resources and information on author and storyteller visits.

Other useful sources of information

The Standards Site

http://www.standards.dfes.gov.uk/

This is an extremely full and rich government site which contains information on the PNS, planning, assessment and useful PDF files on many different literacy initiatives.

Teachers' television

http://www.teacherstelevision
Teachers' television is not just a website but a television channel. It broadcasts weekly programmes for teachers on the Web which cover a range of topical subjects and which, along with the archive, make this a very useful resource for students and teachers.

Children's literature websites

Booktrusted

http://www.booktrusted.co.uk
Booktrusted is the children's branch of The Book Trust, which is a charity set up to promote reading and books. The Booktrusted website includes information on National Book Week, the Nestlé Children's Book Prize, a free Best Book Guide, a list of children's bookshops, links to their websites and a selection of recommended books for children.

The Word Pool and UK Children's Books

http://www.wordpool.co.uk and http://www.ukchildrensbooks.co.uk
Both of these sites are run by Steve and Diana Kimpton. The Word Pool site has a variety of sections which include reviews of big books, choosing books, reluctant readers and author profiles. UK Children's Books is a directory of children's authors and illustrators.

Journals and magazines

Books for Keeps: http://www.booksforkeeps.co.uk
English in Education: available through NATE
Literacy: available through UKLA
The Primary English Magazine: Garth Publishing Services, PO Box 5034, Birmingham, B13 8JA

Children's bookshops

There are many specialist children's bookshops. Here are three of our favourites.

The Willesden Bookshop

http://www.willesdenbookshop.co.uk
This bookshop has a superb range of multicultural books and a very well organised, accessible and informative website.

The Lion and Unicorn Bookshop

http://www.lionunicornbooks.co.uk
Very well informed staff and a correspondingly informative website will give you all the latest award winners, reviews, news of new publications, author visits and much more.

Madeleine Lindley Ltd

http://www.madeleinelindley.com/
  This well established and popular establishment has a large stock of books, including the biggest selection of big books in the country.

Book guides

Tucker, N. (2002) *The Rough Guide to Children's Books 0–5 Years.* London: Rough Guides.
Tucker, N. (2002) *The Rough Guide to Children's Books 5–11 Years.* London: Rough Guides.

Further reading and website

Boyz Own (reading list with needs of reluctant inexperienced boys in mind) available from Books for Students, Bird Road, Heathcote, Warwick, CV34 6TB.
Kropp, P. with Cooling, W. (1993) *The Reading Solution.* Harmondsworth: Penguin.
PCET Publishing: http://www.pcet.co.uk/
Pinsent, P. (ed.) (1992) *Language, Culture and Young Children.* London: David Fulton Publishers.
Powling, C. and Styles, M. (eds) (1996) *A Guide to Poetry 0–16.* London and Reading: Books for Keeps and the Reading and Language Information Centre.
Stones, R. (ed.) (1999) *A Multicultural Guide to Children's Books 0–16+.* London and Reading: Books for Keeps and the Reading and Language Information Centre.

Chapter 7

Monitoring and Assessing Reading

Liz Laycock

INTRODUCTION

Children's progress in reading has always been a matter of great concern, to parents, to teachers, to local authorities and to governments, as well as to the children themselves. Children's reading attainment is one of the major yardsticks by which schools are measured, by which parents judge the effectiveness of a school and by which children judge themselves and their success as learners. Teachers have the enormous responsibility not only of teaching reading, but also of monitoring children's progress and of maintaining careful records of their development.

Because reading is seen as so important, it is the area where most control is exerted by those outside the classroom. Sometimes the means of assessment that are demanded are not those that teachers feel are the most revealing or effective. It is vital that you take the responsibility and control into your own hands and that you are able to provide your own well founded evidence of children's progress and attainment. The record of this evidence not only will demonstrate achievement to those to whom schools are accountable, but, more importantly, will be the basis for your planning of further reading experiences and specific teaching. If you understand, monitor and record each child's reading knowledge, strategies, strengths, difficulties, confidence and skill, you will be able to ensure, through planning appropriate teaching, that progress is maintained.

As we have shown throughout this book, reading is a complex and multifaceted skill. On a day-to-day basis, teachers can observe what children have learnt about letters and phonemes but, depending on the experience of the child, there are other aspects of reading which are important, such as what children have read, the cueing strategies they use, their enthusiasm and confidence, and their strengths and weaknesses.

The task group set up to report on the assessment and testing of the *National Curriculum* (NC) as long ago as 1987 asserted a key principle which remains important today:

> The assessment process itself ... should not simply be a bolt-on addition at the end. Rather, it should be an integral part of the educational process, continually providing both 'feedback' and 'feedforward'. It therefore needs to be incorporated systematically into teaching practices and strategies at all levels.
>
> (DES, 1987)

These ideas of 'feedback' and 'feedforward' are clearly visible in current thinking, which embraces two main purposes of assessment: assessment of learning (AoL) and assessment for learning (AfL). AoL, which used to be known as summative assessment, 'is any assessment that summarises where learners are at a given point in time – it provides a snapshot of what has been learned' (DfES, 2007c). AfL, which used to be known as formative assessment, 'is the process of seeking and interpreting evidence for use by learners and their teachers to decide where the learners are in their learning, where they need to go and how best to get there' (DfES, 2007c).

In this chapter we start with examining how you can collect AfL evidence from a range of contexts. We cover informal observations, conversations with children and structured semi-formal assessments (reading re-enactments, running records and miscue analysis). Then we move to looking at the formal assessments that are needed for AoL which include NC Assessments (SATs).

ASSESSMENT FOR LEARNING (AfL)

Informal observations

A great deal of information about children's interest in and commitment to reading can be gleaned from day-to-day observation of children in the classroom. Some observations can be made during ongoing activities such as play in the home corner. Even unexpected events in the classroom like a note coming round about the school photographer, which a child finds she can read, can be entered in your notebook.

Interactions with books

Some children will choose to read whenever there is an opportunity; others will rarely opt for reading when there are other alternatives. You will need to note and record observations of how children go about selecting a book, whether they explore a range of reading material, whether they choose carefully and seem to know what they are looking for, or whether they pick up a book without much thought. It might also be apparent that some children read a very narrow range of books, either from choice or because there is little alternative. You might also note whether children turn to books confidently when they are seeking information relating to other curriculum areas. Such observations should indicate that some specific teaching is needed.

Behaviour at quiet reading times

Much information can be gathered about children when they have the chance to read quietly. The teacher will note whether they are able to concentrate on and persist with their reading. Such observations might raise questions about the range and suitability of the books available to the children, as well as about the planning, timing and duration of such sessions.

Reading across the curriculum

As we have already said, the ability to read is necessary in every area of the curriculum and not all texts have to be read in the same way. You will need to know, for example, whether a child's inability to cope with mathematical or science activities, presented in books or on the screen, is related to reading problems or to a lack of understanding of the mathematical or scientific concepts. This might be a matter of vocabulary which has a subject-specific meaning (for example, 'mean', 'table', 'current', 'desert') or it might be a matter of diagrams, charts, graphs, tables used in many subject areas which are not 'read' in the same way as continuous text.

Children are also asked to acquire the specific skills of 'skimming', 'scanning' and 'close reading'. You need to observe and record competence in these skills not only in English but in other curriculum areas. Opportunities to read information texts are, of course, present in the literacy hour and these texts should be consistently linked to work in other curriculum areas.

Conversations with children

A key characteristic of AfL is the involvement of the children themselves in the assessment process. When children are involved it helps them to understand what they are learning. Opportunities to review their own work and progress, to reflect on their understanding and needs, in discussion with teachers, enable children to set realistic targets for themselves and to see their learning and achievement in a positive light.

Children's informal comments

When children talk about their preferences, enthusiasms, likes and dislikes, perhaps as a part of discussions following a teacher's reading aloud, much can be learnt which will inform your records of individual children and the choices you make about book provision.

Reading conferences

Surprising insights into children's reading can emerge in the one-to-one conversations that you have with them. Children will talk about a range of interests, such as football and other sports, animals, computers or music, all of which may involve reading in the family context. There may be a wealth of reading material at home, from comics and newspapers, magazines and manuals to websites, CD-ROMs and information books about their interests. Just because children do not appear to be enthusiastic readers of what is available in school, that does not mean that they are not reading at other times and in other places. Particularly by Key Stage 2 (KS2), many children will have discovered, and be reading at home, texts which they suspect may not be approved of at school. Many children who are learning English as an Additional Language should be encouraged to talk about the reading they do in other languages and the classes they attend after school. As we discussed in Chapter 1, Hilary Minns (1990) and Eve Gregory (Gregory and Williams, 2000) have documented the wide range of literacy events in which children from minority communities can be engaged. It is important for you to record that the child is willing and able to share with you her understandings of different scripts and languages. The reading conference is a good context for children's own assessments of their current knowledge and understanding.

Reading aloud to the teacher or other adults

In the *Early Years Foundation Stage* (EYFS) practitioners still read with children on a one-to-one basis but this is much rarer in Key Stages 1 and 2. For these children, guided reading is the principal occasion for making observations of their reading. Your school will have a group record sheet on which to record your observations and the CLPE website has records that you can download. Some group records make links with NC level descriptors; others may operate with prompts such as strategies, responses and attitudes. So, for a child in the EYFS, you may find yourself recording that she has made a coherent story using the pictures and she can identify where the character's name comes up on each page. For an older fluent reader you may record the child's comments on the sad ending of Michael Morpurgo's *The Dancing Bear* and how they had not expected it.

Children with English as an Additional Language (EAL) may feel confident enough to read aloud in their first language. Although it is obviously useful if children can read aloud to someone who shares their language, so that the reading can be more accurately monitored, useful information about a child's reading confidence and competence can still be collected without your understanding a word. You could, for instance, record that the child explained the story to you and read with apparent expression and perseverance.

Teaching Assistants (TAs) are invaluable in providing information: they are better equipped to help children with their reading since the start of the *National Literacy Strategy* (NLS) intervention programmes (ELS, ALS, FLS – see Chapter 8) and can be an invaluable support in helping you with your records. Parents may also offer to read with children. You do, however, need to monitor the records made by others; it is the class teacher's responsibility to know and plan for the learning needs of all the children in the class.

As you will see below, these sessions are occasionally used to make more formal assessments of the children through the use of running records or miscue analysis.

Structured, semi-formal assessments

Re-enactments

The youngest children's interactions with and retellings of familiar texts are a productive site for your observations. Don Holdaway (1979) first highlighted reading-like behaviour as a significant step on the way to reading and showed us how to record it. When a child picks up a familiar book and retells the story page by page, perhaps using the language of the text, we learn much about her understanding of reading. Analysis of such re-enactments reveals that they are much more than repetitions, rote-learned and lacking comprehension; when the actual words are not remembered, the child frequently substitutes his own words which demonstrate real understanding. Table 7.1 shows Neil (three years eleven months) re-enacting *Mouse and Elephant* (An Vrombaut).

Early concepts of print

Marie Clay (1979) devised a procedure for checking whether beginner readers are familiar with the way in which books and print work. The intention is to identify what a young child knows by asking questions as the child and teacher share a book. This will allow you to observe and record the following things:

- whether the child can identify the front of the book;
- whether the child realises that it is the print (rather than the picture) which tells the reader what to say;

Table 7.1 Neil's re-enactment of *Mouse and Elephant*

Words from the book	Re-enactment	Comments
Title on cover: Mouse and Elephant	Mouse and Elephant. He's a very colourful elephant.	Said title from memory. Comments on character.
Title on inside cover: Mouse and Elephant An Vrombaut	*Opens book, points to the words 'Mouse and Elephant' but does not say them.*	Is aware that print says the title of the story but cannot 'read' it yet himself.
Mouse wants to play a game with Elephant. What can they play? Can they …	*Points to picture of Elephant on right-hand side of spread:* There's Elephant. *Looks back to left-hand page:* And there's little mouse.	Looks firstly at right-hand side of page. Does he know that he should be reading from left to right?
… play basketball? Elephant likes basketball. But Mouse does not! Can they …	Elephant likes to play this. He has a sucky trunk. *Pointing to the ball in the net he makes an upward movement with his hand.*	Started on right page again. Is re-enacting the story with accompanying physical actions.
… play football? Mouse likes football. But Elephant does not! Can they …	*Points to elephant:* Elephant does not like football … *Points to mouse in goal:* He can't get any goals.	Beginning to use book language as he picks up the repetition. Draws on his own experience of football to make sense (semantic).
… bounce on the bed? Elephant likes bouncing. But Mouse does not!	*He looks at this page briefly and turns to the next one.*	
What can they play? Can they… … walk on the tightrope? Mouse can (just about). But Elephant cannot!	*Points to helicopter on top right-hand page, then to bird on bottom left:* Mouse likes flying but Elephant does not.	Using picture, shape of story and previous experience of hearing the story read aloud to tell the story. No links made with actual print.
Elephant does not like ballooning.	Mouse likes balloons. Elephant does not.	Repeats the same structure. Has tuned into the repetition. Using written (book) language, e.g. 'does not'.
Mouse does not like flying a kite.	Mouse likes flying but Elephant does not.	
Elephant really does not feel like parachute jumping!	He's crying. *N. frowns.*	Emotional engagement with story.

Words from the book	Re-enactment	Comments
It is no use. Elephant is just too big and Mouse is just too little.	Elephant is big and Mouse is little and they're sad. They're sitting on bugs.	He has spotted the tiny bugs drawn on the hill. Paying close attention to the illustration.
Then Elephant has an idea! Hammer, hammer! Bang, crash, bang, ouch! Elephant has made …	*Excitedly:* He's building something. Making something for Mouse.	Note his enjoyment and engagement.
… a tricycle that is just right …	A trical! With a **big** seat for Elephant and a **little** one for Mouse, and wheels.	Meaning is clear even though he can't articulate 'tricycle'. Note intonation for 'big' and 'little'.
… a mouse-and-elephant tricycle … made for two!	Up they go! *Sweeps his arm up into the air as he says this last sentence.*	Active engagement.
	Closes the book and says: The End	The book doesn't actually say this. He has drawn on previous experience to add this detail.

- where one starts to read and which direction to go in (directionality);
- where one goes at the end of a line (return sweep to left in English);
- whether the child understands 'first' and 'last' (words and letters);
- whether the child notices that the line order is altered;
- whether the child notices incorrect word order (1:1 correspondence);
- whether the child is aware that one reads the left-hand page before the right-hand page (in English);
- whether the child understands the meaning of full stops, commas, question marks, and speech marks;
- whether the child can identify upper-case and lower-case letters;
- whether the child knows the difference between 'word' and 'letter';
- whether the child notices words that have been reversed ('was'/'saw'; 'no'/'on').

Two commercially published booklets, *Sand* and *Stones*, were written so that teachers could survey children's book and print knowledge in a systematic way on a score sheet. Some teachers feel that the booklets, with their deliberate printing errors, are confusing for young children, as well as being rather dull and dated. They prefer, therefore, to draw up their own checklist of the concepts and to use a more appealing ordinary book. Goodman (in Marek and Howard, 1984) reports on a 'bookhandling knowledge task' which has some helpful suggestions as to how you might choose such a book:

- take a picture storybook that is suitable for reading to a preschool child;
- make sure the book has a title page which includes the title of the book and the author's name;
- make sure that the pages have clear, bold print and that there are many pictures in the book. If possible, there should be a page with print on one side and a picture on the other;
- try not to give too much information or direction.

This is followed by a list of questions that focus on the same concepts as those that underpin Marie Clay's list (above). The principles embodied in these observations are now evident in the *Foundation Stage Profile* (see below).

Running record

Many teachers are now familiar with carrying out running records because the NC Assessments (SATs) for KS1 made use of a version of the procedure, although in this context the errors were scored (right or wrong) rather than being analysed as described below. As with the early concepts of print assessment, the running record procedure was also devised by Marie Clay. It is really a simplified version of miscue analysis, which is described below, and it is intended for use with children who have moved beyond the very earliest stages of reading and who are just beginning to read known texts independently. Making a running record is a way of looking in a focused manner at what a child is doing as he reads aloud; you can analyse the child's miscues (errors) to inform further planning for that child. Comments or questions by the child should also be noted, as they frequently provide insights into the child's thinking. The following procedure will help you implement a running record.

Procedure for carrying out a running record

1 Choose a book which is known to the child but not so well known that he can recite it from memory.
2 Decide how the reading will be recorded (see below). You may also want to consider tape-recording the session, especially if you are familiarising yourself with the procedure.
3 Ensure that the child is at ease and is happy about the book to be read.
4 Ask the child to read aloud from the book.
5 Do not intervene or give words too quickly; allow time for the child to think or work it out.
6 Do intervene if the child becomes distressed or cannot read the book: if this happens, simply take over the reading yourself and read to the end, without criticism or negative comment.
7 Allow the reader time to comment, look at pictures, ask questions, if that is what he wants to do.

Recording the miscues

The miscues can be recorded in two ways. Either make a copy of the text or the part of the text you wish to concentrate on and mark this as the child reads or mark the reading on a blank sheet of paper, keeping to the same line arrangement as the text (as in the example below). Mark the reading, using the following symbols:

- a stroke (/) for each word read correctly;
- a 'T' for every word TOLD to the child;
- a substituted word above the actual word of the text
        said (substituted)
  e.g. *shouted* (text)
- a circle for a word missed out;
- the letters 'SC' alongside any error which the child self-corrects.

Leave a column alongside the recording of the reading (or write on the text, if using a copy) to note any comments or questions. Marie Clay offers detailed guidance for interpreting the miscues in the reading. You will need to look back to Chapter 1 to remind yourself of the cue-systems used in reading and use these to decide which cues the child is utilising or ignoring. The child who substitutes 'said' for 'shouted' is using meaning and syntax though he fails to fine-tune the reading with attention to graphic and phonic cues. It is worth quoting Clay's advice to look at every error recorded in the running record:

> To work out whether the child is responding to the different kinds of cues that could be used, you need to look at every error that the child makes and ask yourself 'Now what made him say that?' 'Did he miss out on the visual cues?' 'Was he ignoring meaning?' It is misleading if you do this selectively; you must analyse every error and count those that show this or that kind of cue. You want to be able to conclude, on sound evidence, that 'he pays more attention to visual cues than meaning' or 'he is guided by structure and meaning but does not search for visual cues'. It is only when you go to the trouble of analysing all the errors that you really get any indication of what his strategies are on reading.
>
> (Clay, 1985:56)

In the example of a running record and the analysis shown below, the child's reading strategies are revealed clearly in the miscues. The teacher observes the child's positive strategies but can also see where further support and teaching are needed.

Example of a running record

Child: Elizabeth
Age: 5 years 2 months
Text: *Titch* (Pat Hutchins)
Child's comments are in italics.

Titch was little.	/ / /
	T T
His sister Mary was a bit bigger.	/ / *marry* / / /*digger*
	Mary bigger
	T
And his brother Pete was a lot bigger.	/ / / *Pet* / / / /
	Pete
	SC
Pete had a great big bike.	/ / / *greet* / /
	great
Mary had a big bike.	/ / / / /
And Titch had a little tricycle.	/ / / / / /
	SC
Pete had a kite that flew high above the trees.	/ / / / / / / *over* / /
	above
	We had a kite last Christmas,
	made of plastic. It didn't work.
Mary had a kite that flew high above the houses.	/ / / / / / / / / /
And Titch had a pin-wheel that he held in his hand.	/ / / / / / / / / / / /
	At the end he gets the
	good thing.
Pete had a big drum.	/ / / / /
Mary had a trumpet.	/ / / /
	SC
And Titch had a little wooden whistle.	/ / / / / *wo-oo-den* /
	wooden
Pete had a big saw.	/ / / / /
Mary had a big hammer.	/ / / / /
	SC
And Titch held the nails.	/ / *had* / /
	held
Pete had a big spade.	/ / / / /
Mary had a fat flowerpot.	/ / / / /
	T
But Titch had the tiny seed.	/ / / / *teeny* /
	tiny
And Titch's seed grew	/ / / /
and grew	/ /
and grew.	/ /
	He did – see!

Teacher's analysis

1 marry/Mary: error arose from E sounding out the word, using phonic knowledge. TOLD the correct word

2 digger/bigger: error perhaps arose from confusion of 'b' and 'd' graphemes. TOLD the correct word

3 pet/Pete: error arose from use of phonic knowledge to sound out word; final 'e' not noticed/taken into account? TOLD the correct word

4 greet/great: error arose from use of phonic knowledge to sound out word. SELF-CORRECTION because first reading did not make sense

5 over/above: error arose from prediction of word which made sense; further look at word printed, using phonic knowledge to check, and at the pictures led to SELF-CORRECTION

6 wo-oo-den/wooden: error arose from use of phonic knowledge to blend phonemes, resulting in three syllables. SELF-CORRECTION when this did not result in a word which made sense

7 had/held: error arose from prediction of next word, based on previous use of 'had'. A further look at the word led to SELF-CORRECTION

8 teeny/tiny: error arose from prediction of a word which made sense and partial use of graphophonic cues. TOLD the correct word.

Teacher's comments

'The text was read confidently. She was not afraid to attempt words that were new to her. She was involved in the text, as her comments show. Some expression in her voice, especially when words appeared to be known or easily read.

'She was definitely using her previous knowledge and memory of the text. It was remembered well. She used the pictures to help with words such as "kite" and also drew on her real experience of kites. In many cases mis-read words still made sense (5, 7, 8), so she was drawing on semantic cues. She was using grapho-phonic knowledge (1, 4, 6, 8) to work out unknown words, with some success. She has a strong reliance on phonic knowledge, though she also uses other cues.

'She seemed to enjoy reading the text. When asked, at the end, who the "titch" was in her house, she replied, "me in the people, the stick insects in the pets". This shows she understood the concept behind the story.

'Future support: E is confident and should be guided into tackling a wider range of more demanding texts. Her use of phonic knowledge should not be discouraged in any way but she needs to have additional strategies suggested, e.g. using similar, familiar words as a guide. Encourage her to continue to focus on the meaning and check whether a word makes sense. Guided reading opportunities, where she could read with others and observe others' strategies, would be useful.'

(Mary Thompsett, student at Roehampton University)

Miscue analysis

The psycholinguist Kenneth Goodman (1973) devised a procedure which he called 'miscue analysis' as a way of opening a 'window onto the reading process'. It is a procedure which differs from running records in that it is generally used with older children whose reading is giving you some cause for concern. You do not need to use the procedure with readers who are reading independently, fluently and with good understanding. It is also different from running records in that you work from a book that is unknown to the child. Traditionally, the way of recording miscues looks different from the running records but both share the purpose of diagnosing and analysing errors and both inform your subsequent teaching.

Several variations of Goodman's original procedure have been developed over the years, some of which simplify it, so that it can be used more regularly and is more manageable in the classroom (e.g. Moon, 1984; Arnold, 1982; Campbell, 1983). The version described in the *Primary Language Record* (Barrs, 1988) incorporates an element of silent reading preceding the reading aloud. The version given here draws on all of these.

If miscue analysis is new to you, it can be very helpful, the first few times, to use a recording sheet so that the patterns of the miscues can be seen clearly. Once the procedure is familiar, the miscue patterns will become clearer and you may not need to make a detailed breakdown in order to identify a reader's strengths and areas of difficulty. It is certainly true that once a few careful analyses have been carried out, your ear becomes attuned and you will notice aspects of a child's reading that you have not been aware of before.

Procedure for carrying out a miscue analysis
SELECTING THE TEXT(S)

An analysis of miscues can be carried out on a reading of a text which is unknown to the child and slightly more demanding than his or her current reading material. It could be an extract from a longer narrative or a complete short story. Non-fiction texts do not lend themselves as well to this procedure because of the amount of new vocabulary, proper names and the complexity of the sentence structure. It is important to choose a text that is interesting, flows well and that takes account of the child's literacy, and linguistic and cultural experiences. It is a good idea to have several texts to hand so that if one is too easy and the child makes very few miscues, an alternative can be used. If the child has great difficulty (as a guide, more than one miscue in every ten words) it is likely that he will lose the sense of what is being read, so a different text should be used.

PREPARATION

From the text, select the passage that you intend to analyse and make a copy of this. This copy is for the teacher; the child should read from the original book. The passage should be long enough to provide scope for a substantial number of miscues (about 300 words), though the analysis should not begin until after the first few paragraphs, so that the reader has time to get into the text.

Ideally, have a tape recorder so that the reading can be tape-recorded and analysed later. It is easy to miss things if marking is done during the reading, especially at first when the coding symbols are unfamiliar to you. Listening to the tape more than once allows all the detail to be noted.

THE READING

Ensure that the child is comfortable and fairly relaxed. Explain that while he reads this book you are going to listen very hard and that you want him to try to work out any difficulties and unknown words without your help. You also need to say that this is not a test and that it is going to help you, the teacher, to help the child. Explain the tape recorder, if the child is not used to seeing it used to record reading. Explain that when the reading aloud is finished, you will be asking him to tell you what it was about.

Ask the child to begin reading. He should read the whole text or extract, even though only part may be analysed. Let the child have a go before you intervene: the intention is to see what strategies are being used to deal with difficulties, so thinking time should be allowed. It is surprising how often a child can solve the problem alone when given the chance. If the child gets completely stuck, particularly if there are unfamiliar names in the text, you should give the word. If the child tires or appears very worried by the activity, you should take over the reading and finish the story, rather than allowing the child to struggle on.

After the reading has been completed, ask the child to tell you about what has been read. It is better not to ask testing or closed questions. You could ask whether he enjoyed it, make links with the child's experience and ask for opinions about the characters or events. Make a note of the child's comments, responses, questions and ideas.

MARKING THE MISCUES

If a recording has been made, listen to the tape as soon as possible and mark your copy using the following symbols. These are the standard symbols and the advantage of using them is that the script can be interpreted by others. This is important if the marked script is to be included in the child's records.

- substitution: word substituted written over the text
- omission: phrase, word or part of word omitted is circled in the text
- insertion: word inserted written above omission
- reversal: words reversed marked with a continuous line
- self-correction: the miscue is written above the word in the text, then marked 'SC'
- repetition: words repeated are underlined. Double underlining indicates repeated twice; triple underlining, repeated three times, etc.
- block, or teacher gives help: word(s) given written above, marked by capital 'T'
- pause of over two seconds: oblique stroke or dot before the word paused at
- punctuation ignored: parallel lines above and below punctuation.

ANALYSING THE MISCUES

In general terms, if children's miscues do not change the meaning of the text, they are probably using positive strategies and making sense of the text. Positive strategies include:

- reading ahead in order to help work out a word;
- going back and repeating a previously read phrase or sentence, in order to establish or check the context;

- stopping if what is read does not make sense and self-correcting;
- using the grapho-phonic features of words to confirm predictions.

If children's miscues do change the meaning then they are probably using negative strategies and not reading for meaning. Negative strategies might include:

- reading word by word and not using the context to help work out the meaning;
- sounding out words and settling on a word which may be graphically or phonically similar, but which does not make sense, or is a non-word;
- leaving miscues uncorrected when the sense is disrupted.

If a miscue is uncorrected, but the sense of the text stays intact, it is not a miscue of the same serious order as the other negative strategies mentioned above as it is probable that the reader is attending to the meaning. However, it is not accurate and it is something that needs noting.

The miscue analysis that follows begins with a piece of text on which the miscues have been marked by the teacher. If these are entered on a chart, as shown in Table 7.2, it is easy to see, at a glance, the pattern of the reader's errors and thus the areas that need intervention and further support and teaching.

Example of a miscue analysis

Child: Tom
Age: 9 years 4 months
Text: *Anansi and the Alligator* (traditional tale, out of print)

> Grace is six years old. Every day her mum takes her to school. One day the teacher asked Grace's mum if she would come to school and tell the children a story. When she came she said to the children,
> This is a story I first heard when I was a little girl in Jamaica. It is a story
>   *An – an* T   *farmer's*   *the* SC
> about Anansi the famous spider. In this story we will find out what happened
>   *taste*
> when Anansi teased the alligator. Everyone gather round. This is how the story starts.
> Once there was an alligator who was strong and fierce and very bad
> *tumpered – tampered*
> tempered because he had been covered in paint. Anansi the spider had crept
>   *p-our-d*   *into*
> along the branch of a tree and poured the paint onto him. Alligator was not very pleased. In fact he was very angry with Anansi.
>   *clumbered*   *stamped*
> Alligator climbed out of the river. He had spent a long time washing the paint from his body. He said to himself,
>   *fair*
> 'That spider has gone too far. I think I would like to meet Anansi round about lunch-time'. And he thought of a clever plan.
>   *bad-bo-bostil*
> Now Anansi was a boastful spider who went about telling the other animals

ducked   search
SC

that he was the cleverest of them all. So this is how Alligator decided to catch
him.
'Hey Anansi,'
he called. 'Everyone says you are the cleverest animal. Please help me. I
    troub- SC *touchers*
have a terrible toothache.
      first SC
Anansi was fast asleep in his web when he heard Alligator call his name. He woke up and
said to himself,
'Alligator has never asked for my help before. I wonder what this is all about'.

Teacher's comments

'This shows me that Tom is having great difficulty in reading for meaning. Out of sixteen
miscues, he has only self-corrected three times and made use of meaning cues just
twice. He is heavily reliant on the look of the words (graphic cues) and, whilst using initial phonemes and some consonant clusters, has weak phonic skills. To encourage him
to read for meaning I would suggest some explicit strategies such as reading on and
reading back and remind him to check for sense. In addition, some 'cloze' activities
(where he has to supply missing words) will help him with cross-checking for meaning.
I need to keep reading aloud to the class and make sure that he has a supportive writing partner to whom he can read his writing aloud so as to further develop his sense of
audience. He needs to develop his phonic skills so that he can blend through the words
so I will plan some structured teaching of vowel digraphs (such as 'ea', 'ai' and 'oo').'

THE CYCLE OF OBSERVATION, PLANNING AND ASSESSMENT

A key characteristic of AfL is that it is 'embedded in a view that assessment is an essential part of learning and teaching' (DfES, 2007c). The sort of observations and assessment
that we have discussed above all feed your planning, which in turn guides what you
observe and assess. The PNS offers an online interactive planning tool which allows
schools to download their planning formats into which you can cut and paste activities.
In addition there are many publications to help you plan (e.g. Scholastic *50 Shared
Texts*). However, everything that you use from another source will always need tailoring
to meet the needs of your children and this is where you will need to draw from your
records of children's progress in order to personalise their learning appropriately.

When you are planning, ask yourself:

- Have I set clear learning objectives for the children (i.e. What do I want them to
learn)?
- Have I identified success criteria for the objectives (i.e. How will I know the children
have met the learning objective(s))?
- Have I involved the children in the process (e.g. using 'thumbs up' or smiley faces to
indicate how successful they feel they have been)?
- Have I identified whom I am assessing (e.g. individuals; guided reading group; independent group)?

Table 7.2 Analysis of miscues

Child's name: Tom   Age: 9.4   Title of story: *Anansi and the Alligator* (traditional story o/p)

Miscue no.	Word in text	Word read	Does the miscue sound like the text? (phonic similarity)*	Does the miscue look like the text? (graphic similarity)	Does the word make sense in this context? (semantic)	Is the sentence grammatically acceptable? (syntax)	Was the miscue self-corrected?	Comments
1	Anansi	An-an						Teacher supplies the word. T did not know the character's name.
2	famous	farmer's	✓ Initial, medial and final phonemes	✓	✓	✓	✗	Miscue could make sense at this stage of the story.
3	this	the	✗	✗	✓	✓	✓	Both are same word class (articles).
4	teased	taste	✗	✗	✗	✗	✗	Only the initial phoneme is accurate – meaning lost.
5	tempered	tumpered tampered	✓ vowel only inaccurate	✓	✗	✓	✗	Probably does not know the collocation of 'bad' with 'tempered'.
6	poured	p-our-d	✓ Initial and final phonemes	✓	✗	✗	✗	Pronounced 'our' as in 'our class'.
7	onto	into	✗	✓	✗	✓	✗	Privileges graphic overall – leads to loss of meaning.
8	climbed	clumbered	✓ initial and medial clusters, final phoneme	✓	?	✓	✗	Even though invented, 'clumbered' draws on 'clambered' and 'climbed'.

Miscue no.	Word in text	Word read	Does the miscue sound like the text? (phonic similarity)*	Does the miscue look like the text? (graphic similarity)	Does the word make sense in this context? (semantic)	Is the sentence grammatically acceptable? (syntax)	Was the miscue self-corrected?	Comments
9	spent	stamped	×	×	×	✓	×	Substituted word is also in past tense.
10	far	fair	×	✓	×	×	×	Privileges graphic overall – leads to loss of meaning. Ignores 'air' diphthong.
11	boastful	bad-bo-bostil	✓ initial phoneme, medial cluster	×	×	×	×	'bad' would have preserved meaning but knows there is more – graphic cueing.
12	decided	ducked	×	×	×	✓	×	Word would fit at this point in the sentence but not if he'd read on.
13	catch	search	×	×	×	✓	✓	Although he self-corrects, does not go back to 'ducked'.
14	terrible	troub-	×	×	×	×	×	Loss of meaning.
15	toothache	touchers	×	×	×	×	×	Loss of meaning.
16	fast	first	✓ initial phoneme, final cluster	✓	×	×	✓	Cross-checks and self-corrects.
TOTALS (✓)			6	7	2 (with 1?)	8	3	

* Tick awarded if T has gone beyond using initial phoneme.

- Have I identified how and when I am assessing them (e.g. group record sheet while they are reading; independent group reporting back on their book research in the plenary)?
- Have I planned targeted and differentiated questions for whole-class or plenary sessions which allow me to check individuals' understanding or thinking?

Target setting

Your planning will be framed by the school's targets, which, in their turn, may be determined by the national agenda (expectations for performance in KS2 tests for instance). You need to be clear about the different types of targets and how these impinge on your planning. The most common are:

- quantitative performance targets which the school identifies as a standard to aim for;
- curriculum targets which will cover areas of the curriculum or aspects of teaching and learning;
- learning targets which can be used with classes, groups or individual pupils and which focus on what children know and can do, their progress and areas for future improvement.

(QCA, 1999:5)

Using curricular targets is one of the key ingredients of AfL and these need to be shared with children and parents so that all parties are involved in progress. The setting of whole-school targets is a key mechanism for raising standards and the DfES (2005c) provides examples of how whole-school curricular targets can be broken down appropriately for different age groups and abilities. In their example, a whole-school focus on 'interpretation and response to literary texts' is 'stranded out' into child-friendly targets. So, for Reception children, the target becomes 'I can retell a story using pictures'; for Year 2, 'I can talk about the theme of a story and about why things happen'; for Year 4, 'I can talk about why I think writers have chosen specific words and phrases' and for Year 6, 'I can say whether a writer has been successful in their purpose, e.g. to make me laugh/cry/think'. Differentiated targets, sample questions and success criteria are also given.

ASSESSMENT OF LEARNING (AoL)

Early Years Foundation Stage Profile

For children in the early years of schooling, the *Foundation Stage Profile* (FSP) (QCA, 2003c) provides the vehicle for capturing and summarising children's progress across the six areas of learning. (This will become the *Early Years Foundation Stage Profile* from September 2008.) This summative document is shared with parents at the end of Reception but is built up by practitioners across the EYFS. It comprises thirteen scales which are based on the Early Learning Goals and the Stepping Stones that lead to these. For 'communication, language and literacy' there are four scales, all of which have bearing on a child's reading progress: 'language for communication and thinking', 'linking sounds and letters', 'reading' and 'writing'. Each scale has nine points, the first three of which comprise stepping stones; points 4-8 are Early Learning Goals, with 9 extending beyond the EYFS with aspects of NC level 1 and/or 2c. Practitioners, along with parents and the children, assemble evidence in a portfolio or online record; there is an expectation that this evidence will be succinct and telling and there is no requirement for extensive evidence.

Pupils with English as an Additional Language

Once children move into KS1 they are measured against the NC Level Descriptions. However, for pupils who are in the early stages of learning English and are not yet operating at Level 1 there are extended scales. These scales drop below Level 1, offering two steps and one threshold (i.e. three additional pre-levels). For example, at Step 1 for reading, pupils 'know that print in English is read from left to right' (QCA, 2000). The expectation is that these are used on the child's arrival at school and at regular intervals thereafter until she reaches Level 1 (secure).

A word about 'reading age'

As soon as we move into the area of formal assessments and reading tests the concept of reading age rears its head. How convenient it would be if, as with a child's height or weight, we could determine a child's reading age accurately and match everything we do to that. Reading age was described as long ago as 1975 in the Bullock Report as a 'misleading concept, obscuring more than it reveals'. The Report goes on to say that 'it simply cannot be assumed that children having the same reading age read in the same way, require identical teaching, and will profit from similar books and materials' (DES, 1975:33). Criticisms of the concept persist (e.g. Stierer and Bloom, 1994).

The prevalence of reading age has diminished somewhat as the NC assessments for reading are statutory. The NC has level descriptions which attempt to define the characteristics of readers at different stages, rather than ages, though we feel that the NC's assumption that 'all seven-year-olds should have reached Level 2' implies that this is the description of a 'seven-year-old reader'.

Standardised reading tests

There have always been objective tests for reading; teachers' subjective judgements about their children's reading have not had the same validity or status as these standardised tests. The debate about objectivity and subjectivity is one which continues and lies at the heart of many of the points we make below.

All standardised tests of reading set out to identify and test discrete reading skills (e.g. phonic and graphic knowledge, accuracy, fluency and comprehension) and to provide activities which measure the pupil's ability to use the skills. There is no test which can probe every aspect of reading and each one reflects its compiler's view of what is important.

There are tests that focus on phonic skills (e.g. the *Standard Reading Tests*, Daniels and Diack, 1958). Many of the tests focus on the reader's ability to decode separate words (e.g. the *Schonell Graded Word Reading Test* 1942; restandardised 1972); others offer progressively more difficult sentences to read (e.g. the *Holborn Reading Scale*, Watts, 1948, and the *Salford Sentence Reading Test*, Bookbinder, 1976). In an attempt to assess a reader's understanding of what is read, later tests include sentences (e.g. *Young's Group Reading Test*, Young, 1980) which the reader has to complete with one of several given alternatives. In others, there are paragraphs with gaps (*GAP Test*, McLeod and Unwin, 1970) for which readers have to provide an appropriate word. Some tests, which take considerable time to administer, attempt to assess the child's reading behaviour and skills of comprehension, reading accuracy, use of syntax, ability to sequence as well as decoding, in order to produce a 'profile' of the reader (e.g. *Edinburgh Reading Test*, Godfrey Thomson Unit, 1977–1981).

More recently, the *Effective Reading Tests* (ERT) (Vincent and De La Mare, 1986) have attempted to reflect a wide view of reading, especially of reading for information. They use glossy, illustrated booklets with sections of text which the children have to read and on which they then have to answer questions.

The revised *Neale Analysis* (Neale, 1988), for which children have to read aloud a short narrative, makes use of an approach based on miscue analysis, but the errors are marked right or wrong to provide a summative measure of reading accuracy, comprehension and rate. Accuracy is important as far as the scoring is concerned, though the information available from the child's errors can be analysed to show the pattern of the reader's strategies. The manuals for both the ERT and the revised *Neale Analysis* do warn users that test results should be seen as only part of a picture of a child's reading:

> reading is a complex skill and no test can hope to sample all the various components of the reading process ... The results of any reading test should not be considered as the definitive statement about a child's ability in this area, but rather as samples of the child's reading behaviour.
>
> (Neale, 1988:34)

and 'The progress tests ... should be treated as no more than a component of a cumulative education record' (Vincent and De La Mare, 1986:13).

Whatever their focus, such tests are marked in a way that provides a numerical reading age, a 'reading quotient' or a 'standardised score' (which also raise all the questions about reading ages). Statistically, they enable comparison of one child with another and with national norms. However, it is important to note that different tests may yield different reading ages, as there is no standardisation across tests. For example, one child received a reading age of 5.6 from the *Daniels and Diack* test but, at the same time, was given an age of 7.8 from the *GAP Test* (Laycock, 1989). Many schools still give weight to standardised test scores, using them to supplement NC results in order to secure extra support for pupils with reading difficulties.

Standardised reading tests, if they are used, must be regarded as providing only part of the picture of a particular reader. Few of the most frequently used tests claim to have a formative function, and this is perhaps their greatest weakness, because teachers need to know not only whether a reader is progressing as well as his peers, but also where any difficulties might lie, if appropriate support is to be provided. Teachers need to be very clear about their purposes in deciding to use a test and to look carefully at the test manuals to find out the date of the test and the beliefs about reading current at that time, the compilers' views of what reading involves and what they believe their test will assess. Many of the tests are culturally and linguistically biased so that their content will disadvantage children from Britain's many minority groups, who may be unfamiliar with the material and language used. In deciding whether to use a standardised test of reading, the following questions could provide a starting point for reflection on assessment procedures and the use of tests.

- Why do I want to use this test?
- What is being tested?
- Will I know more about the child's reading ability when I have used it?
- Will it tell me what support or help the child needs?
- What aspects of reading are *not* covered by the test?
- Is there a better way of finding out what I need to know?

(Laycock, 1989:29)

National Curriculum **Assessments**

Although there have been slight variations in the content of the NC Assessments (popularly known as SATs) over the years since they were first introduced, the general form they take now seems to be fairly well established. For the NC Assessments at KS1, the child's performance in several tasks and tests contributes to the teacher's assessment of his level of attainment using the NC Level Descriptions. At KS2, national tests are taken and, along with the teacher's assessment, results determine the level awarded.

Key Stage 1

Since 2005, the assessment of reading at the end of KS1 has given greater weight to teacher assessment, though there is still a requirement to use a task and/or a test.

> The role of national curriculum tasks and tests is to support teachers in making their final judgement of teacher assessment in reading ... Teachers are required to use sufficient tasks and tests for them to be confident that their final judgement is secure.
>
> (National Assessment Agency, 2004:8)

Detailed guidance is also given in this document for teachers' activities with children to enable teacher assessments to be made with specific assessment focuses for the different aspects of reading. All assessment opportunities are located in normal reading/language activities. The tasks/tests for reading at the end of KS1 are a mixture of individual reading to the teacher, for the least independent readers, and pencil and paper tests for the more competent readers, but teachers may decide which ones, from the range of tasks and tests produced since 2005, to use at any time during the year.

Existing reading tasks demand a degree of understanding from teachers about the range of strategies a young reader might employ to make sense of a text, and the ability to judge the appropriateness with which the range is used. Teachers who are familiar with running record and/or miscue analysis procedures will certainly be better prepared to undertake these assessments.

Teacher judgement of a child's current reading level, based on work during KS1, determines which task or test should be used (Table 7.3).

Table 7.3 Determination of the use of tasks or tests using teacher judgement of a child's current reading level

Teacher judgement	Use of tasks or tests
At Level 1	Use a Level 1 reading task. If the child does well, consider letting them attempt a Level 2 task.
At Level 2	Use a Level 2 reading task or a Level 2 reading test. If the child does well, consider letting them attempt a Level 3 reading test.
At Level 3	Use a Level 3 reading test. If Level 3 is not achieved, there is no need to use a Level 2 task or test.

Source: National Assessment Agency, 2004:9

Key Stage 2

As for KS1, teachers must make an initial judgement about the level at which a child is operating. If children are at the earliest stages of reading (Level 1 or 2) they will read with the teacher. Though the selection of books offered will be different, the procedure is the same as that for Levels 1 and 2 at KS1.

Most children judged to have reached Level 3 or above by Year 6 will have to do the full range of tests. These are administered as examinations in one week (May) and all are unseen and strictly timed. For Levels 3–5 the reading test takes one hour: this is made up of fifteen minutes' initial time to read the reading booklet, and forty-five minutes for completing the reading answer booklet. The reading booklet consists of a set of readings linked to a theme and one is an adapted extract from a published book. They consist of two information texts and a semi-fictional extract.

The questions that children must answer mostly require direct identification of specific information, rather in the manner of traditional comprehension exercises, except that the answers do not have to be full sentences. The final section requires some reflection on and comparison of the three texts.

For many children the test procedure can be demanding and sometimes confusing as they have to move back and forth between the two booklets. The number of marks it is possible to get for each answer is printed below each question, and this is also pointed out to them in the instructions, which puts additional pressure on the most conscientious children. Anxiety can be created if they feel they cannot answer a particular question and have to miss it out. After forty-five minutes they must stop even if they have not finished.

Although the test compilers have made an effort to present the reading booklets in an appealing way, with colour illustrations, the test remains a very tough reading experience as the children must switch from one kind of reading to another in a short space of time and must read accurately and rapidly to complete the test.

The completed answer booklets are marked externally rather than by the children's own teachers, though the teacher information booklets explain the mark scheme and show what kinds of answers will earn marks. After the tests have been completed, schools are sent information on how the scores will be converted to NC levels.

These tests take the assessment procedures out of the control of teachers. The teacher's only contribution is in the initial assessment of the level at which each child is working; if the test result differs from the teacher's assessment, the teacher must indicate the two different marks.

As with all tests of reading which assess a child's competence on the basis of a single reading activity, the outcome may not reflect the child's true achievement. This means that teachers' ongoing assessments, even if they have to be modified, still have an important role in providing a fuller picture of a child's reading as well as evidence of what has been accomplished and information on which to base planning for the child's future needs.

MANAGING YOUR RECORDS

Assessments of children's progress need to be recorded carefully and in ways which make the information accessible to all who may be involved with a child. Remember that you need these records in order to inform your planning, to make judgements for NC Assessments and to share with parents (both at parents' evenings and in end-of-year summative reports).

How you record your observations and organise your records will vary from school to school. Recording of observations can be as simple as annotating weekly plans with comments on individuals' or groups' achievement of tasks; these notes then inform further planning. *Building a Picture of What Children Can Do* (National Assessment Agency, 2004) gives examples of such annotated plans. Teachers often use tick-sheets (of lists of books read, phonemes recognised, etc.). Such records give some information about a child's reading but we also need evidence about their attitudes and their own view of their learning. Typically, a school's record-keeping for reading is likely to include guided reading records, individual records and, sometimes, reading diaries that travel between home and school.

You will need to be efficiently organised so that your different types of evidence can be easily accessed. Various record-keeping formats are already in existence which help teachers organise and structure observations. Many of these have been developed by local authorities and by individual schools and several draw on the *Primary Language Record* (Barrs *et al.*, 1988). This was the framework for teacher observation and assessment which was recommended by the first version of the NC as the starting point for the development of such records. Whatever framework you use, it should enable you to observe and sample a child's work, not only to record achievement but also to identify a child's strengths and areas for development in all modes of language. Your framework should allow you to collate evidence from discussions with parents, informal observations of the child, conferences with a child about her reading and regular sampling of individual reading sessions. The role of bilingual TAs and the Ethnic Minority Achievement Grant (EMAG) teachers in contributing to your records should not be underestimated.

Further reading and websites

Black, P., Harrison, C., Lee, C., Marshall, B. and Wilian, D. (2005) *Assessment for Learning: Putting it into Practice*. Maidenhead: Open University Press/McGraw-Hill Education.

Clarke, S. (2005) *Formative Assessment in Action: Weaving the Elements Together*. London: Hodder & Stoughton.

Drummond, M.J. (2003) *Assessing Children's Learning*. London: David Fulton.

CLPE: http://www.clpe.co.uk

DfES Standards site on planning: http://www.standards.dfes.gov.uk/primaryframe works/literacy/planning/

Extended scales for pupils with EAL: http://www.qca.org.uk/3359.html

Chapter 8

Meeting Individual Needs
Judith Graham

INTRODUCTION

You will know, if you have been in schools for any length of time, that the child who finds reading difficult is the child about whom teachers constantly talk and worry. Of all the curriculum areas, reading is seen as the start of sophisticated thinking and the gateway to all future academic learning. If children are not reading by the age of seven or so, fears for their future intellectual development start to be voiced and parents particularly start to panic. Recognition of this situation lies behind the concern of all teachers.

REASONS FOR FAILURE TO READ

The reasons for underachievement in literacy are never straightforward to identify and it is unlikely that there is only one cause behind a child's failure to learn to read. Interrelated reasons, such as a home where the child is not read to, illness and absence at the start of schooling and a teacher whose classroom is not well organised, might contribute to a child's failure to make progress; but for every child who fails in such a set of circumstances there are several others who become successful readers. Some very clever children fail to learn to read whilst others, less clever, succeed. Many children with poor eyesight and poor auditory discrimination become good readers whilst children with no problems in those areas do not. Some children arrive at school having learnt to read from watching advertisements on TV; others, with whole shelves of their own books, seem interested in anything rather than reading. So, whilst we can broadly say that some circumstances are more likely than others to result in reading difficulties, we can never be categorical or forget that children continually surprise us. All this needs to be borne in mind whilst we discuss children with reading difficulties under the headings below.

CHARACTERISTICS OF STRUGGLING READERS

Whilst reasons for underachievement may be multiple and varied, the characteristics of children who are becoming aware (usually around the age of seven) that they cannot read are easier to pin down. These children do not seek opportunities to read, they employ delaying tactics when asked to read, they claim that they do not need to read in their lives, they are afraid of being seen to fail, they blame the book ('it's boring, Miss', 'that book's for babies, Miss') or their previous teacher ('she never taught me the sounds the letters make, Miss'). They tend to overuse one single strategy: some children sound out and believe that accurate decoding is what reading is about and is all they need to get better at it; some guess at words wildly and appear unable to bring grapho-phonic abilities into play. Neither group seems to have access to the pleasure that reading provides and their views of reading are almost always utilitarian. When pushed, they might say that they would like to be able to read because 'it helps you to get a job'.

CHARACTERISTICS OF SUCCESSFUL READERS

Successful readers, even in the first years of school, have much less fear of failure. They know books off by heart, reread favourite books, 'play' at reading texts that others have read to them, talk about books, make cross-connections to other books read, see relevance in books to their own lives, draw on first-hand experience to aid comprehension, enjoy writing and are curious about written language, which they notice everywhere they go. They self-correct when reading aloud, selecting from a full range of strategies as appropriate. Older children are confident enough to read the author's name on a book, to scan the blurb on the back or to assess the contents, using chapter headings or lists of contents, and to use such information in making decisions about whether or not to read. Indeed, knowing that you can choose and that you do not have to read everything is one of the freedoms that successful readers enjoy.

CHARACTERISTICS OF GIFTED AND TALENTED READERS

There are children for whom reading is a challenge; there are children who read successfully and, at the other end of the continuum, there are gifted and talented children (the top 5 to 10 per cent) who are attaining well beyond *National Curriculum* (NC) age-related expectations.

Joe is one such child. He is nine years old and this is the opening of his story written in six chapters. Before the story begins, he writes a note about the author:

> The author was born in London and has lived all his life in Shepherd's Bush. He was inspired to write this book by his English teacher Mr Porter. He also made the book and drew the pictures under the watchful eye of his teacher Miss Patrick. This book is his big break and he hopes to write many more.

The story begins:

> CHAPTER 1 Base Camp
> "You ready to go yet Matt?" asked Charlie.
> The heat was intense as I sat, reflecting over the day's activities. I had been driven out that morning from where I was staying in Brazil in a little village in the jungle. I was going on an expedition after some treasure and I didn't know what to expect. I knew that it was a temple and I was going to find it with just a two-way radio and some supplies between me and the jungle.

On the back of his book, we find a blurb:

> A brave young adventurer, an unexplored jungle and a temple full of death! All these things come together in a story of one man's quest to find lost treasure.
> "Excellent" Morning Chronicle
> "Brilliant" Evening Chronicle

This snippet shows Joe displaying characteristics of a gifted and talented child. He reads 'extensively and voraciously, including books and materials written for older readers' (QCA, 2001:26) and his story provides clear evidence of the impact of Joe's avid reading habit on his writing. His voracious reading of *Lion Adventure* by his current favourite author, Willard Price (an author for teenagers), provided the inspiration for the content and style. Notice the confidence with which he asserts his authorship, adopting the language of blurbs but with an ironic edge (his 'big break'). There is an effortless shift from the third person and passive mood of the author note to the first person and powerful start of the story itself. An opening piece of direct speech draws the reader straight in. Then there's some skilful scene setting with clues dropped as to the action to come. His written language has all the hallmarks of an experienced reader ('the heat was intense'; 'I didn't know what to expect'; 'supplies between me and the jungle').

In its guidance on working with gifted and talented children, QCA offers some useful characteristics that distinguish such children at different stages. Some of its points about reading are included here.

In Years 1 and 2, children can:

- make creative connections between their reading and writing;
- read fluently and accurately, showing independence and enthusiasm;
- respond perceptively to books;
- make comparisons between texts;
- draw conclusions about how particular authors work.

In Years 3 and 4, children can:

- respond creatively and critically to what they read;
- read extensively and voraciously, including texts written for older readers;
- consolidate appreciation of favourite authors.

In Years 5 and 6, children can:

- show critical understanding of texts they read, their structure, language and meanings;
- write formal reviews, pastiches and commentaries, developing their responses to the texts;
- tackle difficult texts;
- undertake personal reading with independence and enthusiasm.

(QCA, 2001:3, 26, 49)

Just as you need to be sensitive to the characteristics of children who struggle, you also need to be alert to these hallmarks of the most experienced readers so that you can accommodate them in your planning as well. As with all areas of individual need, your assessments of the pupils will be at the heart of your success in setting challenging and appropriate tasks. The *Primary National Strategy* (PNS) organises its objectives by both year group and strand and the latter allows you to pick objectives that may fall outside the age range of your children but that are nevertheless appropriate. For Year 6, the progression into Year 7 is invaluable here.

The QCA guidance offers helpful scenarios of work that is 'broader, deeper, faster, and encourages independence and reflection' (QCA, 2001:5). Central to your success with this group of children will be your knowledge of children's books as you will need to be able to offer books that extend these sophisticated and fluent readers. Pullman's *His Dark Materials* and Nicholson's *The Wind on Fire* are two well known trilogies; try also titles by classic authors Ursula Le Guin and Alan Garner, or cult writers Joe Delaney, Garth Nix or Eoin Colfer; Sharon Creech's *Walk Two Moons* will intrigue both boys and girls. Guided reading will be a prime site for developing these children's discerning responses and you will find it helpful to look back at Chapter 5 for guidance on devising questions that will really probe and extend children's thinking. Look too at the NC website for examples of units of work from reception through to Year 6 (http://www.nc.uk.net/gt/).

Each school will have a policy for gifted and talented children, so you may well find much in place already to support you. For example, a primary school in Bristol invited an English teacher in from the local secondary school to run a reading club with gifted readers in Year 6. Watson (2006) reports on the success of pupil learning logs in helping the school develop support for gifted and talented pupils. They found, for instance, that there were occasions when it was appropriate for time on the carpet (both in the introductions and plenaries) to be cut short for these children. Invaluable too were the children's voices in this – getting a sense of what really engaged them and, on the other hand, when they were bored, and recording and following up such observations. We are now going to return to struggling readers.

WHAT INEXPERIENCED READERS NEED

What inexperienced and struggling readers need is what all readers need – but in every case they need more of it. They need much more of someone reading aloud to them and the accompanying opportunity to have their eyes on print. As teachers can never read enough to them, we have to use cassette tapes and helpers, older children and parents, TV and radio programmes to keep up the modelling and exposure to the pleasures and benefits of reading.

As well as listening to much more reading, these pupils need:

- to be given extra time to browse, revisit familiar texts, make their own choices and to come at reading through purposeful activities;
- to experience the power of dramatising a text or of extending a text into make-believe play;
- to be asked their opinion of texts;
- to have responses to their volunteered remarks;
- to have their efforts to create texts of their own taken seriously and to have them put into class or individually published books;
- to have an organised classroom, with the full range of routines employed and easy access to a range of books and other resources;
- to have a teacher who is sensitive to their learning styles, monitors progress and keeps – maybe with the child – an accumulating record of all reading done;
- to have a teacher who praises appropriately and never loses her optimism, enthusiasm and high expectations;
- to know that teacher and carers at home are in agreement over the value of literacy and the activities that support it.

All this sensitive scaffolding contributes towards an improvement in the child's self-esteem and attitude towards reading that is all-important if we are to meet that child's needs.

As the children read aloud, the listener should be ready to take over the reading when they are clearly struggling (errors of more than one word in ten is a handy guide); paired reading (see Chapter 5) has shown itself to be most effective in terms of the extent to which it both challenges and supports. They need to be reassured that approximations which sustain meaning and 'guesses' are not sinful, though both will need to be fine-tuned against the print on the page; for example, to read 'scared' when the text says 'frightened' preserves meaning but the teacher will need to go back after the reading to talk about the miscue with the child. Similarly, they need to be reassured that decoding is commendable but that meaning will help the fine-tuning; for example, to read 'shepherd' as 'sheferd' shows the child trying to use phonic skills but the context should be used to supply the meaning and thus the accurate pronunciation. (The fine judgements that the teacher makes with these miscues are described in Chapter 7.)

Almost certainly, struggling readers require early intervention. It used to be thought that the dangers of labelling a child early on as having literacy difficulties were greater than the task of remedying the problems later. The evidence is clear that early help is not only more humane and productive but also more cost-effective. As you will read in the sections below, it is also now a formal requirement of every school that focused help be provided well before the child reaches Year 3.

WHAT INEXPERIENCED READERS DO NOT NEED

A programme that is mostly exercises, rote learning and non-reading-related games is not likely to make much of a difference to a child's reading progress. A narrowing of focus on to the 'bits and pieces' of reading, the teaching of subskills in a decontextualised form without a rich reading environment, results in, at best, only a temporary improvement in these subskills and no noticeable gain in fluent reading (see Wasik and Slavin, 1993). On the other hand, a programme where the child hesitantly reads from books that are too difficult, or where reading is always of new texts which remain 'cold' because they have not been introduced or discussed, is not helpful either. We can only emphasise again how important it is that you help children choose books with care and skill, that you introduce them in a way that 'warms up' the text and that you leave them with a feeling that the book has been a worthwhile event in their lives.

The children who continue to underachieve in school are often those whom teachers and parents pressurise. In their anxiety, adults forget to commend what the child does well, tending only to see the repeated errors and forgetfulness. A tension can be generated about reading failure that is hugely destructive to progress. Children need praise; they need to know exactly what it is they have done well, whether it is self-correction or a wise prediction or an interesting reflection when the book is finished. They do not need blanket or unmerited praise, any more than they need collusion with their wish to avoid reading.

FORMAL ARRANGEMENTS FOR STRUGGLING READERS

There has been no shortage of initiatives aimed at alleviation of the serious problems that beset a minority of our pupils as far as literacy is concerned. You will see considerable overlap in the provision described in the three sections below and individual schools and local authorities may have introduced yet further programmes. The local authority in Cumbria, for instance, has had most encouraging results from its intervention programme. The results (Hatcher *et al.*, 2006) indicate the importance of linking phonological training with reading, when teaching children to read. One of the most successful support programmes is *Reading Recovery* (we devote a section to this later). Unlike some support initiatives, *Reading Recovery* works with the very lowest-attaining children. Two reports, Sylva and Hurry (1995) and Brooks (2002), describe the dramatic results achieved by those receiving *Reading Recovery* through which children are enabled to reach (and sustain) a reading level appropriate for their age. There is universal recognition that problems should be identified and tackled early so that the familiar sense of defeat that we see in children who are still not reading after the age of seven or eight can be avoided.

Special Educational Needs (SEN) Code of Practice

The *National Curriculum* (NC) is an inclusive curriculum: one to which all pupils, irrespective of ability and achievement, are entitled and in which they have the right to participate. Children's additional needs come in all shapes and sizes and this notion of inclusivity can be a challenging one for a new teacher. In 1981, the Warnock Report established the principle that some pupils should have a statement of 'special need'. The 1993 Education Act tightened up arrangements and set out a Code of Practice (DfE, 1994) which stressed the need for early identification of difficulties, affirmed that children with special educational needs should be educated in the classrooms of mainstream schools and stated that their assessment should be school-based. It also established the notion of an Individual Education Plan (IEP) to be drawn up as part of the school-based assessment. Your greatest support and source of information in all these matters will be the school's SENCO (Special Educational Needs Coordinator). You will liaise with her over any worries you have about an individual's reading and, if it comes to it, you will construct an IEP with her guidance. All schools, early years settings and local authorities must, legally, identify, assess and provide for all children's special educational needs. The SEN Code of Practice (revised in 2001) asks for a continuum of provision – a graduated approach. In the first place, schools meet most children's learning needs through differentiation; teachers tailor their activities, spoken language and written language to match individual pupils' different learning needs and styles. Those children who do not respond to differentiation and do not make adequate progress have to be given additional or different help. This school-based SEN provision is described in the Code as School Action. A similar system is set out for early years settings and described as Early Years Action and Early Years Action Plus. Teachers draw up an IEP which is developed in consultation with parents and involves the pupil as far as possible. The IEP should record strategies used to enable the child to progress, such as the short-term targets set for or by the child; the teaching strategies and provision to be used and put in place; when the plan is to be reviewed; success and/or exit criteria; and outcomes (to be recorded when the IEP is reviewed).

If School Action has not helped the child to make adequate progress, School Action Plus is brought into play and the school asks for outside advice from the local authority's support services, or from health or social work professionals. If a child's needs cannot be met through School Action Plus, the local authority may consider the need for a statutory assessment and perhaps a Statement of Special Educational Need which sets out the child's needs in detail and the special educational provision to be made for them. The statement must be reviewed at least annually. When you hear children described as statemented or 'with a statement' it is this statement that is meant.

The decisive factor for taking School Action, moving to School Action Plus, or considering whether a statutory assessment is necessary is whether the child is making adequate progress. The Code defines adequate progress and lists different kinds of progress, depending on the starting point and expectations for a particular child. Essentially, what is considered to be adequate progress for a particular child is a matter for the teacher's professional judgement.

The Code does not ignore the importance of working in partnership with parents and of the child's right to be involved in making decisions and exercising choice as far as his or her education is concerned. Liaison and consultation help progress.

The *Primary National Strategy*

The PNS describes three 'waves' of support for pupils. The SEN Code of Practice (described above) with its 'graduated response' maps onto the NLS waves.

In the first wave, all the children receive 'high quality teaching' (Quality First Teaching) in literacy work in the classroom. The teacher will make use of the routines and resources we mentioned in earlier chapters and will be ensuring that all the children are actively involved. She will work with individual learning styles and be encouraging independence and self-knowledge. A trained Teaching Assistant (TA) supports the teaching. The hope is that this Quality First Teaching will be effective for most of the class; assessment will identify those children who are struggling. Pupils may be at any point on the graduated response, as defined by the SEN Code of Practice.

The second wave of teaching is for those children who have been identified as struggling and for whom a special programme of support is needed. The children may or may not have special educational needs related specifically to learning difficulties in literacy; however, some may be on School Action or School Action Plus for other reasons. Daily sessions, usually from the TA and usually in small groups, are set up for these struggling readers. Sometimes a local authority will set up such booster classes. Most children are expected to catch up with their peers as a result of these interventions and will need no further support.

The third wave of teaching is for those children who have clear SEN needs. These needs may be related specifically to literacy or they may be more widely based. Specialist advice is sought at this point and the previous aims and styles of teaching may both be changed. The intention is to reduce gaps in attainment and make it possible for the child to benefit from Waves 1 or 2. All the children who are the focus of the *Reading Recovery*, initiated and funded by *Every Child a Reader* (see below), are entitled to Wave 3 support. The child ideally will receive individual teaching, which is often at the beginning of the afternoon, first thing in the morning, or last thing in the afternoon and in preschool clubs. Ideally, work arising from these sessions should be displayed in the classroom alongside other work. It is important that children do not miss the same thing every day and are present for classroom literacy work.

Government-funded literacy support programmes and materials

Three stages of support have been instituted by the government since 1999 which are typically implemented for children in Wave 2. The *Early Literacy Support* (ELS) programme is designed to identify and support children who are clearly not making expected progress in their first term in Key Stage 1 (KS1). The programme usually takes place in term two of Year 1. The rationale for such early intervention is clear: support at this point prevents longer-term and more intractable difficulties later on. At the beginning of the spring term, in the child's first year at school, the teacher and the TA (who will have received special training) will start a programme of support. Soler and Paige-Smith (2005) have evaluated the ELS programme and note that those with mild difficulties do best.

For those children with entrenched difficulties and still needing help in Key Stage 2 (KS2), the *Additional Literacy Support* (ALS) programme is appropriate. ALS is offered to those children who only reach a Level 2c or 1 in their KS1 national assessments but who have currently no other support being offered. These materials are intended for use in classroom group work and rely on close collaboration between the teacher and the TA. The TA should run three guided reading and writing sessions each week and the teacher one. The focus is on reading, writing and phonics.

The *Further Literacy Support* (FLS) programme consists of intervention materials offered to pupils in late KS2. It is designed to offer structured additional support for those children who are still not making the expected progress in literacy. Based on PNS objectives, it offers teachers and TAs practical guidance and resources.

A QUICK CHECKLIST IF A CHILD SEEMS TO BE STRUGGLING

What procedures should you follow if you are concerned about the progress of an individual child? You may, for instance, be concerned that your child is exhibiting signs of dyslexia (see below and Chapter 9). What follows is a checklist for you to use whatever your concerns:

- Look out for early warning signs.
  As well as difficulties specifically associated with tackling texts, accompanying early warning signs may take the form of a range of difficulties such as negative attitudes and poor self-esteem; difficulties in sequencing, remembering, coordinating; discrepancy between language skills and other abilities.
- Carry out appropriate diagnostic procedures.
  As well as your ongoing formative assessment (and ensure that this includes phonological awareness), carry out either a running record or a miscue analysis (depending on the age and experience of the child).
- Implement an initial action plan.
  Use evidence from the above to plan some very specific teaching for the child with well focused targets.
- Liaise with SENCO and parents.
  Discuss your findings with the SENCO and then with the child's parents and share your plan with them. The stronger the partnership between you and the parents the better it will be for the child.

- If the child makes progress – good! Continue with carefully targeted steps.
- If the child does not make progress – keep liaising with the SENCO. You may decide that the child needs additional support as described above and that an IEP should be drawn up.

A note about dyslexia

Dyslexia received its first official recognition in the Code of Practice (1994). For much of the twentieth century, dyslexia (often called 'word blindness') as a particular difficulty with reading was not fully acknowledged or accepted by the teaching profession. As new teachers you need to know how dyslexia is currently defined and how you go about seeking the extra help your pupil will need. Below, we give a brief summary of pertinent aspects but Chapter 9 will enable you to deepen your understanding of this specialist area.

The literal meaning of dyslexia is difficulty with words but the area has been complicated by the inclusion of many other 'symptoms' such as clumsiness, disorganisation, poor short-term memory and bad behaviour. More relevant to the teacher of reading is the understanding that children who are diagnosed as dyslexic have problems with all-important phonological processing. We do know that children whose reading is developing with great difficulty will develop other behaviours (such as truculence in the face of books) but it is not those behaviours that define dyslexia. Because dyslexia is such a broad term, you will find that the term 'Specific Learning Difficulties' is used to pinpoint more precisely the nature of a child's problems. You may however also hear the terms used interchangeably; in either case you will know that you are facing a child with serious literacy difficulties who will need additional specialist support.

There are specific diagnostic assessments that can be carried out for dyslexia but you will not have to administer these yourself; the important thing for you to do is be sure that you have taught, monitored and assessed the children as well as you possibly can so that you can hand on full and well focused information to specialist teachers with whom you liaise.

In the rest of this chapter we look at ways in which you can support the particular reading needs of the children in your class. We start with assessment, where you identify those needs, and then we look at ways of responding to them through out-of-class support and through your own in-class teaching strategies.

ASSESSMENT

As we have said above, when planning to meet the needs of children who are struggling with reading you should start from your observations and assessments of the children. For a full discussion of assessment issues, you need to look back at Chapter 7. Here we want to make some general points as far as they relate to pupils who are finding reading difficult. First of all, you need to ensure that your records contain evidence of the child's achievements as well as his or her difficulties. Notes from parent and child conferences are a useful contribution to your overall view of the child. We have also talked about observing and recording the child's strategies as you read with them.

For most children these records and observations will provide you with sufficient information; however, for the children who are giving you concern, additional information to be gained from methodically employing a running record or miscue analysis and analysing your findings must be obtained. It is at this point that you should be able to decide to what extent you can meet the child's needs in your classroom as these assessment tools will allow you to plan for tailored teaching that is responsive to the child's needs. If you think that you cannot, then you will need to discuss the child with other staff (e.g. the SENCO) in order to establish what additional support is available to you and whether an IEP is needed (see checklist above). Whatever the outcome of your discussions, the running record and miscue analysis will still provide you with sufficiently focused information to allow you to meet the NC's principles for inclusion:

- the provision of suitable learning challenges;
- response to a pupil's diverse needs;
- overcoming potential barriers to learning and assessment for individuals and groups.

(DfEE, 1999a:30–33)

At the heart of these principles lies your secure understanding of the reading process and of appropriate assessment procedures.

We emphasise here the need to reduce pressure on the child when carrying out a test. This is even true in a miscue analysis or running record, which some underachieving children construe as a test. Do tell the child that the analysis will help and that you will share all the findings with him or her. As a rule, one should only use other kinds of tests when there is no other way of obtaining information and when you know that you can use the results to focus teaching. Unfortunately, some testing is officially required of us and you can expect to see your poor readers suffering at these times.

Everything that we have included in the chapters on resources and routines is relevant here. What is good practice for your class in general is good practice for your struggling readers. But, because they are struggling, because they lack experience, uppermost in your planning must be the question 'How am I going to engineer more exposure to print?' Everything we have said about big books is particularly important for poor readers; you must ensure that your poor readers can see the text and that they remain focused. Print everywhere in the classroom, access to computers, TV programmes, the school bookshop (owning a book makes a big difference), the active promotion of books, books chosen with care, reading material that the child has chosen and which he claims he wants to read, time to read, shared reading and writing, responsibilities given and purposes for reading made obvious, consultations with parents – all these should guide your planning and management of the classroom and should support all your readers. You should also consider the pairing of your poor (older) reader with a younger child. As we show in 'Reading partners/buddies' (Chapter 5), the benefits are two-way.

MEETING INDIVIDUAL NEEDS IN AND OUT OF THE CLASSROOM

Since the Warnock Report (DES, 1978), the withdrawal of children from class to receive extra individual support has become less common and in-class support is probably now the norm. There are advantages and disadvantages to both systems. It could be said that mature, competent readers read privately and that retirement to a small, quiet, comfortable room without distractions symbolises the act of reading. It is perhaps easier to build

a relationship with one's tutor in the withdrawal arrangement and to feel that one's difficulties are being taken seriously. But someone who helps in the classroom can more
readily ensure that work is not missed and that the child is not treated so obviously as
special. The helper or extra teacher can keep more children under her eye and can more
easily coordinate and discuss work with the regular class teacher.

Reading out of the classroom – *Every Child a Reader* and *Reading Recovery*

The main support arrangements that do withdraw children are *Reading Recovery* programmes. There are other interventions – *Ruth Miskin Literacy, Supported Reading, 15
Minutes a Day*, to name a few – but, because *Reading Recovery* is regarded as very
effective and because its impact has been the subject of much research, we include
some detail at this point. Brooks (2002) has evaluated nineteen interventions including
Reading Recovery.

It is estimated that 35,000 children, equivalent to 6 per cent of the age group, leave
primary school each year with well below the expected literacy level for their age.
Every Child a Reader was set up to address these children's difficulties. The project is
a collaboration between charitable trusts, the business sector and the government
(www.everychildareader.org). In the first year of operation (2005–2006) the project
extensively funded the training of specialist literacy *Reading Recovery* teachers to provide intensive one-to-one support to those children most in need. An independent
evaluation (Burroughs-Lange, 2006) assessed the success of the first year of the initiative, looking at children in ten London boroughs. Most of the children were poor,
two-thirds of them were boys and all at the age of six had reading ages below that of
five-year-olds. So, the needs of the hardest-to-reach children were being addressed.
The children receiving *Reading Recovery* showed statistically significant gains in reading, ending the year with an average reading age of six years and seven months
compared with the groups not receiving *Reading Recovery*, who had an average reading age of five years five months. More than 75 per cent of the *Reading Recovery*
children returned to the classroom with average or above average reading for their
age.

The initiative has shown that schools can raise their aspirations for the lowest-attaining
children and begin to break the link between poverty, gender and attainment (see
Chapter 2). Obviously a programme on this scale costs a lot but the evidence is that, of all
the interventionist programmes, *Reading Recovery* is the one that produces effects which
last. Similar findings in the USA have also been reported (Pinnell *et al.*, 1994). Those
schools with *Reading Recovery* are in a position to monitor their children (including
through national test results) to lend credence to the sustained benefits of the programme. Because of the importance of this initiative, we include below some detail on
the programme.

Reading Recovery, developed by Marie Clay in New Zealand, was designed to prevent reading failure in young children (six-year-olds). Children thought to be at risk are
withdrawn from class and given one-to-one teaching daily for about half an hour over
twelve to twenty weeks. The hope is that such intensive and early teaching will elimi-
nate some of the enormous costs later, not only in financial terms but also in terms of
pupil stress and poor prospects of progress later on.

The characteristics of *Reading Recovery* are:

- intensive training of teachers (literacy methods, child development and children's books);
- high expectations conveyed to the child;
- a range of child-focused and meaning-based approaches;
- the linking of reading and writing;
- clear evidence of success given to the child.

A typical *Reading Recovery* session as described by Jean Hudson (in Harrison and Coles, 1992:239–241) goes through the following seven stages:

1 rereading of two or more familiar books to practise reading skills and to develop reading fluency;
2 practice in letter identification using plastic letters on a magnetic board;
3 shared writing of a story to be read and reread;
4 rearranging a cut-up story to provide many opportunities to study individual words and their structures;
5 practice in analysing the sounds in words;
6 introduction and attempted reading of at least one new book;
7 individual variations depending on a child's needs, e.g. prediction, letter identification.

The clear benefits for children are:

- increased confidence that they will be able to read;
- an enthusiasm for books;
- a willingness to take risks and a corresponding reduction in the fear of failure;
- a wider range of strategies used;
- more independence;
- an early return to the normal work of the classroom.

The clear benefits for teachers and schools are:

- in-service training with clear practical outcomes;
- raised standards of literacy as *Reading Recovery* children are no longer held back;
- better monitoring of all children;
- easier planning as there is less differentiation to consider.

Reading in the classroom

The *Reading Recovery* programme takes children out of the classroom in the early stages of reading but it offers principles for working with children, in KS1 and KS2, within the classroom too. Indeed, the research evaluation of *Reading Recovery* mentioned above (Burroughs-Lange, 2006) showed that a trained literacy expert in the school helped improve overall literacy throughout the school, not just in the children being withdrawn. Some children who 'qualified' for *Reading Recovery* help but for whom there was no space still improved far more than expected. Key features of *Reading Recovery* – the volume of reading, the choice of appropriate texts, creating personal texts, the explicit discussion of strategies for getting at words, and the focus on what the child already knows – are all key aspects of appropriate provision for struggling readers.

There are programmes intended to provide in-class support for KS2 children (e.g. *Catch-Up*) and the NLS materials specifically for use with children in KS2, the ALS and FLS materials described above, can be downloaded.

Whether you are organising additional support programmes or not, there are still key principles that should guide your planning of in-class support and we look at these below.

Word recognition

Children who are over-reliant on the meaning of a text and do not use phonic knowledge in their reading will need the kind of careful teaching we discussed in Chapter 3 and you will need to revisit that section to support your planning in this area for struggling readers. Again we stress the importance of keeping such teaching firmly contextualised for the child.

Work that you do in the context of the child's writing or during shared writing can contribute to his or her graphic knowledge. You could use the shared writing of a story to demonstrate, for instance, past tense verb endings. In this extract from some writing with Year 1 children, the teacher took the opportunity to point out the consistently spelled though differently pronounced 'ed' endings as they arose in the shared composition: 'Red Riding Hood liv*ed* in a forest and every week she walk*ed* to her granny's cottage …'.

In another example of work on graphic knowledge, a Year 3 class teacher wanted to target some work on plurals with a particular child as she had noticed him ignoring such word endings in his reading. She suggested he make a number book for a younger child (as part of a unit of work on bookmaking for different audiences). They planned the book together, firstly talking about the kind of items that would appeal to a younger child. Settling on the fruits from *Handa's Surprise* (Eileen Browne), the teacher wrote the list of fruits: 'banana, passion fruit, pineapple, guava, etc'. Then they listed them again putting them into the traditional counting format: '1 banana, 2 passion fruits, 3 pineapples, 4 guavas …'. As she wrote each item the teacher asked the child 'How do I show there's more than one passion fruit, pineapple...?', thus drawing his attention to the 's' ending in each case. You could of course carry out such an activity with either the whole class or a group of children.

For many children multisensory approaches to letter recognition work well: writing letters in the sand, trailing a finger over a letter cut out of sandpaper, feeling for wooden letters in a bag, having the letter written on your back, manipulating magnetic letters all make a positive contribution to some children's learning of letters. Alphabet charts and books are important so look out for interactive/multisensory examples or make your own. These can be made to meet the needs and interests of particular children: for instance, a football alphabet could be constructed by cutting the letters out of differently coloured cloth representing different teams.

Children's word recognition skills will be supported by the environmental print that you provide as well as by more specifically tailored activities. These might include cloze procedures; name dominoes (which some teachers extend to topic words); a version of

Pelmanism (maybe based on book characters: wolf, pig, house, sticks, straw, etc.); class-made dictionaries (e.g. of favourite foods); short personal lists of words to learn that the children select themselves from their writing or from a favourite book.

A particularly useful activity for developing word recognition is one in which sentences are cut up and reassembled by the child. It works in this way. Take a book that the child knows well, for example *Not Now Bernard* (David McKee), and either read it to the child or read it together. Then take a memorable page such as '"Not now, Bernard," said his mother'. The child watches as you write this out on a strip of paper and cut it up into the six words. Then the child reassembles the words, matching them to the printed page. The activity can be developed either at this point or in a subsequent session by asking the child to rearrange the words without the support of the book. You could then provide additional nouns (e.g. other children's names, 'father', 'monster') and use these to generate new sentences: '"Not now, Sunil," said his mother'; '"Not now, Miles," said his father'. This activity works well because it keeps the words contextualised for the child and draws attention to one-to-one correspondence. It also encourages children to draw upon the structure of the sentence itself, the syntax, which children need to use when employing grammatical knowledge. It is to this key skill that we now turn.

Comprehension

Children who are over-reliant on the letters and words and lose the meaning of what they are reading will need support in developing grammatical awareness and contextual understanding.

These children are using graphic-phonic strategies well enough, so it is important that you work to strengthen the other areas. Then the fine-tuning of the decoding that has to go on can be made more rapidly. This, after all, is our aim with poor readers; we want rapid and automatic orchestration of all the cue-systems.

We pay particular attention to contextual understanding through our later points in this chapter about familiarity with texts and stories (the big shapes again) so we will spend some time now considering grammatical awareness.

To explore this we will consider possible responses to grammatical confusion in two teaching contexts: with the individual child and with the whole class.

A child misreads, 'I shall be a detective. I shall walk around and find some terrible crime going on' as 'I shall be a detective. I shall walk around and find some trouble crime going on'. She does not self-correct the miscue. In English the juxtaposition of these two nouns, 'trouble' and 'crime', is syntactically impossible and most readers would do a double-take at this point, checking, amongst other things, the punctuation, the graphic arrangement ('terrible/trouble') and the general meaning of the sentence.

What are you going to do to teach the child to use a range of strategies? Obviously, encourage her to have another run at the sentence; if she gets it right this time you could end the session by discussing the grapho-phonic differences between the two words. If she repeats the miscue you would need to read the sentence back to her correctly and ask her to identify the difference. You would want to talk to her about the importance of using context and of whether the sentence makes sense. This is something that you could reinforce when she later makes a similar mistake in the sentence 'She remembered an arrow', which she reads as 'She remind an arrow'. If in this case she does self-correct you could ask her, 'How did you know that it was "remembered" and not "remind"?' If her answer only refers to the grapho-phonic differences, encourage her to reflect on the fact that she made it make sense. If her answer is that 'remind' does not make sense, get her to reflect on the different configuration of 'remember' and 'remind'.

As well as the work you do in one-to-one reading sessions like this on reminding children to reread and to read ahead, you could also model thought processes aloud when you are working with the whole class in shared reading and shared writing sessions. You might, for instance, say, 'I'm going to read ahead now and see if that helps me with this word.'

Another context for developing such whole-class awareness can arise as you prepare children for sessions when they are going to read with a younger child (see 'Reading partners/buddies' in Chapter 5). One teacher gave her Year 5 class quite specific lessons in this. In groups they discussed questions (on 'prompt' cards) that were specifically designed to increase understanding about using the different cue-systems in reading. The teacher's intention here was twofold; she wanted to develop the quality of the interactions in the reading partnerships by giving her older class some effective strategies for supporting their younger partners, and she also wanted to take the opportunity to make such strategies very clear for the struggling readers in her class. For instance, one card asked the question, 'What would you do if your reading partner was trying to read "the pumpkin seed grew a pumpkin sprout" and she read it as "the pumpkin seed *green* a pumpkin sprout"?' (from *Pumpkin Pumpkin* by Jeanne Titherington). The children were able to verbalise that their pupil would need to see that the sentence disintegrated because 'green' did not fit; in other words, it was syntactically inappropriate. They also said that they would draw their pupil's attention to the ending of the word 'grew' and show how it was different from the ending of the word 'green'. After accepting the children's suggestions, the teacher added her own, which included suggesting that they ask their pupil to reread the sentence. All the suggestions were collated on to a class list entitled 'Ways of Helping our Reading Partners'. In this way awareness and reading ability grow hand in hand.

Texts

The question of which books to have in the classroom is explored in general terms in Chapter 6. We will try to make points more specifically related to children with difficulties, though if the books are valuable for such children they should be valuable for all.

Margaret Meek (1991) speaks of the struggling reader's 'misalignment' with the text. Undoubtedly many children are given texts to read that for one reason or another are neither attractive nor supportive to them. Maybe they never encounter anybody remotely like themselves. We know of an older poor reader from a black family who angrily rejected any more of the *Little Tim* books (Edward Ardizzone), which have all the middle-class assumptions of their time of writing (pre and post World War II). Many children's books assume a readership that is comfortably-off, middle-class, white, two-parented and amply grandparented. Eventually this may alienate those children who already feel marginalised and unsure of their place in this activity of reading. Conversely, and ironically, children may feel that they never have books that take them beyond their immediate environment. (A reading scheme designed especially for working-class inner-city children, *Nippers*, was found to be less popular with its intended audience than the 'exotic' *Keywords* (Peter and Jane) Ladybird books.) What is probably essential is that the books have emotional truth. Children need to glimpse in them something of how they have felt and feel about life and its ways.

Many older readers are convinced that animal characters are babyish and will feel demeaned by a diet of such books (unless the teacher seeks out and promotes the more subtle examples, such as *The True Story of the Three Little Pigs* (John Scieska and Lane Smith) or *Tusk Tusk* (David McKee) or *Fred* (Posy Simmonds)). Sadly, there is, in some schools, a prejudice against picture books for older children despite the vast numbers of such books that are suitable throughout the age range. In our view, illustrated texts not only welcome the child to the book and give clues about and a context for the written text, but also teach essential lessons about character, plot, setting and theme. They can add a sophistication to the whole book that keeps an older but less experienced reader involved. You might think that a picture book where the text and the illustrations seem to contradict each other, or where the narrator seems unaware of what is going on in the picture, would be the last thing a struggling reader needs, but books such as those by Anthony Browne and Pat Hutchins bestow the pleasure of being 'in the know', and that superior feeling is rewarding enough to make the child return to the book to experience the pleasure again. Rereading is when the most important reading lessons are learned.

If we accept the idea that readers with difficulties have simply not had enough exposure to text then we will want to make sure that they have books they care about reading. The use of narrative texts in schools for early readers has a long and honourable history. In many ways the chronological, time-based ordering of events centring around characters is perhaps quite close to how we all see life. Thus, narrative texts present fewer disjunctions and difficulties to those coming new to reading. This is not to say that non-narrative texts will not be sought out, especially by older boys, but you will need to provide even more support for the reading of non-fiction if your pupil is not to be downcast by the textual challenges.

We have stressed in earlier chapters that rhyming texts are the texts that children quickly get off by heart and which give enormous, almost sensual, pleasure. Texts in verse or picture books of well known songs have a secret support system: children find themselves able to read almost by magic as the rhyme reduces the possibilities. The fact that rhyming texts strengthen appreciation of onset and rime, so important to literacy development, makes them of central importance for the struggling reader. Ideally, all children would have experienced rhyme in nursery rhymes and songs before school; unfortunately, this is not always the case and it is not easy to share nursery rhymes with a reluctant nine-year-old. Fortunately, there are many rhyming texts, often in picture books, that are suitable, engaging and thought-provoking, and which, in a pleasurable way, aid phonological awareness and reveal how our written language encodes the rhymes. Collections of poems by Michael Rosen, Allan Ahlberg, Kit Wright, Charles Causley and the subversive Roald Dahl yield many witty and accessible poems for you to share and enjoy with less experienced readers. When you want to move into classic poetry, seek out in the first instance ballads and narrative poems, as these provide the support of story.

Many children who find reading a problem will turn to humour very willingly; it gives a purpose to the struggle. The Ahlbergs, Jill Murphy, Quentin Blake and Tony Ross consistently come near the top of favourite author/illustrators in this respect. Look out also for the work of Colin McNaughton, Nicholas Allen and Dav Pilkey, whose hugely popular *Captain Underpants* series has rescued many a poor reader.

Traditional tales make good reading for the struggler because, unless they are very inexperienced, they know 'how they go'. It is worth seeking out retellings from around the world; John Steptoe's *Mufaro's Beautiful Daughters*, for instance, is the Cinderella story set in Zimbabwe. Once readers have a store of these texts they will enjoy books which play around with traditional tales, such as many picture books by Tony Ross and the Ahlbergs or *Snow White in New York* (Fiona French). James Marshall's witty and streetwise retellings of traditional tales also have great appeal.

Finally, a word on comics and, for older children, graphic novels, is in order. Many children would love to belong to the 'club' that reads comics and graphic novels and they may well want to read such texts with you in class. They are not always easy to read aloud together: which bit do you look at first? do you read every bit of print? in which order? Comics, comic strip books and graphic novels are probably best for poring over in private; there are reading lessons to be learnt within and children are seldom 'just' looking at the pictures. We should not dismiss their efforts if they seem to be directed towards comics more than towards other texts for a limited period.

We need to give some thought to the role of told stories. For poor readers, the lessening of tension involved in listening to a story is usually such that they can relax and reflect on some of the most significant reading lessons. They can start to contemplate and store in their minds narrative conventions such as openings, endings, characters, settings and the ups and downs of events in the plot, and they can begin to glimpse the pleasures of story and of language: all features of written narrative but in this mode supported by eye contact, facial expression and intonation. They can hold their own in classroom discussions that may follow. In our experience, some of the best comments on story and some of the best retellings have come from those who are still struggling with the print on the page. The told story gives them confidence and understanding of story conventions, and, with appropriate support, this eventually feeds into reading ability.

PARENTAL INVOLVEMENT

One of the relatively underexplored areas in education is what parents actually do at home when they are enlisted to help with their child's reading in a PACT scheme. As we said in Chapter 5, we know that, in various monitored projects, most children whose parents read with them and listened to them made greater progress than those children whose parents were not involved. What has been less appreciated is that some children whose parents had received insufficient guidance and resources did not make progress and that those children were usually the very ones most in need of extra help (see Toomey, 1993, for a full discussion of this). We suggest that if, as we hope, you are seeking to enlist parental involvement with your poor readers, it is important to talk regularly with the parents to ensure that you share the same views of what works for the child. You should recognise that the older the child the harder it is to sustain parental contact over reading but the more imperative it actually is to do so. The ELS programme, whilst recognising the importance of parents and carers and accordingly making provision for home activities, is designed to be self-standing and is not reliant on children completing activities at home. Look out for materials for parents and carers that are translated into community languages.

CONCLUSIONS

It may appear that our view of the poor reader contains a protective element. In your experience, the poor reader may be a tricky, disruptive boy (most of the children with literacy difficulties are boys) who rejects all your efforts and whose attention span is of seconds, not minutes. But our feeling is that no child does not want to read. Angry, rejecting behaviour when it comes to reading lessons is a symptom of the grave realisation that fills the child of his incompetence in an area that society considers so essential and that he can see brings so much pleasure, knowledge and satisfaction to those around him. The anger is compounded by the evidence that it is so easy for some of his classmates. Most children with difficulties have missed vital early literacy experiences, have been confused by information that lets them down and have been allowed to slip through countless nets, ranging from inadequate resources to badly managed classrooms. We have stressed that collusion with defeatism or unconditional acceptance of the reader's low opinion of himself is not helpful, but a situation where we *blame* the victim is unforgivable. There is a great deal that can be done to help the poor reader, especially if it is done early enough. We are confident that if you can use some of the advice given here then your sullen/terrified/indifferent/aggressive child will start to experience success and you will know the rewards of helping him to become a reader.

At the beginning of your career, listening to a stumbling beginner may seem monotonous and unrewarding, but we hope you can draw inspiration from this book so that your increasing knowledge and repertoire of approaches, activities and strategies will enable you to respond creatively to your pupils' struggles and to hear their reading with a fresh ear. The message of this chapter and of the book as a whole is that as a teacher of reading you need to be fully informed about reading processes and practice. You will then be free to enjoy your teaching and to respond constructively to all your pupils' varying and multiple needs.

Further reading and website

Bates, J. and Munday, S. (2005) *Able, Gifted and Talented*. London: Continuum.

Bentley, D. and Reid, D. (1995) *Supporting Struggling Readers*. Widnes, Cheshire: UKRA.

Berger, A. and Gross, J. (eds) (1999) *Teaching the Literacy Hour in an Inclusive Classroom: Supporting Pupils with Learning Difficulties in a Mainstream Classroom*. London: David Fulton.

Reason, R. and Boote, R. (2004) *Helping Children with Reading and Spelling: A Special Needs Handbook*. London: Routledge.

Every Child a Reader: The Results of the First Year is published by Every Child a Reader. It contains case histories of individual children who have benefited from *Reading Recovery*: copies of the report are available from http://www.everychildareader.org

Chapter 9

Dyslexia and Reading

Cathy Svensson

INTRODUCTION

Most children learn to read with relative ease. However, for a minority the act of reading presents immeasurable difficulties. The reading difficulties experienced by some children were first described by Dr Pringle Morgan in the nineteenth century (Morgan, 1896). He reported on a fourteen-year-old boy, Percy, who could 'with difficulty spell out words of one syllable … wrote his name as "Precy" and did not notice his mistake until his attention was called to it more than once' (Morgan, 1896:1378). Percy was nevertheless described as one of the cleverest boys in the school. Hinshelwood (1900) later coined the term 'word blindness' to account for the discrepancy between the specific reading problems Percy and some otherwise normally developing children experienced and their intelligence. Traditionally, this discrepancy (between intelligence and expected reading attainment) has long been associated with dyslexia. However, difficulties with reading can occur at all levels of intellectual ability; interestingly, children of high ability who do not read very well can have very special abilities and talents (and so can any child), particularly in the field of visual and spatial skills (Singleton, 1999). It is also striking that some children of low intellectual ability have no problems with reading. The discrepancy model of dyslexia has been disputed; children with dyslexia are not necessarily seen as all that different from other poor readers (sometimes labelled 'garden-variety').

DEFINING THE CONDITION

Understanding the roots of the word 'dyslexia' helps define the condition. It originates from the Greek words *dys* (difficulty) + *lexis* (written word). This would indicate that dyslexia is a specific difficulty associated with the written word. Despite its common association with problems in reading, dyslexia has been differently defined over the last thirty years with each definition giving greater or less weight to various features of the condition. However, central to all definitions, the difficulty with reading is widely acknowledged.

The British Psychological Society locates the reading-related difficulty at 'word' level:

> Dyslexia is evident when accurate and fluent word reading and/or spelling develops very incompletely or with great difficulty. This focuses on literacy learning at the word level and implies the problem is severe and persistent despite appropriate learning opportunities.
>
> (1999:68)

The British Dyslexia Association's definition goes further in listing the potential difficulties and abilities which may be characteristic features of dyslexia. Peer (1994) specifies the breadth of underlying problems which are affected and claims these may extend to numeric skills and music:

> A combination of abilities and difficulties which affect the learning process in one or more of reading, spelling and writing. Accompanying weaknesses may be identified in areas of speed of processing, short-term memory, sequencing, auditory and/or visual perception, spoken language and motor skills. It is particularly related to mastering written language, which may include numeric and musical notation.
>
> (Peer, 1994:68)

Despite the lack of agreement about what constitutes dyslexia, there appears to be a growing consensus that dyslexia is a language-based difficulty (Lundberg, 1994; Lyon, 1994). De Fries (1991) provides convincing evidence that dyslexia runs in families and that it affects more males than females. Boys whose father is dyslexic have a 40 per cent chance of inheriting the condition while for girls the risk is only 20 per cent. Opinions about the percentage of the population affected by the condition vary. Stein (2001) claims that it affects up to 10 per cent of the population and severely affects 4 per cent (Miles and Miles, 1999; Peer, 1994). For classroom teachers this means that they may expect to teach between one and three children with dyslexia in each class group of thirty children. For the country as a whole this means that 350,000 children are affected. Characteristics of the condition at different developmental stages will vary so that no two children with dyslexia will present identical characteristic features, and yet common to all dyslexic pupils is their well documented and 'specific' difficulty in learning to read. Snowling (1987) describes dyslexia as a spectrum or a continuum of difficulties to reflect the diverse forms it may take. Children can present mild to severe symptoms which interfere to a greater or lesser extent with their literacy skills.

Research into dyslexia and reading contributes to an enduring debate between educationalists and cognitive psychologists and it also finds voice in social research, where the existence of a 'condition' called dyslexia is considered to be a social construction. Educationalists have traditionally centred their interest on wide, holistic approaches to the teaching of reading associated with 'top-down methods' which focus on offering a breadth of teaching approaches beyond the scope of single words (Smith, 1978; Goodman, 1967). Cognitive psychologists, on the other hand, have focused their attention on single-word reading and in analysing the subskills that are involved in the reading process. Theirs is most commonly perceived to be a 'bottom-up' approach which focuses on the development of word reading. Both groups embrace a different body of knowledge; both influence our understanding of the reading process.

In giving their account of the dyslexic condition, cognitive psychologists have been particularly influential. Their quest has traditionally been to discover the underlying source of the reading difficulties associated with dyslexia. In this chapter we will draw from the work of cognitive psychology. We will discuss Frith's reading model (1985) in order to set a context for single-word reading and to explore the skills that underpin the reading process. We will give careful consideration to the potential barriers to reading that are strongly present in dyslexia. Two case study pupils – one a pupil in Year 2 and the other in Year 5 – will be discussed and reviewed against the framework of the 'simple' view of reading (DfES, 2006a). The chapter will conclude by considering the personalised learning needs of the two pupils and the wider implications for classroom practice.

Over the last thirty years, research into dyslexia has focused on identifying and isolating those skills that predict a child's success in learning to read. This is by no means an easy task as there are numerous factors that may influence reading, many of which extend beyond the scope of studies on dyslexia. For example, a child's exposure to texts, family experiences and expectations related to reading, and the child's interest and motivation to read all may have an impact, to a greater or lesser extent, on reading (Wade and Moore, 2000; Hannon, 1999).

LINES OF ENQUIRY INTO DYSLEXIA

In an effort to explore the serious reading difficulties traditionally associated with dyslexia, researchers have explored three different lines of enquiry:

- the visual theory: how readers make sense of the written words on the page;
- the automaticity theory: the role of motor timing skills in supporting or inhibiting the reading process;
- the phonological theory: how a reader's underpinning sound-based knowledge system impinges on the reading process.

The visual theory

The act of reading requires the child to process a wide range of visual information. The child needs to hold the shape of the word in memory (visual memory) for recall, to visually discriminate individual words one from another, to follow the sequential procedure of reading by tracking print from left to right and top to bottom of a page. Stein *et al.* (2001) propose that associated difficulties may include coordination, left/right confusion and poor sequencing in the visual and spatial domains, each of which is important to reading.

Children with specific reading problems frequently report that they have problems in copying words from the board and following text on the page. They may describe words as 'jumping off the page' as they read. Their confusion in discriminating similarly shaped words and letters such as 'was' and 'saw', 'b' and 'd', is well documented in the literature and supports the view that the reading problem associated with dyslexia is part of a wider problem with visual processing. Proponents of the visual theory emphasise the importance of the visual processing system in reading (Stein, 2001). Evans (2001) proposes that there is convincing research evidence to suggest that about two-thirds of dyslexic people experience problems in processing and interpreting visual information. Garzia (1993) suggests that these anomalies may be related to subtle problems in the transmission of visual information between the eye and the brain. Interestingly, associated strengths in visual and spatial skills have also been documented in the literature on dyslexia. This serves to remind the reader that there is not one single manifestation of dyslexia that is universally agreed on in the research literature.

The automaticity theory

Fawcett and Nicholson (1992, 2001) claim that some of the reading difficulties associated with dyslexia may be due to more generalised problems with motor timing. They report on the often subtle differences in the speed with which children with dyslexia complete motor skill activities, including reading, when compared with their non-dyslexic peers. They claim that tasks such as tying shoelaces, throwing a ball, learning times tables and retrieving words from memory take longer for the child with dyslexia. In a similar way, the sophisticated information processing required for fluency in reading relies on highly efficient and synchronised word decoding, retrieval and speech processing skills (Wolf and O'Brien, 2001). Where these skills are not automatic, reading may be compromised. Brain imaging studies support their findings and locate the source of the problem at the site of the cerebellum (Brown *et al.*, 2001).

The phonological theory

According to Snowling *et al.* (2001), children's phonological skills – their ability to process and represent speech sounds – can determine the ease with which they learn to read. A strong claim for the inextricable link between language and reading has been made by many researchers (Ehri, 1992; Snowling *et al.*, 2001; Stanovich and Siegel, 1994; Muter *et al.*, 2004) who suggest that language underpins all areas of reading, notably speech perception and production. Speech perception and production may affect the reader's ability to retrieve words from memory and to name words at speed. It can affect such diverse language-based skills such as learning a modern foreign language, following oral classroom instructions and sequences and learning times tables. The reader's ability to map the sound structure of words onto letter shapes and to detect and manipulate sounds in decoding is considered to be closely linked with phonological development.

The sound units of the syllable, onset/rime and the phoneme have come under particular scrutiny in research on phonological awareness. Difficulties with blending, segmenting and analysing these sound units have been strongly linked with problems in learning to read. For example, a number of studies have highlighted the importance of a child's sensitivity to rhyme and alliteration in predicting his future success in learning to read (Bradley and Bryant, 1983). Later studies have argued for the predictive quality of other phonological skills. For example, the ability to segment words into onset and rime (h/at and fr/og) is considered to have an important place in learning to read by analogy (Goswami, 1994; Ehri, 1992). The predictive quality of phoneme knowledge has more recently been acknowledged (Muter, 2003; Hatcher *et al.*, 2004). Separately and together, these studies make a strong case for the important role of competent phonological awareness in fluent reading and also for the corollary of this, that poor levels of phonological knowledge are strongly associated with poor reading. Figure 9.1 demonstrates the behavioural signs associated with phonological processing difficulties.

A unifying theory for dyslexia?

The quest for a unifying theory which can give a plausible account of the reading difficulties associated with dyslexia presents an ongoing challenge for research. There is some recent consensus that the role of motor timing may offer some solution. Stein and Walsh (1997) propose that associated visual and phonological problems may be regulated by motor timing, which in turn is regulated by the cerebellum, at the base of the brain. Both are two sides of a similar difficulty and are strongly implicated in the development of single-word reading, as the following discussion of Frith's model (1985) of single-word reading demonstrates.

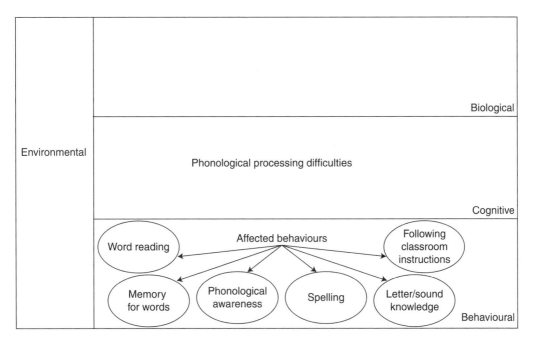

Figure 9.1 Model showing the behavioural signs of dyslexia that are linked to phonological processing skills (adapted from Frith, 1997)

Frith's model of the reading process

In studies of single-word reading and in the domain of dyslexia, Frith's model of the reading process has particular authority, although it is not without its critics, in part because of its simplicity and because it fails to take account of factors outside reading and spelling that may influence single-word reading (Snowling and Hulme, 2005; Goswami and Bryant, 1990). Frith sets out the three developmental phases through which a child proceeds in becoming a skilled reader: these are the logographic, alphabetic and orthographic phases (Figure 9.2). She highlights the significance of alphabetic knowledge within the reading process and the difficulty dyslexic pupils may experience in learning

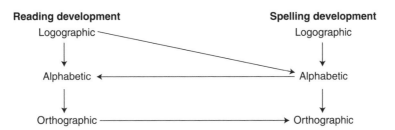

Figure 9.2 Frith's model of single-word reading: the three phases within reading and spelling (adapted from Frith, 1985)

to map letter shapes onto letter sounds during this vital reading stage. In this way, her developmental model of reading is influential both as a starting point for a discussion on reading, and in opening up a discussion of the skills that underpin the reading process, particularly those involved in acquiring the alphabetic principle.

Logographic phase

The earliest phase is marked by children's ability to recognise images and words based on a few prominent visual features. The child attends to both the image or word shape and the semantic association of the word, rather than to print/sound correspondence (Byrne, 1992). For example, the child may be able to 'read' advertising logos and images, personal names on coat pegs, familiar characters' names in stories, and, in this way, she develops an early reading repertoire. In making these early connections between symbols and spoken language, the child is essentially engaged in 'primitive' reading (Stuart, 2006). Typical reading errors reflect readers' reliance on the visual features of a word. For example, the child may read 'yellow' for 'children', as they are both visually similar long words with tall letter shapes in the middle. According to Gough and Hillinger (1980), this stage places heavy demands on a child's visual memory and, as a system, it breaks down after storing around forty words unless the child has acquired an additional reading strategy to distinguish the different visual features of words. From this point on, the child needs to establish letter/sound links to make progress from using only visual cues to using an alphabetic reading system as well.

Alphabetic phase

The child with dyslexia frequently finds the transition to the alphabetic phase problematic (Frith, 1985). As a reading phase, it is underpinned by the child's application of letter/sound knowledge and the developing understanding that there is a consistent link between letters and sounds. The dyslexic reader who has traditionally not established a secure phonological processing system may be severely disadvantaged in proceeding through the alphabetic phase. According to Ehri (1995), the phase emerges as the child begins to make some connections between the sound values of words. She refers to this stage as 'partial alphabetic', preferring, as Ehri does, to break down these processes into partial and full alphabetic stages to represent more closely developmental progression within each phase.

The alphabetic phase is important in establishing the sequential left-to-right order of reading and in providing the child with an additional strategy with which to decode words. Throughout this phase, decoding is established and becomes fine-tuned. Knowledge of the alphabet and the link between sounds and letter shapes allows the child to sound out simple regular words following the left-to-right sequence, for example h-o-p spells 'hop'. As the skill becomes fine-tuned, the child learns to decode more complex word structures; for example, he learns that when another 'o' is inserted into the word 'hop' the vowel sound changes from a short to a long vowel sound ('hoop'). Eventually, the knowledge of the sound–symbol correspondence becomes sufficiently sophisticated to accommodate subtle features: for example, the child knows that 'c' makes a soft sound similar to a 's' when followed by 'e', 'i', or 'y' as in 'city' and 'cyclops', and a hard 'c' sound when followed by 'a' and 'u' in 'cup' and 'cap'. Thus, the alphabetic phase facilitates a rapid increase in sight vocabulary. However, if a child is relying too much on the alphabetic principle because his phonological development is delayed, his reading progress will be challenged.

Orthographic phase

The orthographic phase is the fluent reading phase marked out by the automatic recognition of printed words. It relies on the amalgamation of logographic and alphabetic skills which indicates that the child has to draw selectively from a knowledge base of the sound structure of words while remembering a visual sequence of letters which may have little or no bearing on the sound structure of the word. This allows the child to read words that do not conform to regular sound patterns, for example 'island', 'enough', 'yacht' and 'bough'. The need to rely on both sound and visual processing systems that is required by orthographic reading is challenging for dyslexic children.

Frith's model provides some insight into the developmental stages of single-word reading. It highlights the need for secure phonological skills for decoding. It also highlights the important role of visual processing from the logographic to the orthographic phases in reading and the potential problems a child with a specific reading difficulty may experience. It does not claim to give any account of the processing skills that underpin reading for meaning or comprehension. The simple model of reading (Gough and Tunmer, 1986) does that and further strengthens the claim that reading is inextricably linked with language, as it is the sum of the two parts: comprehension and decoding.

The simple model of reading

The simple model of reading (Gough and Tunmer, 1986; Hoover and Gough, 1990) has received much attention and has replaced the earlier searchlights model of reading as the favoured approach in the *Primary National Strategy* (DfES, 2006b). It emphasises the fundamental role of language in the reading process and helps to illuminate the specific nature of the difficulty that is traditionally associated with dyslexia.

Stated simply, this model proposes that fluent readers must be able to read and understand the words on the page. Two skills are essential to this: the skill of decoding and the skill of understanding the written word. Reading, according to this model, is the product of word recognition and language comprehension. Word recognition or 'decoding' refers to the ability to map letter shapes onto sounds without the aid of context. Comprehension is the ability to understand language and therefore applies to both reading and spoken language comprehension. The reading comprehension element in this model therefore is synonymous with language comprehension, whether written or spoken. An important consideration here is that reading comprehension is either strengthened or limited by the quality of a child's spoken language comprehension (Stuart, 2006). Both are essential components of the reading process and, separately and together, they place demands on both phonological skills and language comprehension.

In their own diagrammatic representation of the simple model of reading (Figure 9.3), Snowling and Stackhouse (2005) locate children with reading disorders, those that attract the term 'dyslexia', in the right-hand side of the model in the upper quartile.

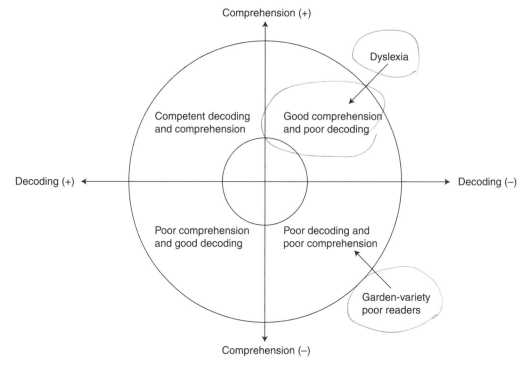

Figure 9.3 The simple model of reading (adapted from <u>Snowling and Stackhouse, 2005</u>)

Traditionally, Snowling and Stackhouse suggest, this group of readers will have poor phonological skills and the extent of their difficulties will determine where they lie on the phonology (or decoding) continuum. They propose that, as a group, they may have unidentified subtle or more persistent speech problems. However, their language comprehension, whether written or spoken, is considered secure and is reflected by their position on the comprehension continuum. Unlike the traditionally described dyslexic readers, the 'garden-variety poor readers' are, on the other hand, characterised by poor levels both of decoding and of comprehension. It is this that has conventionally set them apart from the group of readers with specific reading difficulties and it is this discrepancy that has been challenged recently.

A CASE HISTORY OF DAVID IN YEAR 2

David, in Year 2, is a reader with specific reading difficulties. According to the simple model of reading, David would be located in the right-hand upper quartile of the model. His reading is characterised by his articulate response to stories read, his keen interest in books, and yet cracking the code and applying letter/sound knowledge to words for reading is proving particularly challenging for him. Recently, he has been experiencing growing frustration about his ability as a reader. He is concerned that he will never learn to read. David's parents are aware of this and in an interview they offer some insight into his reading history.

David's mother reported that when he was two years old they had some early concerns about his speech development, mostly about his pronunciation of words. He was late to learn to talk, and although this did not surprise his mother, as his older sister did all the talking on David's behalf, he was nevertheless referred for speech therapy in nursery and discharged nine months later. The speech therapist assured his mother that his speech was beginning to develop along normal lines. David apparently settled well into school. He was a sociable boy and popular with his peers. Both David's parents and his reception class teacher describe David as spending much time 'poring over books' of special interest such as dinosaur books and more general animal and transport books. He clearly enjoyed sharing books with adults in the nursery and at home. Reading with his parents was part of a special bedtime routine. It was therefore quite a surprise for his teachers and parents to learn that his efforts to decode were interfering with his reading pleasure and progress. By the end of Year 1, a concern was raised for David's progress and in Year 2 he was placed on the Special Needs Register. It was only when working in a one-to-one situation with David that his subtle language-related problems became evident.

In conversation David was chatty, engaging and expressed firm views. However, in attending closely to his speech, one could detect subtle mispronunciations of everyday words. These were related to his articulation and not to accent. His articulation reflected the developing speech pattern of a younger child. He had not confidently mastered the blending of sounds in his spoken speech and in this way he sounded like a younger child. For example, he spoke of 'gasbetti' for 'spaghetti', 'sool' for 'school' and 'nake' for 'snake'. When talking about his favourite book, David said, 'I 'member whe(n) I we(nt) to ge(t) a boo(k) farm the libry'. He also spoke about his '(com)puter ga(me)', which, in the context of spoken language, was completely intelligible to both his peers and parents; nevertheless, his speech did not offer him a secure base from which to recognise, for example, rhyme in words or to hear subtle differences between words – 'bat' and 'bag' – and between sounds 'i' and 'e' and 'j' and 'ch'. It will therefore come as no surprise to the reader to learn that when the focus of reading in school moved from the overarching pleasure of sharing a book (and the conceptual engagement that this involves) to attending to the decoding and the essential mapping between letter sounds and letter shapes, David's phonological structures let him down. The simple model of reading offers a helpful framework against which to highlight the gap between David's decoding and comprehension skills and is discussed below.

Unwrapping reading: comprehension and decoding

Comprehension

At the start of Year 1, David's comprehension skills offered him a secure starting point for reading.

He demonstrated:

- a clear understanding of the mechanics of how a book works;
- a sophisticated engagement and response to stories read to him and a frequent use of personal experiences to make links with the story;
- a confident ability to interpret meaning beyond the literal words on the page.

Decoding

A different profile of David's decoding emerges. His phonological development lagged behind his comprehension. He had not yet established the essential link between letters and sounds, between spoken words and their written representation, and he therefore relied heavily on making visual and semantic cues. For example, he could read 'mummy', 'daddy', 'school', 'home', and his name, 'David'. Any letter names he knew were based on their visually distinctive appearance and not on any link between letter sound and shape and their place in spoken words. He could name 's', 'm', 'o', 'p', 'z' and 'a'. David was in Frith's logographic phase or what Stuart describes as 'primitive' reading (2006). In order to progress to the alphabetic phase, he needed to make the link between letters and sounds. The challenge presented by the alphabetic phase seemed to be symptomatic of a more fundamental problem that had its roots in phonological development, as the following information indicates.

David's phonological skills were most secure at the level of the rhyme. He could suggest a rhyming word to go with a given word, for example 'mat' to rhyme with 'cat'. He could not, however, reliably complete a series of rhyme recognition, generation and manipulation tasks. His ability to clap out beats in a word (syllable count) was unreliable. When invited to count the beats for the word 'elephant' he said it contained two beats which, on the basis of his fuzzy articulation, it did. Tasks at the level of the phoneme were the most challenging for David. He was beginning to identify the first sound in words. On the basis of these findings, his phonological skills seemed to be the source of his reading difficulties.

The gap between both phonological and comprehension skills meant that David presented a somewhat jagged reading profile which is accurately expressed by his location on the simple model of reading quartiles. It was important therefore that any support programme devised for David would play to his strengths whilst tackling his weaknesses. This was the strategy adopted in considering his personalised learning needs and in setting up David's Individual Education Plan (IEP).

Planning for support

The focus of David's support programme in his Year 2 class was to harness his interest in reading while supporting his decoding skills. His reading programme was guided by two principles:

- the importance of separating out the decoding and comprehension elements of reading so that each could be appropriately supported in different ways and at different levels;
- the importance of selecting reading material so that it matched the desired reading outcome of independent or supported reading.

Comprehension

Real, rich and varied books were chosen to support David's comprehension. Reading aloud every day to him and providing alternative opportunities for reading with a taped story or with other children, parents or TAs was recommended. This strategy would:

- maintain David's focus on comprehension and take pressure off decoding;

- offer conceptually and linguistically challenging reading material which would extend his language and thinking;
- help maintain his self-esteem.

In addition, the best of reading scheme books would:

- offer a reassuringly familiar structure;
- offer reinforcement of key sight words through a different medium;
- provide ample opportunities for learning high-frequency vocabulary that is consistently supported both in the text and in the support material used alongside the text;
- provide some sense of achievement for David as he progressed through the scheme.

His parents were reminded of the importance of matching reading opportunities and expectations to levels of text difficulty. For example, texts selected for independent reading should be read at a comfort level of at least 95 per cent accuracy, while more challenging texts, read with 90 per cent accuracy, would be shared and supported by being read with 'a more knowledgeable other'. Parents' and teachers' sensitivity to David's reading choices, would, it was hoped, help maintain David's self-esteem and offer him an wide reading opportunities.

Decoding

At word level, a synthetic phonics programme with a strong focus on phonological development was implemented. This makes explicit the teaching of the forty-four phonemes in the English language in a multisensory, multimodal manner. Such a programme helps with the demands of the alphabetic principle, representing forty-four sounds of the language in twenty-six letters. The strength of such a programme lies in isolating the specific skill that needs support, in this case the phonological skills needed for decoding.

Table 9.1 Classroom strategies to support David's phonic knowledge

Phonological awareness	Strategies
Rhyme	• Listen to nursery rhymes • Sing and say nursery rhymes • Identify rhyming words from a series of pictures • Identify rhyme in spoken words • Generate rhyme from a suggested word • Spot the 'odd one out' from a series of four or five rhyming words • Support the child's spoken language in thinking about rhyme
Syllable	• Clap syllables in own name/friends' names, familiar items • Count the syllables in a given word • Suggest a word with a simliar number of syllables
Phoneme	• Count the phonemes in a given word (cvc) • Isolate and suggest the first sound in a given word • Suggest the final sound in a given word • Say the word without the final/first sound • Make up a new word of a similar pattern • Create a character for this new word and build a rhyming story around him *(continued)*

Table 9.1 Continued

Phonological awareness	Strategies
Letter knowledge	Multisensory letter sound learning strategies
	• Make a letter shape memorable: it may take on the shape and name of a favourite character
	• Trace over the shape. Make the shape in the sand. Make the shape on a friend's back with your finger, all the time saying its sound
	• Check how many times you can write the given letter in thirty seconds
	• Track a line of writing and highlight the given sound every time it is spotted
	• Find the given letter amongst an arc of alphabet letters
	• Match the letter to an object that begins with the same sound
	• Select the letter from some similarly shaped letters ('p' and 'q' and 'd' and 'b', for example)
	• Clap your hand when you hear the given sound: at the start of a spoken word; at the end of a spoken word
	• Suggest some words that begin with the given sound
	• Create a word bank of words that begin with the same sound

A CASE HISTORY OF GARY IN YEAR 5

Unlike David, our next pupil, Gary, has reading difficulties such that he was issued with a statement of special educational needs in Year 4. In this statement, he was described as having 'severe' and 'specific' difficulties that extended beyond the confines of reading. The statement also raised a concern for Gary's self-esteem, which at the point of his statement was a cause for concern. When Gary was diagnosed with dyslexia by the school, his reading was almost four years behind his chronological age. He was developing a history of poor attendance at school and had, despite his statement and the remedial activity it prompted, not made the desired progress in reading.

The school, for its part, had identified Gary's reading difficulties since Year 1. His teachers' responses from these early days were to add him to the list of children who were to be heard reading on a daily basis. Detailed records and reading logs of Gary's reading were kept. The TA closely monitored his responses to texts. Despite additional reading on a one-to-one basis and receiving extra reading support in a guided group programme three times a week, Gary made little progress in reading. By Year 5, the gap between his reading and that of his peers had grown. He felt alienated from his friends because he could not share the same stories, computer magazines and reading from the screen that they all participated in.

Gary's parents expressed concern that his reading was confined to sports and computer hobbies. They also expressed grave concern about his negative attitude to school. His earlier interest in reading had, they added, not been maintained. Art, maths, and design and technology, his considered strengths, no longer seemed to hold any interest for him.

A discussion with Gary confirmed that his self-esteem had indeed taken a battering. He felt stupid, isolated and deskilled and was constantly confronted with his failure to learn to read. Everything he had to do in class, he said, involved reading. 'If you can't read you can't do it. You just sit there and begin to fiddle around, just to pass the time'.

The school responded. All were aware that, as Gary approached Year 6, his support programme needed revising and his interest in reading rekindling. In the multidisciplinary discussion that followed, it became evident that the narrow diet of reading which Gary followed might in itself present a barrier to his progress in reading. The strategy of providing 'more of the same', that is, merely providing extra opportunities for reading, was not working. Two reasons for this lack of progress were proposed: firstly, Gary's extra reading was isolated from the context of the classroom setting. This had little transfer over into the classroom and therefore seemed to have little relevance to Gary. Secondly, his reading lessons failed to address or target his underdeveloped skills. The school was, in essence, dealing with the manifestations of the problem rather than the problem itself.

A whole-school approach

Following the annual review meeting, a number of changes were initiated within the school. The staff agreed to adopt a whole-school approach to reading that was both inclusive and multisensory. The school acknowledged that it was necessary not just to tinker on the peripheries with individual support programmes but also to initiate a far-reaching whole-school policy. Such an approach would enhance the reading opportunities for all children, including pupils with English as an Additional Language (EAL). After discussion with his teachers and his parents and with Gary, some general principles of classroom support for reading were established. The class teacher agreed to extend the range of teaching approaches she used when working from texts in order to accommodate different learning styles. She agreed to:

- play to strengths (in Gary's case, art, DT and maths and his visual learning channel):
  - use visual stimuli to support reading and discussion of any texts read;
  - provide opportunities for use of multimedia as a way of enhancing access to reading and as a medium of response;
  - use mind maps as a way of representing information while minimising the demands of reading and spelling;
  - use overhead transparencies or the interactive whiteboard to ensure everyone had access to texts being read;
  - use visual aids to make explicit the timetable of the day, the learning intention of the lesson and the organisation of the classroom;
- encourage use of phone or dictaphone to dictate notes or record information to support topic work or homework instructions.

In reading:

- ensure access to a rich diet of texts which challenge thinking and support decoding;
- ensure texts are differentiated for decoding but are conceptually challenging;
- provide individual lists of words to support reading of new specialist vocabulary across all the curriculum topics;
- use talking books to rekindle interest in reading;
- teach study skills, starting with alphabetical order;
- support any expectation of copying from the board by writing each line on the whiteboard, using a different colour so it is easy to 'copy write' from the board.

Table 9.2 Gary's Individual Education Plan

Name: Gary		Class: Year 5	Parent/Guardian:	
DOB			**Teacher:** **Stage:**	**Date:**
December 1996	**Key focus** Gary to make six months' reading progress in one month: to ensure success in all tasks he undertakes		**Statement**	**December 2006**

Start date	Targets	Criteria for success	Possible resources and strategies	Ideas for support teacher
December 2006	To research the Romans	Improved study skills Alphabetical order of letters known	Provide home with reading material on the Romans which is strongly supported by images	Use wooden letters to reinforce alphabetic order by making the alphabetic arc
	To ensure continued access to quality reading material	Ability to use scanning techniques to locate key words Successful documentary on the Romans produced by Gary and Sarah Gary rediscovers reading for pleasure researching his favourite hobby	Establish the relevance of enhancing alphabetical order with parents to support Gary's study skills Make a Romans 'fact file' Use dictaphone support, as a strategy for recording information on the Romans Provide 'shared reading' opportunities for Gary to challenge his thinking whilst supporting his decoding	Use tracking activities to find a given word in a set piece of text Ensure Gary can successfully use the dictaphone and save his digital recording onto his computer file. Listen, discuss and consider editing his report, as necessary
	To know topic words by sight	Words relevant to topic on Romans accessible to Gary and known by sight	Ensure home have list of key words to support reading around this topic. Invite parents to add extra words to the high-frequency words already on this list Provide home with word list	Remind Gary to start each topic session with reference to his word list – to generate his own computer word lists and to agree font size and colours, etc. to help make words memorable for him Gary to monitor his own success

Start date	Targets	Criteria for success	Possible resources and strategies	Ideas for support teacher
	To learn by sight ten new words weekly from high-frequency word list	Ten words weekly learnt by sight from high-frequency word list	Make words using individual wooden letters in a fixed time and working against the clock. Use highlighter pen to highlight tricky letters, those seen in the word but not heard	Words of the week; focus on one particular vowel digraph weekly. Collect words with the given sound and agree a minimum target number of words to collect
	To have fast recall of vowel digraph	Vowel digraphs read on sight. He can hear the long vowel sound in words; match the given long vowel sound to the letter representation of the sound; suggest a word with the given sound	Sets of images and list of long vowel digraph words. Games, e.g. bingo or spot the odd one out from a series of sounds and pictures based on vowel digraphs	
	To answer a question directed to him by a teacher	Gary's engagement in the lesson is monitored	Teacher and class assistant to actively encourage and monitor Gary's engagement in whole-class lessons	Monitor engagement and quality of interaction
	To maintain a diary to organise homework and daily schedule	Gary has what he needs, when he needs it for every lesson	To be agreed in discussion with Gary	Discuss and agree possible options for diary – clip art images set out as a weekly timetable; use of dictaphone or setting of alarm-timed phone message

Gary's IEP prioritises multisensory learning strategies; it identifies the importance of supporting study skills and of providing quality reading opportunities to develop higher-order thinking skills. According to OFSTED (1999), highly structured and well targeted support linked to multisensory approaches to reading offered effective support to pupils with specific learning difficulties (SpLD). OFSTED underlines the importance of teaching study skills to pupils and engaging their higher-order skills through the provision of rich reading opportunities. The benefits of synthetic phonics teaching for pupils with SpLD are, it claims, 'likely to be considerable' (1999:32).

CONCLUSION

The debate about dyslexia will continue. For many educationalists, the label dyslexia is considered to be at odds with current understandings of inclusion and therefore it is a trigger for a much wider political debate. Many question the value of the label dyslexia, particularly when there is no single uniform definition of the syndrome. They rightly challenge the assumption that somehow pupils with dyslexia are a 'special' group and quite distinct from 'garden-variety' poor readers (non-dyslexic struggling readers). One can argue that dyslexic readers are special: they represent a particular learning style at different ends of a continuum. They challenge our understanding of the reading process and the numerous assumptions on which the teaching of reading is based. In terms of equity, they are similar to all pupils, in that they have special and personalised learning needs that must be met.

Research into dyslexia has contributed to our understanding of both topics: reading and dyslexia. Dyslexia is no longer regarded as a simple discrepancy between IQ and reading performance. Many educational psychologists have abandoned the discrepancy definition of dyslexia and argued that it is culturally biased (Deponia *et al.*, 1999) and that it no longer accurately reflects current research on dyslexia or reading (Share, 1996; Stanovich, 1996; Mansell, 2005). Instead, phonological processing and the gap between the child's reading comprehension and listening comprehension are recognised as having a central role in reading. The ideas represented in the simple model of reading (Gough and Tunmer, 1986) reflect this current understanding and the important role of phonological processing, which we now see expressed in the *Primary National Strategy*. A drawing together of a wealth of research evidence helps us to work productively to meet the personalised needs of all pupils, whether we call them late developers, dyslexics or precocious readers.

Further reading and websites

Miles, T. and Miles, E. (1999) *Dyslexia a Hundred Years On*. Buckingham: Open University Press.
Snowling, M. (2000) *Dyslexia*. Oxford: Blackwell.
Stuart, M. (2006) *Learning to Read*. Professorial lecture. London: Institute of Education.
British Dyslexia Association: http://www.bdadyslexia.org.uk/
Dyslexia Handbook 2007/8: http://www.bdadyslexia.org.uk/news26.html
Professional Association of Teachers of Students with Specific Learning Difficulties: http://www.patoss-dyslexia.org/
DfES website on dyslexia: www.dfes.gov.uk/readwriteplus/understandingdyslexia/

References

Adams, M.J. (1990) *Beginning to Read: Thinking and Learning about Print.* Cambridge, MA.: MIT.

Alexander, R. (2006) *Towards Dialogic Teaching: Rethinking Classroom Talk* (2nd edn). Cambridge: Dialogos.

Anderson, M. (2003) 'Reading violence in boys' writing', *Language Arts* 80 (3), 223–230.

Arnold, H. (1982) *Listening to Children Reading.* London: Hodder & Stoughton.

Arts Council (2003) *Drama in Schools.* London: Arts Council England.

Ashley, B., Pullman, P., Fine, A. and Gavin, J. (2003) *Meetings with the Minister: Five Children's Authors on the NLS.* Reading: National Centre for Language and Literacy.

Bain, R., Fitzgerald, B. and Taylor, M. (1992) *Looking into Language.* London: Hodder & Stoughton.

Baker, C. (2000) *The Care and Education of Young Bilinguals.* Clevedon: Multilingual Matters.

Barrs, M. (1988) 'Maps of play', in M. Meek and C. Mills (eds) *Language and Literacy in the Primary School.* Lewes: Falmer Press.

Barrs, M. (2000) 'Gendered literacy', *Language Arts* 77 (4), 287–293.

Barrs, M. and Cork, V. (2001) *The Reader in the Writer.* London: CLPE.

Barrs, M. and Meek Spencer, M. (2005) 'Essay review, inquiry into meaning', *Literacy* 39 (1), 46–53.

Barrs, M. and Thomas, A. (eds) (1991) *The Reading Book.* London: CLPE.

Barrs, M., Ellis, S., Hester, H. and Thomas, A. (1988) *The Primary Language Record Handbook for Teachers.* London: CLPE.

Beard, R. (1987) *Developing Reading 3–13.* Sevenoaks: Hodder & Stoughton.

Bielby, N. (1999) *Teaching Reading at Key Stage 2.* Cheltenham: Stanley Thornes.

Bradley, L. and Bryant, P. (1983) 'Categorising sounds and learning to read: A causal connection', *Nature* 301, 419–421.

Brice Heath, S. (1983) *Ways with Words.* Cambridge: Cambridge University Press.

Brice Heath, S. (2004) *Visual Learning in the Community School.* London: Creative Partnerships.

Brice Heath, S. (2005) *Dramatic Learning in the Community School.* London: Creative Partnerships.

British Psychological Society (1999) *Dyslexia, Literacy and Psychological Assessment: Report of a Working Party of the Division of Educational and Child Psychology.* Leicester: BPS.

Brooks, G. (2002) *What Works for Children with Literacy Difficulties: The Effectiveness of Intervention Schemes.* London: DfES report 380.31.

Brooks, G. (2003) *Sound Sense: The Phonics Element of the NLS: A Report to the DfES*. London: DfES.

Brown, W., Eliez, E., Menon, V., Rumsey, J., White, C. and Reiss, A. (2001) 'Preliminary evidence of widespread morphological variations of the brain in dyslexia', *Neurology* 56, 781–783.

Bryant, P. and Bradley, L. (1985) *Children's Reading Problems*. Oxford: Blackwell.

Bunting, J. (2005) 'Making the most of TA talent', *Primary English Magazine* 11 (2), 8–10.

Burroughs-Lange, S. (2006) *Evaluation of Reading Recovery in London Schools: Every Child a Reader 2005–2006*. London: Institute of Education, University of London.

Bussis, A., Chittenden, E., Amarel, M. and Klausner, E. (1985) *Inquiry into Meaning: An Investigation of Learning to Read*. Hillsdale, NJ: Lawrence Erlbaum Associates.

Byrne, B. (1992) 'Studies in the acquisition procedure for reading: Rationale, hypotheses and data', in P.B. Gough, L. Ehri and R. Treiman (eds) *Reading Acquisition*. Hillsdale, NJ: Lawrence Erlbaum Associates.

Byrne, B. and Fielding-Barnsley, R. (1989) 'Phonemic awareness and letter knowledge in the child's acquisition of the alphabetic principle', *Journal of Educational Psychology* 81, 313–321.

Campbell, R. (1983) *Miscue Analysis in the Classroom*. Royston: UKRA.

Chall, J. (1967) *Learning to Read: The Great Debate*. New York: McGraw-Hill.

Chambers, A. (1990) *Booktalk*. Stroud: Thimble.

Clark, M. (1976) *Young Fluent Readers*. London: Heinemann.

Clay, M. (1985) *The Early Detection of Reading Difficulties* (3rd edn). Auckland: Heinemann.

Clay, M. (1998) *By Different Paths to Different Outcomes*. Portland, ME: Stenhouse Publishing.

CLPE (1988) *The Primary Language Record Handbook for Teachers*. London: CLPE.

Collier, V. (1995) 'Acquiring a second language for school', *Directions in Language and Education*, 1 (4). Accessed online at http://www.ncela.gwu.edu/pubs/ directions/04.htm (9/04/07).

Collier, V. and Thomas, W.P. (2001) *A National Study of School Effectiveness for Language Minority Students' Long-Term Academic Achievement*. Washington, DC: National Clearinghouse on Bilingual Education. Accessed online at http://crede.berkeley.edu/ research/llaa/1.1_references.html

Collins, F.M. (2005) '"She's sort of dragging me into the story!" Student teachers' experiences of reading aloud in Key Stage 2 classes', *Literacy* 39 (1), 10–17.

Collins, F.M. and Svensson, C. (in press) 'If I had a magic wand I'd magic her out of the book: The rich literacy practices of competent early readers', *Early Years*, 28.

Collins, F.M., Svensson, C. and Mahony, P. (2005) *Bookstart: Planting a Seed for Life*. London: Booktrust.

Cook, M. (2002) (ed.) *Perspectives on the Teaching and Learning of Phonics*. Royston: UKRA.

Cox, B. (1991) *Cox on Cox, An English Curriculum for the 1990s*. London: Hodder & Stoughton.

Crystal, D. (1987) *Cambridge Encyclopedia of Language*. Cambridge: Cambridge University Press.

Cummins, J. (2000) *Language, Power and Pedagogy: Bilingual Children in the Crossfire*. Clevedon: Multilingual Matters.

De Fries, J.C. (1991) 'Genetics and dyslexia', in M. Snowling and M. Thompson (eds) *Dyslexia: Integrating Theory and Practice*. London: Whurr.

Deponia, P., Landon, J., Mullin, K. and Reid, G. (1999) 'An audit of the processes involved in identifying and assessing bilingual learners suspected of being dyslexic. A Scottish study'. Paper presented at the Multilingual and Dyslexia BDA International Conference, Manchester, 17–19 June.

DES (1967) *Children and their Primary Schools* (The Plowden Report). London: HMSO.

DES (1975) *A Language for Life* (The Bullock Report). London: HMSO.

DES (1978) *Special Educational Needs* (The Warnock Report). London: HMSO.

DES (1987) *Report of the Task Group on Assessment and Testing (TGAT)*. London: HMSO.

DfE (1994) *English in the National Curriculum*. London: HMSO.

DfEE (1998) *The National Literacy Strategy Framework for Teaching*. London: DfEE.

DfEE (1999a) *English in the National Curriculum*. London: HMSO.

DfEE (1999b) *The National Literacy Strategy, Phonics: Progression in Phonics*. London: DfEE.

DfES (2000) *Curriculum Guidance for the Foundation Stage*. London: DfES.

DfES (2002) *Birth to Three Matters*. London: DfES.

DfES (2003a) *Excellence and Enjoyment: A Strategy for Primary Schools*. London: DfES.

DfES (2003b) *Speaking, Listening and Learning: Working with Children in Key Stage 1 and Key Stage 2*. London: DfES.

DfES (2003c) *Guided Reading: Supporting Transition from Key Stage 1 to Key Stage 2*. London: DfES.

DfES (2004a) *Primary National Strategy, Playing with Sounds: A supplement to Progression in Phonics*. London: DfES.

DfES (2004b) *Every Child Matters: Change for Children*. London: DfES.

DfES (2005a) *Ethnicity and Education: The Evidence on Ethnic Minority Pupils*. London: DfES.

DfES (2005b) *Understanding Reading Comprehension* (Flyers 1–3). London: DfES.

DfES (2005c) *Exemplar Whole School Curricular Targets*. London: DfES.

DfES (2005d) *The Independent Review of the Teaching of Early Reading Interim Report*. London: DfES.

DfES (2006a) *Independent Review of the Teaching of Early Reading* (*The Rose Report*). London: DfES.

DfES (2006b) *Primary National Strategy, Primary Framework for Literacy and Mathematics*. London: DfES.

DfES (2006c) *Primary Framework for Literacy and Mathematics: Supporting Guidance for Headteachers and Chairs of Governors*. London: DfES.

DfES (2006d) *National Statistics for Key Stage English Tests*. London: DfES.

DfES (2007a) *Statutory Framework for the Early Years Foundation Stage*. London: DfES.

DfES (2007b) *Guidance for Practitioners and Teachers on Progression and Pace in the Teaching of Phonics* (Annex B: Outline of Progression). London: DfES.

DfES (2007c) *Assessment*. Accessed online at http://www.standards.dfes.gov.uk/primaryframeworks/mathematics/assessment/ (4/03/2007).

DfES (2007d) *Letters and Sounds: Principles and Practice of High Quality Phonics*. London: DfES.

Diack, H. (1965) *In Spite of the Alphabet: A Study of the Teaching of Reading*. London: Chatto & Windus.

Ehri, L.C. (1987) 'Learning to read and spell words', *Journal of Reading Behavior,* 19, 5–31.

Ehri, L.C. (1992) 'Reconceptualising the development of sight word reading and its relationship to decoding', in P.B. Gough, L.C. Ehri and R. Treiman (eds) *Reading Acquisition*. Hillsdale, NJ: Lawrence Erlbaum Associates.

Ehri, L.C. (1995) 'Phases of development in learning to read words by sight', *Journal of Research in Reading* 18 (2), 116–125.

Ellis, S. and Safford, K. (eds) (2005) *Animating Literacy: Inspiring Children's Learning through Teacher and Artist Partnerships*. London: CLPE.

Evans, J.W. (2001) *Dyslexia and Vision*. London: Whurr.

Fawcett, A. and Nicholson, R. (1992) 'Automatisation deficits in balance for dyslexic children', *Perceptual and Motor Skills*, 75, 507–529.

Fawcett, A. and Nicholson, R. (2001) 'Dyslexia and the role of the cerebellum', in A.J. Fawcett (ed.) *Dyslexia: Theory and Practice*. London: Whurr.

Ferguson, J. (2002) 'Journeys to, from and around the text: an examination of young children's individual responses to picture story books'. London: University of Surrey Roehampton (MA dissertation, unpublished).

Frith, U. (1985) 'Beneath the surface of developmental dyslexia', in K. Patterson, J. Marshall and M. Coltheart (eds) *Surface Dyslexia*. Hillsdale, NJ: Lawrence Erlbaum.

Frith, U. (1997) 'Brain, mind and behaviour in dyslexia', in C. Hulme and M.J. Snowling (eds) *Dyslexia: Biology, Cognition and Intervention*. London: Whurr.

Garzia, R. (1993) 'Optometric factors in reading disability', in D.M. Willows, R.S. Kruk and E. Corcos (eds) *Visual Processes in Reading and Reading Disabilities*. NJ: Lawrence Erlbaum.

Gibbons, P. (1993) *Learning to Learn in a Second Language*. Portsmouth, NH: Heinemann.

Gibbons, P. (2002) *Scaffolding Language, Scaffolding Learning*. Portsmouth, NH: Heinemann.

Gilborn, D. and Gipps, C. (1996) *Recent Research on the Achievement of Ethnic Minority Pupils*. London: OFSTED.

Gilborn, D. and Mirza, S. (2000) *Educational Inequality: Mapping Race, Class and Gender*. London: OFSTED.

Goodman, K.S. (1967) 'A psycholinguistic guessing game', *Journal of the Reading Specialist* 6, 126–135.

Goodman, K.S. (1973) 'Miscues: Windows on the reading process', in K.S. Goodman (ed.) *Miscue Analysis: Application to Reading Instruction*. Urbana, IL.: ERIC Clearing House on Reading and Communication, NCTE.

Goodman, K.S. (1982) *Language and Literacy: The Selected Writings of Kenneth S. Goodman*, Volume 1. London: Routledge and Kegan Paul.

Goswami, U. (1994) 'The role of analogies in reading development', *Support for Learning* 9, 22–25.

Goswami, U. (1995) 'Rhyme in children's early reading', in R. Beard (ed.) *Rhyme, Reading and Writing*. London: Hodder & Stoughton.

Goswami, U. (2002) 'Rhymes, phonemes and learning to read', in M. Cook (ed.) *Perspectives on the Teaching and Learning of Phonics*. Royston: UKRA.

Goswami, U. and Bryant, P. (1990) *Phonological Skills and Learning to Read*. Hove: Lawrence Erlbaum.

Gough, P.B. and Hillinger, M.L. (1980) 'Learning to read: an unnatural act', *Bulletin of the Orton Society* 30, 179–196.

Gough, P.B. and Tunmer, W.E. (1986) 'Decoding reading and reading disability', *Remedial and Special Education* 7, 6–10.

Gravelle, M. (2000) *Planning for Bilingual Learners*. Stoke-on-Trent: Trentham Books.

Gregory, E. (1996) *Making Sense of a New World: Learning to Read in a Second Language*. London: Sage.

Gregory, E. and Williams, A. (2000) *City Literacies*. London: Routledge.

Hall, K. (2003) *Listening to Stephen Read*. Buckingham: Open University Press.

Hannon, P. (1999) 'Rhetoric and research in family literacy', *British Educational Research Journal* 7, 6–10.

Harris, R. (1997) 'Romantic bilingualism: Time for a change?', in C. Leung and C. Cable (eds) *English as an Additional Language: Changing Perspectives*. Watford: NALDIC.

Harrison, C. and Coles, M. (eds) (1992) *The Reading for Real Handbook*. London: Routledge and Kegan Paul.

Hatcher, P.J., Hulme, C. and Snowling, M.J. (2004) 'Explicit phoneme training combined with phonic reading instruction helps young children at risk of reading failure', *Journal of Child Psychology and Psychiatry* 45, 338.

Hatcher, P.J., Goetz, K., Snowling, M.J., Hulme, C., Gibbs, S. and Smith, G. (2006) 'Evidence for the effectiveness of the Early Literacy Support Programme', *British Journal of Educational Psychology* 76, 351–367.

Hinshelwood, J. (1900) 'Congenital word blindness', *Lancet* 1, 1506–1508.

Hobsbaum, A. (ed.) (2000) *Book Bands for Guided Reading: Organising KS1 Texts for the Literacy Hour*. London: Reading Recovery National Network, Institute of Education.

Hobsbaum, A., Gamble, N. and Reedy, D. (2006) *Guiding Reading: A Handbook for Teaching Guided Reading at Key Stage 2* (first published 2002). London: Institute of Education, University of London.

Holdaway, D. (1979) *The Foundations of Literacy*. Sydney: Ashton Scholastic.

Holden, C. (1999) 'I'm not good at holding a pencil: The underachievement of Year 4 and 5 boys in English.' Exeter: Project JUDE, School of Education, Exeter University.

Holland, P. (2003) *We Don't Play with Guns Here: War, Weapons and Superhero Play in the Early Years*. Milton Keynes: Open University Press.

Hoover, W. and Gough, P. (1990) 'The simple view of reading', *Reading and Writing* 2, (2), 127–160.

House of Commons Education, Science and Arts Committee (1990) *Standards of Reading in Primary Schools* (Select Committee Report). London: HMSO.

House of Commons Education and Skills Committee (2005) *Teaching Children to Read*. London: HMSO.

Hudson, J. (1992) 'Reading delays', in C. Harrison and M. Coles (eds) *The Reading for Real Handbook*. London: Routledge and Kegan Paul.

Hulme, C., Hatcher, P.J., Nation, K., Brown, A., Adams, J. and Stuart, G. (2002) 'Phoneme awareness is a better predictor of early reading skill than onset–rime awareness', *Journal of Experimental Child Psychology* 82, 2–28.

Hunt, P. (ed.) (1995) *Children's Literature: An Illustrated History*. Oxford: Oxford University Press.

Johnston, R. and Watson, J. (1998) *Accelerating Reading and Spelling with Synthetic Phonics: A Five Year Follow Up*. Edinburgh: Scottish Education Department.

Johnston, R. and Watson, J. (2005) *The Effects of Synthetic Phonics Teaching on Reading and Spelling Development: A Seven Year Longitudinal Study*. Edinburgh: Scottish Executive Education Department.

Kelly, C. (2004) 'Buzz Lightyear in the nursery', in E. Gregory, S. Long and D. Volk (eds) *Many Pathways to Literacy*. London: RoutledgeFalmer.

Kress, G. (2003) *Literacy in the New Media Age*. London: Routledge.

Laycock, L. (1989) 'Testing reading – an investigation', in M. Barrs and L. Laycock (eds) *Testing Reading*. London: CLPE.

Liberman, I.Y., Shankweiler, D., Fischer, F.W. and Carter, B. (1974) 'Reading and the awareness of language segments', *Journal of Experimental Child Psychology* 18, 201–212.

Lloyd, S. (1998) *The Phonics Handbook* (3rd edn). Chigwell: Jolly Learning.

Lundberg, I. (1994) 'Reading difficulties can be predicted and prevented: A Scandinavian perspective on phonological awareness and reading', in C. Hulme and M. Snowling (eds) *Reading Development and Dyslexia*. London: Whurr.

Lunzer, E., Gardner, K., Davies, F. and Greene, T. (1984) *Learning from the Written Word*. Edinburgh: Schools Council/Oliver and Boyd.

Lyon, G.R. (1994) 'Towards a definition of dyslexia', *Annals of Dyslexia* 45, 3–27.

McKay, D. (ed.) (1970) *Breakthrough to Literacy*. Harlow: Longman.

McKenley, J., Power, C., Ishani, L. and Demie, F. (2003) *Raising Achievement of Black Caribbean Pupils: Good Practice in Lambeth Schools*. London: Lambeth Research and Statistics Unit.

MacMillan, B. (1997) *Why Children Can't Read*. London: Institute of Economic Affairs.

McWilliam, N. (1998) *What's in a Word? Vocabulary Development in Multilingual Classrooms*. Stoke-on-Trent: Trentham Books.

Mansell, W. (2005) 'Dyslexia Storm Brews', *Times Educational Supplement*, 2 September, p.1.

Marek, A. and Howard, D. (eds) (1984) *A Kid-Watching Guide: Evaluation for Whole Language Classrooms*. Program in Language and Literacy, Occasional Paper No. 9, Tucson, AZ.

Maynard, S., Mackay, S., Smyth, F. and Reynolds, K. (2007) *Young People's Reading in 2005: The Second Study of Young People's Reading Habits*. LISU, Loughborough University, and National Centre for Research in Children's Literature, Roehampton University.

Meek, M. (1988) *How Texts Teach What Readers Learn*. Stroud: Thimble Press.

Meek, M. (1991) *On Being Literate*. London: Bodley Head.

Miles, T. and Miles, E. (1999) *Dyslexia: A Hundred Years On*. Buckingham: Open University Press.

Millard, E. (1997) *Differently Literate: Boys, Girls and the Schooling of Literacy*. London: Falmer Press.

Millard, E. (2006) 'Transformative pedagogy: teachers creating a literacy of fusion', in K. Pahl and J. Rowsell (eds) *Travel Notes from the New Literacy Studies*, Clevedon: Multilingual Matters.

Minns, H. (1990) *Read It to Me Now!* London: Virago.

Minns, H. (1999) 'Pathways into reading: Five young people and the development of the English curriculum', *Curriculum Studies* 7 (3), 493–505.

Mobbs, M. (1997) 'EMA Project, Lancashire', *NALDIC News* 13 (5), 11.

Moon, C. (published annually) *Individualised Reading*. Reading: Reading and Language Information Centre.

Moon, C. (1984) 'Making use of miscues when children read aloud', in *Children Reading to their Teachers*. Sheffield: NATE.

Morgan, R. (1976) 'Paired reading tuition: A preliminary report on a technique for cases of reading deficit', in *Child: Care, Health and Development* 2, 13–28.

Morgan, W.P. (1896) 'A case of congenital word-blindness', *British Medical Journal* 2, 1378.

Moss, G. (1999a) *The Fact and Fiction Project*. Southampton: University of Southampton School of Education.

Moss, G. (1999b) 'Texts in context: Mapping out the gender differentiation of the reading curriculum', *Curriculum Studies* 7 (3), 507–522.

Muter, V. (2003) *Early Reading Development and Dyslexia*. London: Whurr.

Muter, V. and Snowling, M. (1998) 'Concurrent and longitudinal predictors of reading: The role of metalinguistic and short-term memory skills', *Reading Research Quarterly* 33, 320–337.

Muter, V., Snowling, M. and Taylor, S. (1994) 'Orthographic analogies and phonological awareness: Their role and significance in early reading development', *Journal of Child Psychology and Psychiatry and Allied Disciplines* 35, 293–310.

Muter, V., Hulme, C., Snowling, M. and Taylor, S. (1997) 'Segmentation, not rhyming, predicts early progress in learning to read', *Journal of Experimental Psychology* 65, 370–396.

Muter, V., Hulme, C., Snowling, M. and Stevenson, J. (2004) 'Phonemes, rimes, vocabulary and grammatical skills as foundations of early reading: Developmental evidence from a longitudinal study', *Developmental Psychology* 40 (5), 665–681.

Myhill, D. (1999) 'Boy zones and girl power: Gender perceptions and preferences in English', *Curriculum* 10 (2), 86–99.

NAA (2004) *Building a Picture of What Children Can Do*. London: NAA.

National Literacy Trust (2005) *Young People and Reading Survey*. London: NLT.

National Reading Panel (2000) *Report of the National Reading Panel: Reports of the Subgroups*. National Institute of Child Health and Human Development Clearing House, Washington, DC.

New Zealand Ministry of Education (1997) *Reading for Life: The Learner as a Reader*. Wellington: Learning Media.

O'Brien, J. and Comber, B. (2000) 'Negotiating critical literacies with young children', in C. Barratt-Pugh and M. Rohl (eds) *Literacy Learning in the Early Years*. Crows Nest, NSW: Allen & Unwin.

OFSTED (1993) *Boys and English*. London: OFSTED.

OFSTED (1996) *The Teaching of Reading in 45 Inner London Primary Schools*. London: OFSTED.

OFSTED (1999) *Raising the Attainment of Ethnic Minority Pupils*. London: OFSTED.

OFSTED (2002) *The National Literacy Strategy: The First Four Years 1998–2002*. London: OFSTED.

OFSTED (2003) *Expecting the Unexpected: Developing Creativity in Primary and Secondary Schools*. London: OFSTED.

OFSTED (2004) *Reading for Purpose and Pleasure. An Evaluation of the Teaching of Reading in Primary School*. London: OFSTED.

OFSTED (2005) *Ensuring the Attainment of White Working Class Boys in Writing*. London: OFSTED.

Peer, L. (1994) *The Training and Awareness of Teachers*. Reading: British Dyslexia Association Handbook.

Pennac, D. (2006) *The Rights of the Reader*. London: Walker Books.

Pinnell, G.S., Lyons, C.A., DeFord, D.E., Bryk, A.S. and Seltzer, M. (1994) 'Comparing instructional models for the literacy education of high risk first graders', *Reading Research Quarterly* 29 (1), 8–39.

QCA (1999) *Target Setting and Assessment in the National Literacy Strategy*. London: QCA.

QCA (2000) *A Language in Common*. London: QCA.

QCA (2001) *Working with Gifted and Talented Children*. London: QCA.

QCA (2003a) *Year Five Writing Test and Assessment Framework (Space Boots)*. London: QCA.

QCA (2003b) *Creativity: Find It, Promote It!* London: QCA.

QCA (2003c) *Foundation Stage Profile*. London: QCA.

QCA (2004) *More than Words: Multimodal Texts in the Classroom*. London: QCA.

Rapple, B. (1994) 'Payment by results: An example of assessment in elementary education from nineteenth century Britain', *Education Policy Analysis Archives* 2 (1). Accessed online at http://epaa.asu.edu/epaa/v2n1.html (9/04/07).

Reay, D. (1991) 'Intersections of gender, race and class in the primary school', *British Journal of Sociology Education* 12 (2), 163–182.

Robson, S. (2006) *Developing Thinking and Understanding in Young Children*. London: Routledge.

Safford, K. and Barrs, M. (2006) *Many Routes to Meaning: Children's Language and Literacy Learning in Creative Arts Projects*. London: CLPE.

Safford, K., O'Sullivan, O. and Barrs, M. (2004) *Boys on the Margin: Promoting Boys' Literacy Learning at Key Stage 2*. London: CLPE.

Safford, K., Collins, F.M., Kelly, A. and Montgomerie, D. (2007) 'Exploring the field', *Primary English Magazine* 12 (3), 11–14.

Share, D.L. (1996) 'Word recognition and spelling processes in specific reading disabled and "garden variety" poor readers', *Dyslexia* 2 (3), 167–174.

Simpson, A. (1996) 'Critical questions: Whose questions?', *The Reading Teacher* 50 (2), 118–127.

Singleton, C. (1999) *Dyslexia in Higher Education: Report of the National Working Party*. Hull: University of Hull.

Skinner, B. (1953) *Science and Human Behaviour*. Basingstoke: Macmillan.

Smith, F. (1978) *Understanding Reading: A Psycholinguistic Analysis of Reading and Learning to Read*. New York: Holt, Rinehart and Winston.

Snowling, M.J. (1987) *Dyslexia: A Cognitive Developmental Perspective*. Oxford: Blackwell.

Snowling, M.J. (1995) 'Phonological processing and developmental dyslexia', *Journal of Research in Reading* 18 (2), 132–138.

Snowling, M.J. (2000) *Dyslexia*. Oxford: Blackwell.

Snowling, M.J. and Hulme, C. (eds) (2005) *The Science of Reading*. Oxford: Blackwell.

Snowling, M.J. and Stackhouse, J. (2005) *Dyslexia, Speech and Language: A Practitioner's Handbook*. London: Whurr.

Snowling, M.J., Adams, M., Bishop, D. and Stothard, S. (2001) 'Educational attainment for school leavers with a preschool history of speech-language impairments', *International Journal of Language and Communication Disorders* 36, 173–183.

Soler, J. and Paige-Smith, A. (2005) 'The Early Literacy Support Programme (ELS) and the blend and clash of national educational policy ideologies in England', *Early Years* 25 (1), 43–54.

Somekh, B. (2006) *The Pedagogies with E-Learning Resources Project*. Manchester: Manchester Metropolitan University.

South, H. (ed.) (1999) *The Distinctiveness of English as an Additional Language: A Cross-Curricular Discipline*. Watford: NALDIC.

Southgate, V. and Arnold, H. (1981) *Extending Beginning Reading*. London: Heinemann, for the Schools Council.

Stanovich, K.E. (1996) 'Towards a more inclusive definition of dyslexia', *Dyslexia* 2 (3), 154–166.

Stanovich, K.E. and Siegel, L.S. (1994) 'The phenotypic performance profile of reading disabled children: A regression-based test of the phonological core variable difference model', *Journal of Education Psychology* 38, 175–181.

Stein, J. (2001) 'The magnocellular theory of dyslexia', *Dyslexia: An International Journal of Research and Practice* 7, 12–30.

Stein, J. and Walsh, V. (1997) 'To see but not to read: The magnocellular theory of dyslexia', *Trends in Neurological Science* 20 (4), 147–152.

Stein, J., Talcott, J. and Witton, C. (2001) 'The sensorimotor basis of developmental dyslexia', in A.J. Fawcett (ed.) *Dyslexia: Theory and Good Practice*. London: Whurr.

Stierer, B. and Bloom, D. (1994) *Reading Words*. Sheffield: NATE.

Street, B. (1997) 'The implications of the "New Literacy Studies" for literacy education', *English in Education* 31 (3), 45–59.

Stuart, M. (1999) 'Getting ready for reading: Early phoneme awareness and phonics teaching improves reading and spelling in inner-city second language learners', *British Journal of Educational Psychology* 69, 587–605.

Stuart, M. (2006) 'Learning to read'. Professorial Lecture, London: Institute of Education.

Sumbler, K. and Willows, D. (1996) 'Phonological awareness and alphabetic coding instruction within balanced senior kindergartens', Paper presented at National Reading Conference, Charleston, SC, December.

Sylva, K. and Hurry, J. (1995) 'Early intervention in children with reading difficulties'. SCAA Discussion Papers No. 2. London: SCAA.

Tolkien, J. (1964) *Tree and Leaf*. London: Allen & Unwin.

Toomey, D. (1993) 'Parents hearing their children read: A review. Rethinking the lessons of the Haringey Project', *Educational Research* 35 (3), 223–236.

Topping, K. and Wolfendale, S. (eds) (1985) *Parental Involvement in Reading*. London: Croom Helm.

Treiman, R. (1985) 'Onsets and rimes as units of spoken syllables: Evidence from children', *Journal of Experimental Child Psychology* 39, 161–181.

Tucker, N. (1981) *The Child and the Book*. Cambridge: Cambridge University Press.

Turner, M. (1990) *Sponsored Reading Failure*, Warlingham, Surrey: IPSET.

Twist, L., Sainsbury, M., Woodthorpe, A. and Whetton, C. (2003) *Reading All Over the World: The Progress in International Reading Literacy Study*. Slough: NFER.

Vellender, A. (1989) 'Teacher inquiry in the classroom: What's in a name? Literacy events in an infant classroom', *Language Arts* 66 (5), 552–557.

Vygotsky, L. (1978) *Mind in Society*. Cambridge, MA.: Harvard University Press.

Wade, B. and Moore M. (1993) *Bookstart*. London: Booktrust.

Wade, B. and Moore, M. (2000) 'A sure start with books', *Early Years* 20, 39–46.

Wasik, B. and Slavin, R. (1993) 'Preventing early reading failure with one-to-one tutoring: A review of five programs', *Reading Research Quarterly* 28 (2), 179–200.

Waterland, L. (1985) *Read with Me*. Stroud: Thimble Press.

Watson, K. (2006) *Hearing the Voice of Gifted and Talented Pupils through the Use of Learning Logs in Order to Improve Teaching Provision*. Accessed online at http://www.nagty.ac.uk/research/practitioner_research/documents/dr_keith_ watson.pdf (15/04/07).

Wells, G. (1987) *The Meaning Makers*. London: Hodder & Stoughton.

Wegerif, R. and Dawes, L. (2004) *Thinking and Learning with ICT: Raising Achievement in Primary Classrooms*. London: Routledge.

Wolf, M. and O'Brien, B. (2001) 'On issues of time fluency and intervention', in A.J. Fawcett (ed.) *Dyslexia: Theory and Good Practice*. London: Whurr.

Wood, D., Bruner, J. and Ross, G. (1976) 'The role of tutoring in problem solving', *Journal of Child Psychology and Psychiatry* 17 (2), 89–100.

CHILDREN'S BOOKS

Agard, J. and Nichols, G. (2004) *From Mouth to Mouth*. London: Walker Books.

Ahlberg, A. (1980) *Mrs Wobble the Waitress*. London: Puffin.

Ahlberg, A. and Ahlberg, J. (1978) *Each Peach Pear Plum*. London: Kestrel/Viking.

Ahlberg, A. and Ahlberg, J. (1988) *Starting School*. London: Viking.

Aiken, J. (1962) *The Wolves of Willoughby Chase*. London: Cape.

Aiken, J. (1984) *The Fog Hounds and Other Stories*. London: Hodder & Stoughton.

Aiken, J. (1995) *The Winter Sleepwalker*. London: Red Fox.

Alborough, J. (1992) *Where's My Teddy?* London: Walker Books.

Alborough, J. (1994) *It's the Bear!* London: Walker Books.

Almond, D. (1999) *Skellig*. London: Hodder Children's Books.

Andreae, G. and Parker-Rees, G. (2000) *Giraffes Can't Dance*. London: Orchard.

Andreae, G. and Wojtowycz, D. (2002) *Rumble in the Jungle*. London: Orchard.

Ardizzone, E. (1936) *Little Tim and the Brave Sea Captain*. Oxford: Oxford University Press.

Arlon, P. (2007) 'eye know' books e.g. *tree*. London: Dorling Kindersley.

Armitage, R. and Armitage, D. (1977) *The Lighthouse Keeper's Lunch*. London: Deutsch.

Beake, L. and Littlewood, K. (2006) *Home Now*. London: Francis Lincoln.

Beck, I. (2004) *The Enormous Turnip*. Oxford: Oxford University Press.

Bee, W. (2005) *Whatever*. London: Walker Books.

Biet, P. and Bloom, B. (1998) *The Cultivated Wolf*. London: Siphano Press.

Blackman, M. (1993) *Hacker*. London: Corgi.

Body, W. (1998) *A Collection of Classic Poems*. London: Pelican Longman.

Brown, R. (1981) *A Dark Dark Tale*. London: Andersen.

Browne, A. (2006) *Silly Billy*. London: Walker Books.

Browne, E. (1994) *Handa's Surprise*. London: Walker Books.

Browning, R. and Amstutz, A. (1993) *The Pied Piper of Hamelin*. London: Orchard Books.

Burningham, J. (1970) *Mr Gumpy's Outing*. London: Jonathan Cape.

Butterworth, C. and Lawrence, J. (2006) *Seahorse: The Shyest Fish in the Sea*. London: Walker Books.

Byars, B. (1970) *The Midnight Fox*. London: Faber.

Cameron, A. (1982) *The Julian Stories*. London: Gollancz.

Carle, E. (1970) *The Very Hungry Caterpillar*. London: Hamish Hamilton.

Carroll, L. (1954) *Alice's Adventures in Wonderland*. London: Collins.

Cleary, B. (1985) *Dear Mr Henshaw*. London: Puffin.

Cottrell Boyce, F. (2004) *Millions*. London: Macmillan Children's Books.

Creech, S. (2001a) *Love that Dog*. London: Bloomsbury.

Creech, S. (2001b) *Walk Two Moons*. London: Macmillan Children's Books.

Dodd, L. (1983) *Hairy Maclary from Donaldson's Dairy*. London: Puffin.

Dodd, L. (2002) *Scarface Claw*. London: Puffin.

Doherty, B. (1995) *Children of Winter*. London: Mammoth.

Donaldson, J. (1999) *The Gruffalo*, London Macmillan Children's Books.

Douglas, D. (2005a) *Itching for a Fight*. Leamington Spa: Scholastic.

Douglas, D. (2005b) *Going out with a Bang*. Leamington Spa: Scholastic.

Douglas, D. (2005c) *They Think It's All Over!* Leamington Spa: Scholastic.

Fine, A. (1989) *Goggle Eyes*. London: Mammoth.

Fine, A. (1993) *The Angel of Nitshill Road*. London: Mammoth.

French, V. and Prater, J. (2000) *The Gingerbread Boy*. London: Walker Books.

French, V. and Robins, A. (2000) *The Three Billy Goats Gruff*. London: Walker Books.

Gavin, J. (2000) *Coram Boy*. London: Mammoth.

Gray, K. (2007) *006 and a Bit*. London: Red Fox.

Grey, M. (2005) *Traction Man is Here*. London: Cape Children's Books.

Hayes, S. and Craig, H. (1986) *This is the Bear*. London: Walker Books.

Heapy, T. (1997) *Korky Paul: Biography of an Illustrator*. Oxford: Heinemann Educational Publishers.

Henderson, J., Donaldson, J. and Docherty, T. (2006) *Fly Pigeon Fly*. London: Little Tiger Press.

Hill, E. (1980) *Where's Spot?* London: Heinemann.

Hoffman, M. and Binch, C. (1995) *Grace and Family*. London: Francis Lincoln.

Hoffman, M. and Littlewood, K. (2002) *The Colour of Home*. London: Francis Lincoln.

Hughes, S. (1977) *Dogger*. London: Bodley Head.

Hughes, S. (1981) *Alfie Gets In First*. London: Bodley Head.

Hughes, T. (1989) *The Iron Man*. London: Faber.

Hutchins, P. (1972a) *Rosie's Walk*. London: Bodley Head.

Hutchins, P. (1972b) *Titch*. London: Bodley Head.

Innocenti, R. and McEwan, I. (1985) *Rose Blanche*. London: Jonathan Cape.

James, S. (1997) *Leon and Bob*. London: Walker Books.

James, S. (2004) *Baby Brains*. London: Walker.

Jeffers, O. (2004) *How to Catch a Star*. London: Collins.

Kerr, J. (1971) *When Hitler Stole Pink Rabbit*. London: Collins.

Kerr, J. (1984) *Mog and Me*. London: Collins Picture Lions.

King-Smith, D. (1978) *The Fox Busters*. Harmondsworth: Penguin.

King-Smith, D. (1983) *The Sheep Pig*. London: Gollancz.

McGough, R. (2005) *Sensational!* London: Macmillan.

McKee, D. (1978) *Tusk Tusk*. London: Andersen Press.

McKee, D. (1980) *Not Now Bernard*. London: Andersen Press.

Magorian, M. (1981) *Goodnight Mister Tom*. London: Kestrel.

Mark, J. (2006) *Road Closed*. London: Hodder Children's Books.

Mitchell, A. (2004) *Daft as a Doughnut*. London: Walker Books.

Morpurgo, M. (1977) *Friend or Foe*. London: Macmillan.

Morpurgo, M. (1994) *The Dancing Bear*. London: Collins.

Morpurgo, M. (1995) *The Wreck of the Zanzibar*. London: Mammoth.

Morpurgo, M. (1996) *The Butterfly Lion*. London: Collins.

Morpurgo, M. (1997) *Farm Boy*. London: Pavillion.

Morpurgo, M. (2002) *Billy the Kid*. London: Collins.

Naidoo, B. (2000) *The Other Side of Truth*. London: Puffin.

Passes, D. (1993) *Dragons: Truth, Myth and Legend*. London: Artists and Writers Guild Books.

Patten, B. (ed.) (1997) *The Puffin Book of Utterly Brilliant Poetry*. London: Puffin.

Pearce, P. (1958) *Tom's Midnight Garden*. Oxford: Oxford University Press.

Prater, J. (1995) *Once Upon a Time*. London: Walker Books.

Price, W. (1967) *Lion Adventure*. London: Cape.

Pullman, P. (1995) *Northern Lights*. Leamington Spa: Scholastic.

Pullman, P. (1996) *The Firework Maker's Daughter*. London: Corgi Yearling.

Richter, H.P. (1978) *Friedrich*. London: Heinemann.

Rosen, M. (2006) *Mustard Custard Grumble Belly and Gravy*. London: Bloomsbury.

Ross, T. (1987) *Oscar Got the Blame*. London: Andersen Press.

Ross, T. (1991) *A Fairy Tale*. London: Andersen Press.

Sachar, L. (2000) *Holes*. London: Bloomsbury.

Sachar, L. (2001) *There's a Boy in the Girls' Bathroom*. London: Bloomsbury.

Scieszka, J. and Smith, L. (1989) *The True Story of the Three Little Pigs*. New York: Viking Penguin.

Sendak, M. (1963) *Where the Wild Things Are*. London: Bodley Head.

Simmonds, P. (1987) *Fred*. London: Jonathan Cape.

Steptoe, J. (1988) *Mufaro's Beautiful Daughters*. London: Hamish Hamilton.

Swindells, R. (1980) *The Ice Palace*. London: Young Lions.

Titherington, J. (1986) *Pumpkin Pumpkin*. London: Julia MacRae Books.

Tomlinson, J. (1968) *The Owl who was Afraid of the Dark*. London: Methuen.

Trivizas, E. and Oxenbury, H. (1993) *The Three Little Wolves and the Big Bad Pig*. London: Heinemann.

Voake, C. (1997) *Ginger*. London: Walker Books.

Voake, C. (2006) *Hello Twins*. London: Walker Books.

Vrombaut, A. (1998) *Mouse and Elephant*. London: Hodder & Stoughton.

Waddell, M. and Benson, P. (1992) *Owl Babies*. London: Walker Books.

Waddell, M. and Firth, B. (1988) *Can't You Sleep, Little Bear?* London: Walker Books.

Waddell, M. and Firth, B. (1989) *The Park in the Dark*. London: Walker Books.

Westall, R. (1989) *Blitzcat*. London: Macmillan Children's Books.

White, E.B. (1952) *Charlotte's Web*. London: Hamish Hamilton.

Willis, J. and Ross, T. (2003) *Tadpole's Promise*. London: Andersen.

Wilson, J. (1999) *The Illustrated Mum*. London: Corgi.

Wilson, J. (2007) *Jacky Daydream*. London: Doubleday.

Zephaniah, B. (2001) *Refugee Boy*. London: Bloomsbury.

Books in series

(no dates given as these cover a range)

Colfer, E. *Artemis Fowl*. London: Egmont Books.

Higson, C. *The Young James Bond*. London: Puffin.

Horowitz, A. *Alex Rider*. London: Walker Books.

Nicholson, W. *The Wind on Fire*. London: Mammoth.

Pilkey, D. *Captain Underpants*. Leamington Spa: Scholastic.

Pullman, P. *His Dark Materials*. Leamington Spa: Scholastic.

Rowling, J.K. Harry Potter series. London: Bloomsbury.

Snicket, L. *A Series of Unfortunate Events*. London: Egmont Books.

Stine, R.L. *Goosebumps*. Leamington Spa: Scholastic.

Point Horror. Leamington Spa: Scholastic.

Reading schemes

1, 2, 3 and Away (1966) Glasgow: Collins.
Bangers and Mash (1975) Harlow: Longman.
Collins Big Cat (2004) London: Collins.
Janet and John (1949) London: James Nisbet.
Ladybird Key Words Reading Scheme (1964) Loughborough: Ladybird Books.
Letterland (1973) London: Collins Educational.
Oxford Reading Tree (1985) Oxford: Oxford University Press.
Story Chest (1981) London: Kingscourt.

Phonic schemes

Davies, A. (1998) *THRASS: Teaching Handwriting Reading and Integrated Phonographic Program for Teaching Building Blocks of Literacy: Teacher's Manual.* Chester: THRASS.
Hiatt, K. (2006) *Collins Big Cat Phonics Handbook.* London: Collins.
Lloyd, S. (2002) *Jolly Phonics.* Chigwell: Jolly Learning.
Miskin, R. (2004) *Read Write Inc. 2: An Inclusive Literacy Programme Handbook.* Oxford: Oxford University Press.

CD-ROMs

Nursery Rhyme Time. Sherston Software.
Oxford Reading Tree Rhyme and Analogy. Sherston Software.
Ridiculous Rhymes. Sherston Software.

Reading tests

Bookbinder, G. (1976) *Salford Sentence Reading Test.* Sevenoaks: Hodder & Stoughton.
Daniels, J.C. and Diack, H. (1958) *The Standardised Reading Tests.* London: Hart-Davies Educational.
Godfrey Thomson Unit (1977–1981) *Edinburgh Reading Test.* London: Hodder & Stoughton.
McLeod, J. and Unwin, D. (1970) *GAP Reading Comprehension Test.* London: Heinemann.
Neale, M. (Christophers, U. and Whetton, C., British adaptors and standardisers) (1988) *Neale Analysis of Reading Ability, Revised British Edition.* Windsor: NFER Nelson.
Schonell, F.J. and Schonell, F.E. (1942, restandardised 1972) *Schonell Graded Word Reading Test.* Harlow: Oliver and Boyd.
Vincent, D. and De La Mare, M. (1986) *Effective Reading Tests (ERT).* Basingstoke: Macmillan.
Watts, A. (1948) *Holborn Reading Scale.* London: Harrap.
Young, D. (1980) *Group Reading Test.* London: Hodder & Stoughton.

Author index

CHILDREN'S AUTHORS AND ILLUSTRATORS

PHONIC SCHEMES AUTHORS

READING TESTS AUTHORS

Subject index